D0325314

"Dr. Pimental-Habib has written a book that needs to be read, not only by the gay community but by the straight community as well. I wish such a book had been in print when I have had to deal with gay men and women who were struggling with their low sense of self-esteem, or when I have had to confront and work with the members of their families and others who, knowingly or unknowingly, made it so difficult for them to find fulfillment. I heartily endorse this wonderful book. It will make me a more sensitive minister and university professor."

Dr. Laurence C. Keene, Ph.D.
Senior Minister, The Church of the Valley (Van Nuys, California)
Professor of Sociology, Pepperdine University (Malibu, California)

"As we sail into the new millennium, the life force of the gay and lesbian tribe can only be secured by each individual's quest for enhanced self-esteem. Dr. Pimental-Habib is on a mission to provide us with a blueprint for self-improvement. His heartfelt book, written intimately and with great insight, is a how-to for soul preservation. Refreshingly void of psychobabble, EMPOWERING THE TRIBE is designed to jump-start your evolutionary journey."

Michael Kearns
Artist/Activist involved in the gay and lesbian rights movement for over 25 years

"As a mother, grade-school principal, and Doctor of Education, I am heartened that someone cares enough about members of our society who are the last acceptable targets of hatred, bigotry and the misuse of the term "family values." It is the responsibility of each of us, especially parents and educators, to teach our children how to replace bigotry with tolerance, and ignorance with knowledge. EMPOWERING THE TRIBE provides families with a recipe for understanding, growth, compassion and love."

Dr. Juliann Kerrigan, Ed.D., University of Massachusetts, Amherst
Professor of Education

EMPOWERING THE TRIBE

A Positive Guide to Gay and Lesbian Self-Esteem

Richard L. Pimental-Habib, Ph.D.

KENSINGTON BOOKS
http://www.kensingtonbooks.com

KENSINGTON BOOKS are published by

Kensington Publishing Corp.
850 Third Avenue
New York, NY 10022

Copyright © 1999 by Richard L. Pimental-Habib

Excerpt from ON THE PULSE OF MORNING by Maya Angelou copyright ©
1993 by Maya Angelou. Reprinted by permission of Random House, Inc.

Excerpt from CREATIVE VISUALIZATION by Shakti Gawain copyright © 1995.
Reprinted with permission of New World Library, Novato, CA 94949.

Excerpt from THE FAMILY HEART by Robb Forman Dew copyright © 1994
by Robb Forman Dew. Reprinted by permission of Perseus Books.

Excerpt from WHEREVER YOU GO, THERE YOU ARE by Jon Kabat-Zinn ©
1994 by Jon Kabat-Zinn. Reprinted with permission of Hyperion, New York,
NY 90011

All rights reserved. No part of this book may be reproduced in any form or
by any means without the prior written consent of the Publisher, excepting
brief quotes used in reviews.

Kensington and the K logo Reg. U.S. Pat. & TM Off.

ISBN 1-57566-424-0

First Printing: June, 1999
10 9 8 7 6 5 4 3 2 1

Printed in the United States of America

This book is dedicated to my friends, colleagues, and clients who are no longer with us, but whose tireless devotion to furthering our empowerment lives on, in every heartbeat, with every breath.

I send my heartfelt thanks to the following people, for helping to make this book a reality.

To Owen, who's loved me in a way that means the world to me.

To Deidre Knight, agent extraordinaire, for believing in a book of a different sexual orientation, and for her continual support, advice, and friendship.

To Tracy Bernstein and John Scognamiglio, my fabulous editors, and the others at Kensington who believed in this first-time author.

To Dr. Laurence Keene, Dr. Juliann Kerrigan, and Michael Kearns, for their sensitive and flattering endorsements.

To my friends and colleagues for their particular brand of support, confidence, and guidance, and whose personal experiences grace these pages . . . you know who you are.

To all those who, over this past decade, have come to my office for my help and allowed me access into their worlds. A professor of mine once said that first we learn from our teachers, then we learn from our patients. I want to thank my patients for teaching me how to be a better therapist.

To Bob and Bonita, who have raised meditation to new heights.

And especially to Julie, the mother of all supportive mothers. You've come a long way, baby.

To love oneself is the beginning of a lifelong romance.
—Oscar Wilde

If you can't love yourself, how the hell *are you gonna love someone else?*
—RuPaul

Contents

Introduction: This Is Not Just Another How-To Book   xi

Part One: Understandings and Beginnings

1. On Self-Esteem and the Roots of Homophobia   3
2. On Meditation and Coming Out   17
3. Everyday Life, Part I: Altered States of Consciousness   24
4. Everyday Life, Part II: Self-Esteem Messages   30
5. Progressive Relaxation   51
6. The Sailboat Visualization   61
7. The Safe Place Image   67

Part Two: Challenges to Healthy Self-Esteem

Childhood and Family

8. Why Is My Room Blue?   77
9. Parent-Pleasing/People-Pleasing   91
10. Kids Say the Darndest Things, Revised   102
11. Re-parenting for Parents   117

Adulthood and Relationships

12. What a Difference a Gay Makes   131
13. A Thing of Beauty Is a Boy Forever   151
14. What Was I Thinking?   164
15. Surviving Grief   183

Society

16. The Religious Right Is Neither   192
17. Slum-Thinking   205
18. The Road to Wholeness: A Path, Not a Pill   221

Part Three: Growing on from Here

19. Self-Nurturance   239
20. Self-Assessments   249
21. Unity in the Community: Resources   258
22. Conclusion: Whose Choice Is It, Anyway?   263

This Is Not Just Another How-To Book

Paradise is where I am.

—Voltaire

The idea for this book was born in the sun, on a warm wooden deck within earshot of the ocean's pounding surf in Carmel, California: a meditative, soothing and therapeutic setting, to say the least. This is the home of two friends of mine, a gay female couple, and don't you know I visit as often as possible!

For me, spending a few days in such a setting is about serenity and creativity. My mind clears, my body feels alive, and my soul refreshes. With and without my friends I write, walk, meditate, play music, laugh, cry, listen, think, feel . . . in short, I live. But being there is about even more: It is also about having experiences conducive to healthy self-esteem, and about filling up on all the good feelings that come attached to that. Treating myself to a getaway weekend in such a gorgeous corner of the world is, on some level of consciousness, an acknowledgment of deservingness, of worthiness. It's subtle, but it's there. It doesn't feel like, *Hey, look at me, aren't I deserving!?* It feels more peaceful, more internal, as when you've made a choice you feel good about, without guilt or shame, without the need to do anything more with it than simply experience its rewards in the moment.

As someone who meditates on a fairly regular basis, I find it blissfully easy in this type of setting to slip into an altered state where nothing exists but the warmth of the deck, the sun and breeze on my skin, and the lulling sounds of the waves. Not only do I feel good with this moment in time, but if I were to leave my immersion in delicious hedonism—albeit reluctantly—to go to a more cerebral place in my mind, I might admit that I also feel good *about myself*. In thinking about this fact, I might realize, *Of course I do!* How could I give this gift to myself without absorbing, on some level, the underlying message that I'm worth spending a few relaxing moments right here, right now. And so, it becomes a message about self-worth. Feeling soothed yet creative; calm yet alive; connected to all living things, yet contentedly happy with my oneness. Nothing else to do, nothing else to be. Just this, this moment of feeling utterly at peace and totally content.

Ahhhhhhhhh . . .

Empowering the Tribe is a lot about moments and messages. In meditation, we learn that all that exists is this moment, a moment very pure, without goals, agendas or bias, without past or future getting in the way of the present. The very nature of meditation is, in fact, a place where relaxing waves and good feelings are the specials of the day and make the day feel special.

Messages, particularly the sometimes subtle, sometimes harsh societal messages which confront gay people with notions of acceptance versus rejection, are constant reminders of the importance of treating oneself, of helping oneself to warm and comforting feelings about . . . well, simply about *being;* existing on this planet, rightfully and proudly side by side with all other creatures. How important it is that we learn to provide these moments, and these feelings, *for ourselves*. I strongly believe that any message from within can overcome any message from external sources.

It is the goal of *Empowering the Tribe* to marry the ancient, time-honored benefits of the practice of therapeutic meditation with raising the self-esteem of gay men and lesbians. This book, however, and as you will see, is not only of benefit to gay people, and it's certainly not only about meditation. It has been my attempt to organize it in such a way that it is also helpful for loved ones, family members, friends and colleagues of gays, in their understanding of what some of the self-esteem struggles might be like in the life of a gay person. It is, I hope, a palatable way to improve on empathy. Everyone in this country, if not on most of this planet, knows a gay person, directly or indirectly, with or without their knowledge of this fact. There is at least one gay person in absolutely *everyone's* family tree. And yet, not everyone empathizes or fully appreciates what gay people have historically suffered, or continue to suffer, that interferes with the building of healthy self-esteem. Even more dangerous, they may not even know how they themselves are contributing to the problem. Well, this book is for them, too.

Furthermore, there's no reason that these pages cannot speak to anyone who wishes to improve the quality of his own self-esteem. While I believe the following chapters are particularly geared to the challenges to healthy self-esteem that are faced by gay men and lesbians, I am aware that, to a degree, many of these issues are potent and fitting to the lives of non-gay people. In the self-esteem and relationship seminars I lead, I tell the heterosexuals in the audience to simply change a pronoun or two here and there, and they, too, will see themselves and their lives in the presentation. That holds true for much of this book as well.

Bottom line is, when it comes to self-esteem, we're really not all that much different from each other. Although the particulars of everyone's lives are different, and the individual and/or collective histories are unique to each person and each group, we all want to feel good about ourselves. We all want to love and to feel loved. We want to be able to have our feelings and know that they're okay to have, they are valid. We want the same basic, decent respect that ought to be afforded all humans, without bias and without prejudice, and all the sociopolitical rights that come with such respect. We all want to know that we matter.

Perhaps the most important connection among us all is the desire to feel love. No matter what prejudice we may harbor against each other, no matter what form that prejudice may take, we are united in this way: We want to feel love. This desire surpasses; it cuts through homophobia, heterophobia, racism, sexism and all the rest. If only we could keep this awareness in our consciousness at all times.

Be forewarned, however: This book is not a how-to on meditation. It would be presumptuous of any author to claim to know the way for another person to meditate, just as it would be presumptuous for any therapist to think he or she has the "right" answers for a client's difficulties. One can only hope to explore and discover the most beneficial ways to meditate *for oneself*. Meditation is a personal, individual process; a journey that is perhaps not taken by any two people in the exact same way. Each person's style of meditation is different, just as the type of meditation that works best for each person is different. Often, meditation serves to open the emotional pathways which provide the answers to an individual's highly personal questions. I can only hope to help you along your own journey, offering what I believe to be of benefit.

My advice to my private-practice clients is my advice to you now: Let in what works for you, throw away the rest. Or, perhaps just set aside the rest for a later time . . . the teacher never knows when the student within may be ready!

In Part One of this book, we'll look at understanding self-esteem in a way that is original, manageable, and far healthier than how we tend to think of it. As self-esteem is intimately connected to the concepts of homophobia, coming out, and the obstacles we face in day-to-day living, we'll take an in-depth look at these issues as well. An understanding of these issues is essential, I believe, before any further discussion about what goes into a journey toward greater self-esteem.

All along in this book, you'll find affirmations and meditations that coincide with the issues presented in that chapter. These meditations are designed for greater self-awareness, heightened focus, emotional healing, and personal empowerment. As such, many of them pose thought-provoking questions for you, to help you shed some light on those corners of yourself that may be in darkness. Additionally, in Chapters 5, 6, and 7 you'll find some relaxation and creative visualization ideas that I believe facilitate whatever meditative therapies you choose, allowing for maximum benefit. I've always found relaxation techniques to be most helpful prior to engaging in *any* meditation, even if that means taking just a few simple, deep breaths to heighten your focus and relax body and mind as you begin. Relaxation aids greatly in the process of insight and discovery as well.

In Part Two of this book you will read more about the coming-out process, and some of the many challenges to healthy gay and lesbian self-esteem, organized into the areas of Childhood and Family, Adulthood and Relationships, and Society. These cover everything from life on the playground to grieving for the loss of a loved one; from religious persecution to being obsessed with going to the gym. There is discussion of gay and lesbian relationships—friendships as well as sexual involvements—family relationships and professional relationships. Although most of the information is designed to speak directly to gay men and women, some topics are especially geared toward parents and friends. All along the way are Real-Life Stories to help illuminate and elaborate on the issues at hand. Actual names and identifying characteristics are altered in these stories, however, to protect confidentiality.

You may find your own story, or parts of it, throughout the book; you may see stories similar to those of people you know or work with, family members, significant others, loved ones. Hopefully you'll read and feel, at least some of the time, that the words are speaking directly to your experience, that they stir up your own thoughts and feelings in a way that allows for a closer look at them, and that you can benefit from participating in each chapter's concluding meditations.

Toward the end of this book, in Chapter 20, you'll find self-assessment exercises, created to help you achieve a greater understanding of your specific issues. I highly recommend them if you wish to experience increased insight, movement, and further growth through improved clarity. Also, at the end we close with some discussion about nurturance—the healing power of love and self-acceptance–and a listing of gay and HIV/AIDS agencies and national hotlines.

I believe there are many paths to healthier self-esteem. Being a psychotherapist and clinical hypnotherapist, trained in what is called psychoanalytic, developmental psychology, and psycho-dynamic psychotherapy, I am, as you might expect, a firm believer in the benefit of "talk therapy." As part of the (usually) long-term psychotherapy in which I engage with my clients— largely a gay and lesbian, HIV-affected, or gay-supportive popu-lation—I've noticed the enormous benefits to the mental and physical well-being of clients, during the course of treatment, achieved through hypnosis, guided imagery/visualization and meditation. It was not a part of my training in psychology to utilize such techniques, but it was the focus of my doctoral train-ing as a hypnotherapist wanting preparation for further work in the field of mind-body medicine and HIV care. By bringing the two together, psychotherapy and hypnotherapy, as deemed use-ful and timely by a professional, I feel they pose extremely hope-ful possibilities for growth and transformation, in a wide array of issues, for both gay and non-gay people alike.

I do not use hypnotherapy with all clients who come to me for counseling or psychotherapy. And not all hypnotherapy cli-ents want psychotherapy; some come for specific mind-body work (wonderfully helpful with life-threatening conditions such as HIV, cancer, diabetes, etc.), age-regression work, or past-life work. Some may just want to learn self-hypnosis for what they see as a behavioral disorder such as smoking or overeating. (Although I don't agree that these are simply behavioral disor-ders, I do see a way for an individual to gain some degree of mastery over certain problems through behavior modification.) At any rate, knowing the appropriate times and situations in which to utilize a combination of these treatment choices can lead to remarkable, curative effects. I've seen it time and again with my own eyes! In fact, some of these success stories are illustrated in the following chapters so you can see with your own eyes what I consider an all-important message: *There is always hope.*

And so I offer this book to you, dear reader, trusting you to know if it is the right time for your own mental, physical, and spiritual journey into healing and growth, and if this is the right path for you to embark on in this chapter of your life. If you've picked it up off the shelf, chances are your curiosity can be counted on to be an accurate indication of your readiness.

So ... let the journey begin! As Goethe put it, *Whatever you can do, or dream you can, begin it. Boldness has genius, power, and magic in it.* Or, for the more theatrically minded, *Sing out, Louise!*

Warmly,

Dr. Rick

PART ONE

Understandings and Beginnings

We must cultivate our garden.

—Voltaire

PART ONE

Understandings and Beginnings

We must cultivate our garden.
—Voltaire

Chapter 1

On Self-Esteem and the Roots of Homophobia

Just trust yourself, then you will know how to live.
—Johann Wolfgang von Goethe

Self-esteem is not an "either-or" proposition.

It would be a disservice to your personal growth to think of self-esteem in black-and-white, all-or-nothing terms. It simply isn't true that you have *either* good self-esteem (which we'll also refer to as self-worth) *or* poor self-esteem. Such thinking presupposes that there are no gray areas to your opinions and feelings about yourself, or no areas of your life that are in flux, organically on the rise or on the wane.

It is perhaps more helpful—and more accurate—to think of the different parts of your life, and how your self-esteem fares in each part. We all have many parts, or areas, to our lives, which, for purposes of simplicity, can be visualized as pieces of a pie. A person's life may include, say, some basic areas like *home, work, school, a significant love relationship, friendships,* and *family of origin* (the family into which he or she was born). Each piece of the pie requires a different amount of time and energy, and each fulfills a different need: the need to be a student, a lover, a best friend, a son or daughter, and so on.

Each part of your life also carries with it the feelings you have about yourself in that area. For instance, perhaps you think of yourself as a good friend, a great lover, a so-so employee, and feel pretty guilty about being—in your opinion, anyway—a lousy daughter. Or maybe you see yourself as an accomplished career person, a devoted son, but feel just awful about the quality of your friendships and your string of transient love relationships. Perhaps you think very highly of yourself as a dad, but poorly of yourself as a son to your own father. Maybe previously you felt that you were an awful, cruel sibling to your sister, and now that you've grown older, you feel that you're a terrific sibling, but feel a sense of failure regarding the relationship with your parents. Maybe you believe you don't have anything to offer anyone, except your unique and fabulous sense of style. Get the idea? These are pieces of your pie, each with its own degree of self-esteem, each with a set of feelings you have *about yourself.*

Further, the different feelings that you have regarding your self-worth can be seen as though they exist along a continuum, and can change over different periods—or moments—in your life. Do you feel that you are excellent, very good, pretty good, fair, or poor in your role as a son or daughter? Have you always felt that way? Are you a terrific, boring, clumsy, or accomplished lover, according to your own opinion? Were you always? Do you notice that your opinions and feelings about yourself change over the years? Do you feel differently about yourself after you gain weight? Lose weight? And if you find yourself drinking "a bit too much," do you feel differently about yourself than when your drinking feels more in control? What about having a golden tan in the summertime versus how you may look during winter? Perhaps you feel critical or judgmental about yourself if you leave the house without makeup. Or if you haven't gone to the gym in two weeks. Or when you're at parties. Or stressed. Or tired. Maybe you feel fat and unattractive when you wear plaid!

Take a moment and think about yourself: Are there times when you feel especially good about who you are? Under what circumstances? What is that feeling like for you? How often do you have it? How long does it usually last? And conversely, when do you *not* feel good about yourself? Under which circumstances?

During, say, certain previous chapters of life? Perhaps right now? Has something happened to you recently that has adversely affected your self-worth? Do these feelings involve other people . . . your parents, your siblings, your partner(s), your colleagues or boss? How do you feel about yourself when you think of your ex-lover?

Several people I know have extraordinarily successful careers and feel quite empowered in their work lives. One friend in particular who was recently promoted at his company has begun to feel very accomplished with that part of himself, what he calls his "career-self," and believes that he is quite worthy, of great value to his own life and to the lives of others, at least in regard to the work he does. In this area of his life he experiences very high self-esteem but ask him if he thinks of himself this highly when it comes to love relationships and he becomes miserable with feelings of low self-worth, bemoaning himself as someone who is totally unable to emotionally commit to another human being. He has more meaningful and honest conversations with his dog, he says, than he's ever had with a lover.

In contrast, another acquaintance of mine considers herself "lucky in love." When asked to elaborate, she will tell you that she's in a relationship with a terrific partner, is herself the best lover she's ever been, and expects that the two of them will be together for the rest of their lives. She's even hard-pressed to think of a past lover with whom she did not have a successful relationship. But when it comes to her feelings about her abilities in the work force, she feels quite badly, in fact she feels worse as the years go by, and believes that she has no marketable skills, nothing of value to offer society, that she never has and never will. She seems quite stuck in this belief: This is an area where her self-esteem is quite low.

One of the benefits to thinking about self-esteem in this way, as pieces of a pie, is that although there may be some parts of yourself about which you do not feel positive or hopeful, there are other parts where you do. Even if your immediate response is that you don't feel good about yourself in any aspect of your life or in any identity you may have, that just means you need to look more closely. What is it about you from which you can derive some positive regard, whether in the present, or even in the past? We each possess some gift, be it modest or grand, few or many, some aspect to who we are that is commendable, even to the harshest critic (which is usually yourself!). Think about it. Then realize that it is from that aspect of yourself where you experience positive self-esteem that you can gather the strength to help you in your process of working on the rest. This is one approach to self-esteem work and it can be a highly effective way to begin.

For example: You feel that you're too heavy and your weight has been a source of low self-esteem your whole life. You don't know if you have the ability or strength to make the healthier lifestyle changes you'll need in order to feel better about yourself physically. If you were sitting across from me in my office, one question I would ask you is in what areas of your life have you experienced success? Perhaps you put yourself through school, or have kept yourself successfully employed. Maybe you've excelled at some creative hobby, or have developed several long-lasting, satisfying friendships. The point is, you undoubtedly have reason to feel good about yourself right now, overweight or not!

But—and here is where the battle is great—you may not feel able to acknowledge or accept those reasons as worthy, *of value*. They very likely may be overshadowed by your feelings about yourself as a heavy person. Potentially, there could be many areas of pride and esteem to your life, minimized, unfortunately, by one overwhelming, potent area of low self-esteem. Think about this: You've shown your unique and considerable capabilities to undertake challenges as witnessed in the areas of your life where you've felt successful. You've displayed strength, courage, creativity, resourcefulness, responsibility . . . who knows what else? From this fact you can honestly ascertain that you certainly deserve to feel positive about *these* aspects of who you are. Self-esteem is not all-or-nothing. Look closely. Remember: Your accomplishments are real and valid no matter where you are in your process.

Throughout this book you'll hopefully find that your confidence can be bolstered, and your inner strength shored up for, perhaps, any challenge. Self-esteem work is often the process of "borrowing" the positive and empowered feelings from one area of your life, then learning to apply that confidence in another area. The parts of you that you feel need work can benefit from the healthy parts. It is a process. Therapy and various forms of meditation are extremely helpful toward such an end.

The point is that you'll be more successful on your weight-loss or exercise program, for instance, if you're in touch with those areas of yourself that you are proud of, that help you feel worthy, that offer you feelings of positive self-regard. You're heavy? So what? Good for you that you want to improve your health. Understanding and believing in your very heart of hearts that you're a valid and worthwhile person *right now*, a person *in process*, will help you achieve your goals, whatever form your goals may take. Other examples . . .

You feel that you're not intelligent and you want more education, but fear failing in school. Or you think you're too skinny, and want to buff up at the gym, even though you feel far too intimidated to go. Or you feel that you're too shy, or too serious, or not serious enough, or unpersonable, undesirable, unlovable, and on and on. The same way of thinking about self-esteem applies, no matter what particular challenges you might face. You have reason to feel good about yourself right now, as a work in progress. (After all, each of us is a work in progress.) The reasons may be hard to find at first, so look carefully. Ask a close friend, a confidant, to help you start the ball rolling, to help you with a fresh perspective about yourself. It is often hardest to look into our own mirrors and honestly accept what's there, both positive and negative.

Part of the journey you're embarking on right now, by reading this book, is to find out why it might be hard to feel good about yourself. What has gone on for you personally, and what do you face as part of a community, that you need to address in order for you to fully understand the obstacles you face? And then what must you face to learn what to do about these obstacles? Let's look further at this.

We see now that self-esteem is specific to each area of life, and that it looks different on different people. Also, we see that it can fluctuate—as along a continuum—during different stages or even different moments in life. Just as self-esteem can vary tremendously from one area of life to another, so too it can vary from one chapter, or time, of life to another. Understanding self-esteem requires us to go even deeper than this: We're not only talking about *parts of life;* we are also talking about *parts of ourselves,* our different identities.

In other words, the perception of oneself as not being able to do well in a certain aspect of life can translate into adopting a negative identity, and therefore, lead one to feel depressed, discouraged, hopeless, helpless, frustrated . . . all sorts of painful possibilities. So, for example, "I feel badly about the fact that I haven't yet learned how to be a good student," which may be a simple truth, translates to a harsh, "I'm a *bad person* for being a bad student." Or, coming up short on job skills—a highly learnable and therefore fixable proposition—becomes a hopeless, "I'm a no-good worker. I'm a bum. I'll never amount to anything." Having not been taught helpful skills for basic decision-making can lead to a general confusion about life, and an identity that proclaims, "I don't even know what's good for me! I'm such a dummy!" Tell a kid enough times that he doesn't have any common sense and guess what he'll have to contend with? "I'm someone who doesn't have the sense God gave a tree! I'm useless!" A frustrating, depressing belief—and *identity*—to overcome each time he attempts to do well in school, get a job, or develop a meaningful relationship.

As human beings we have a tendency, as we connect our different identities and feelings of worth to our different areas of life, to continue these ways of thinking and feeling about ourselves in a manner that becomes almost a cruel habit, exacerbating the problem as it gains momentum. For example, if someone feels that he or she cannot hold down a job, the internal belief may become more than, simply, "I'm no good at holding a job." It becomes, *"I am such a loser* because I can *never* hold a job." This powerful and destructive identity becomes one that this person may believe forever! Further, he or she may apply this self-belief to *other* parts of him- or herself as well. The negative identity generalizes, spreading from one piece of the pie to another. Now it's about a job, then it's about not being able to find a good apartment, then a relationship . . . on and on it continues. Of course, given this belief, it will undoubtedly be harder and harder to gain employment (or an apartment, or a lover), seeing as how they expect *not* to be able to! So, maybe this person ends up feeling okay about some parts and identities, his or her ability, say, to be good with animals, or to be a successful gardener, but feels like a "loser" everywhere else. What an insidious and shame-filled belief! And such an emotionally painful, burdened way to go through life.

Just how could such a vicious cycle have begun?

Any number of scenarios—and everyone's scenarios are different—could be possible. Imagine something like this: Perhaps the word "loser" was a common one in this person's family of origin, and was something that people were referred to with derision and shame whenever they failed at doing something. Picture a young boy who maybe had a learning difficulty and had trouble doing his math homework, so his impatient father, standing over him and tapping his foot, called him a *worthless loser.* These feelings of frustration, shame, and scorn went on night after night. Or maybe his brother laughed at him and called him a loser whenever he wasn't picked for the sports teams at school. Get the idea? The specifics are speculative, but all with similar devastating results.

Such criticisms, especially when they occur early in life, become what is called a *self-fulfilling prophecy:* When a person is repeatedly told something about himself, and it takes hold, eventually he grows to believe it, and then consequently makes choices which fulfill what he understands to be true about himself. He internalizes the label and makes it his own. If, in the above example, "loser" was indeed an early label, then not surprisingly, this person would all too easily (and unconsciously) start to live up (or down) to it, still thinking of himself this way, and still feeling quite badly about himself for it many years later. What a different outcome it would have been if he had been told, say, that he was a bright and wonderful young man! How happy with himself he would have felt, how hopeful and deserving of the healthy, rewarding things in life! Unfortunately, he is now quite likely to unconsciously make life choices which, to him, continue to prove the identity, continue to fulfill the prophecy: I am a loser.

Self-fulfilling prophecies, while usually born in childhood, are certainly not felt only during early chapters of life. The echoes from the past that cause a person to experience low self-worth, can—and often do—develop even further in all sorts of very common adult circumstances. If a spouse or partner is told, for instance, time and time again, what a terrible and unsatisfying lover he is, he may come to accept it, believe it, and behave accordingly ... the words undoubtedly resonating from some tucked-away earlier self-belief ("You're a terrible child!" "You're a terrible student!"). It may be a very difficult identity to fight, too, given that these words came from trusted adults earlier, and are coming from someone trusted now; given that this person is probably feeling pretty depressed and worthless; and given that these feelings are like familiar old skeletons re-emerging from a dark, hollow, and lonely closet. Who can be a good lover when his ego, already shaky from childhood, is being trampled on?

These are just a few blatant examples of negative internal dialogue (sometimes called self-talk), harsh labels, and perpetuating beliefs that feed low self-worth. In reality, the beliefs one has about one's own worth come from a full and complex past, can be quite subtle and therefore confusing, and are frequently accompanied by depression, anxiety, physical ailments, stress, personality changes, destructive behavior, or even life-threatening illness. As you might imagine, if left unexamined, these kinds of internal beliefs can have horrendous, lifelong effects, sabotaging happiness at every turn.

For gay men and lesbians, the messages that contribute to low self-esteem can, and frequently do, begin in childhood with the subtle comments heard around the house, the playground, and throughout perhaps all areas of society. On top of whatever *other* negative messages may come the child's way, there is the battering club of homophobia to contend with. If a visiting uncle tells homophobic jokes and everyone in the family laughs, but no one points out the cruelty, then a message about homosexuality comes across to the child loud and clear: It's bad, it's laughable, it's not worth our respect. When "fag" is the very worst thing you can be called in the schoolyard, again, the message is clear: whatever you do, do not become a fag. When a book in the town library is pulled because it contains a scene depicting a lesbian kiss, we learn that romantic affection between women is wrong. (Later on we'll find out, in a real-life example, that similarly Chrysler pulled its sponsorship during an important, historic television episode: *Ellen*'s coming out. At least when we're adults, we can boycott the purchase of Jeeps . . . but the message is still received, loud and clear.)

Perhaps less subtle words come from the pulpit, with Mom and Dad sitting in rapt attention in their Sunday finery, listening as gays, murderers, prostitutes, and thieves are lumped together as a group that is harmful and threatening to our children, family, and society at large. Gay people are in the same theological category as murderers? (And they must repent!) Conveniently forgotten are the warm and poetic Bible passages that teach of Jesus's unconditional love for the prostitute Mary Magdalene. Or the fact that as society has changed, so too have scholarly interpretations of all major religious tomes. More about this in a later chapter.

Is it any wonder, then, that the seeds of self-loathing are often planted in the mind and heart of a young gay person from childhood, taking root throughout adolescence and blossoming right up into adulthood? It is not surprising that the national organization PFLAG (Parents, Family, and Friends of Lesbians and Gays) has recently released the statistic that the gay teenage suicide rate is thirty percent higher than the national average. If our country is so concerned about America's youth, why aren't there more Gay and Lesbian Studies programs in our schools so that gay youth can proudly see their roots in history, making contributions in every field imaginable? Why don't we teach courses in health education devoted to safer sex for young gays and lesbians? The message is not lost on the adolescent: As a gay person, I don't matter.

Almost all of the teens I talk to in Los Angeles know of someone in their age group who has been kicked out of his own home for being gay or lesbian. The variable isn't the city of Los Angeles, it's homophobia. It happens in all communities, urban, suburban, or rural. Young people aren't on the streets of Hollywood, hustling tricks and suffering the devastating blows to their self-esteem because they felt it was a promising career choice. They're there because they were kicked out, they have no place else to go. They told the wrong person that they're gay.

The collective blows to gay and lesbian self-esteem continue throughout society.

In the media: When Elizabeth Taylor, upon receiving a special award from the Screen Actors Guild union, loudly and strongly declared, "If it weren't for homosexuals, there would be no Hollywood!" gays and lesbians shouted in gratitude in front of their television sets all across the country. Ms. Taylor, however, was later derided by many of her peers and received unkind press in some of this country's major mainstream publications for her statement. You mean, homosexuals abound in Hollywood? *Hellooo.*

A couple who are friends of mine, Eric and Jon, are planning a trip to Hawaii, to celebrate their union and commitment to each other in a ceremony with their close friends and relatives, overlooking a glorious waterfall. "Do people stop and think of the irony," Jon pondered, "that gays are reputed to be promiscuous and unable to maintain long-term relationships, but our own government keeps us from getting legally married? From sanctioning our long-term relationships?"

"And the other thing that burns me," added Eric, "is that we can die for our country in the armed services, but can't mention that we may have a boyfriend at home waiting for us, because we 'can't tell' anyone that we're gay."

"We can also pay taxes like everybody else," Jon said, "but aren't allowed the same spousal benefits as straight couples." As a medical doctor, Jon works right alongside other doctors—repairing the same wounds, handling the same hospital emergencies—who, because they are heterosexual, can arrange to have their spouses covered with what is perhaps one of the best medical insurance plans in the nation. As Jon's significant other, Eric is not allowed the same benefits, simply because they are a same-sex couple. These two men are just as committed to each other as any other couple they know, gay or straight. (By the way, Eric's parents are refusing to attend the ceremony.)

All this emotional pain, all these lifelong, harmful, esteem-lowering messages, are sent to gay people from the schoolyard right up to our own government, in the media as well as at home, simply because of a fear of the differences in sexual identity.

Where exactly does all this fear come from?

The roots of homophobia lie in our society's devaluing of women. That's a strong statement, but think about it: If our society held in regard that which we consider "female" or label as "feminine" as highly as that which we consider "male" or "masculine," then the feminine in each of us would be held in the same high esteem as the masculine. We would embrace *all* of the person, the creative, nurturing "earth mother" as well as the protective "hunter-gatherer." In every individual, these parts, far from being shamed or ridiculed, would be nurtured and encouraged, would be valued as equally important and necessary, in whatever degree they exist and whether in the body of a man or a woman. A society that has been dedicated, for so many centuries, to suppressing The Woman, the archetypal life-giver, cannot simultaneously glorify or even appreciate that which is characteristic of woman.

When a male displays characteristics traditionally viewed as masculine, he is praised. Whether it is absorbed during his first understanding of heterosexual intercourse (The Talk), or during a boast session in the high school locker room, a boy is taught to "act like a man" and he is rewarded highly, with the acceptance and admiration of his peers. Women are least threatening in a patriarchal society when they "act like women," when they "know their place," which, as we all know, is several professional, personal, and socially sanctioned steps behind men. (Of course, the fact that "acting like a woman" has boundaries defined by men is not lost on any of the women I know!)

But let a woman be assertive in her field (assertiveness being traditionally a male value) and she will undoubtedly be harangued by male colleagues, perhaps even referred to in derogatory terms, even at this point in our history . . . or *her*story. Or let a man excel at nurturing, or in a creative art, and the natural assumption, more times than not, will be that he is gay. (In a word-association test, it would go something like this: Unenlightened society, think of the first sexual identity that comes to your mind. Ready? Hairdresser . . . gay man. Florist . . . gay man. Male flight attendant . . . gay man. Female truck driver . . . lesbian. Doctor . . . straight man. Lawyer . . . straight man. Provider . . . straight man. Nurse . . . straight woman. Schoolteacher . . . straight woman. Nurturer . . . straight woman. Liberace . . . flamboyant gay man. Barbra Streisand . . . pushy broad.)

Why do some people assume that sensitivity will only be found in a man who's gay, or that it *should* be found in women? Then, think about this: Why are budgets for arts programs in our schools (creativity) constantly under attack, while the national budget for military spending and weapons development (about as phallic as we can get) is limitless? Are these the actions of a society that values, honors, and rewards that which is creative in all of us? Is this a society that rewards the feminine as it rewards the masculine? What kind of collective, permeating, government-sanctioned misogyny (and therefore homophobia) is this?

It's no wonder, then, that little boys learn that being called a "girl" or "sissy" is akin to being called a "fag." What are we teaching our children about the value of each human being, about kindness, compassion, open-mindedness and open-heartedness, about tolerance for people's differences and about the lifelong importance of developing healthy self-esteem . . . their own and that of others?

Of course, not all kids are mean. Some are open-minded and compassionate and will make wonderful leaders of tomorrow. Not all families laugh at homophobic jokes. Many embrace with love the different sexual identities of others. Not all preachers are anti-gay. More and more are standing up for equality of God's love and perform same-sex unions despite resistance from their superiors. Not all arts programs are being cut from our schools, and not all gay teenagers are kicked out into the street or even feel unwanted. Times are changing, they say, and yes, that pretty much has to be true: The one thing time does is change. In most respects, we've come a very long way from the Stonewall riots of 1969. But perhaps times are changing too slowly for the gay teens who have committed suicide. Perhaps the homophobic messages that throw such tremendous obstacles in the way of healthy self-esteem for young gays and lesbians are still being sent loud and clear, at home, in the media, in church, at school. These messages are insidious and seductive, often too overwhelming for a young ego, already frightened of being different, to take a stand against, to reject. The messages are everywhere and they attack, bash, discriminate, and reduce the healthy self-esteem of beautiful, creative, talented young people, perpetuating a self-fulfilling prophecy that being gay is bad.

What is the antidote?

The answer lies within you, and begins with the commitment to your own process, your own growth. *Whatever negative or painful messages that now come from within are the result of internalizing the false and unkind messages you've heard, perhaps building one upon the other, since childhood.* (Read that sentence again, please. Say it out loud. Write it down. *Internalize* it!) We must learn to develop an emotional immune system to counter the effects of negative societal messages. Remember: You were not born thinking yourself a loser, or a bad lover, or a bum, or a terrible daughter or son. You were not born hating yourself. You were born loving yourself (and everyone else). Your commitment to growth is the path to getting that love back. Your commitment to growth is the way to recover your self-esteem. All is not lost or hopeless; you are not doomed to feeling unworthy; you do not have to take on the burdens of the world; you do not have to sacrifice your creativity; you do not have to hide who you are.

You simply need to commit to yourself, *whoever you are at this moment*—however you look, however you feel, whatever you think of yourself. The answer lies in committing *right now*.

That is the ultimate message—to yourself!—that you believe you are worthy.

(*Note:* There is a self-assessment exercise in Chapter 20 of this book to accompany the issues discussed in this chapter. You may wish to go there now to further your understanding of your specific issues around self-esteem, or you may want to consider taking all the assessments after you've completed the book.)

The Affirmations

Try repeating these morning, noon, and night . . . whenever and wherever your self-esteem requires a shot in the arm. Consider taping them to your bathroom mirror or on the dashboard of your car. Is your self-esteem low at work? Frame them and put them on your desk. Let them become your *new* self-fulfilling prophecies!

I began in love.
If I want to believe any message about myself, it is this:
I . . . am . . . lovable.

Whoever I am right now, at this very moment,
I am unique, I am worthy, I am lovable.

I am worth whatever I make up my mind to be worth.

I can believe me when I say,
I am a fabulous, unique, highly valuable, and gifted work in progress.

Chapter 2

On Meditation and Coming Out

*Lift up your faces, you have a
piercing need
For this bright morning dawning
for you.*

—Maya Angelou,
On the Pulse of Morning

M editation is a process.
Through meditation we go about deepening our attention, our awareness, and our self-understanding . . . one moment at a time. It is a way for us to awaken and sharpen our sense of ourselves, not only to who we are, but also to what we are capable of. It helps us to see the unfolding of our emotional lives, and how each moment influences what happens next.

Thoreau, in writing about his experiences at Walden Pond said, "Only that day dawns to which we are awake." Buddhism teaches that without meditation, we are not really awake; rather, our conscious state is more like an extended dream state than a place of awareness. Our conscious state has limits when it comes to self-understanding. Meditation helps us to unfold beyond those limits, to be more awake within ourselves, thereby helping us to live our lives more fully, with all the richness and possibilities for growth, transformation, and healing.

Meditation, it is said, is a way to evoke the relaxation response (more about this in Chapter 5). It is a method of centering and focusing the self; a way to relax mind and body; it is known to calm the physiological systems of the body; a way to relieve stress, ease anxiety, and alleviate depression; it is a way to bolster self-esteem. Meditation has been clinically demonstrated to do all of this, and much more.

Meditation is something to come to in your own time, at that point in your life when you are ready to look inward and listen carefully to yourself—when you are ready for the kind of gentle growth that emerges out of quietness. Meditation is very much about listening and witnessing, breathing, and being present. It is very little about doing. (In fact, two of the central concepts in Zen meditation are called "nothingness" and "non-doing.") This is not to say, however, that meditating doesn't require something of you. It requires a great deal of commitment, actually: a commitment that you make to yourself, to your own ability to witness and participate in the blooming of who you are, and who you can be. This is not unlike the coming-out process, but we'll get to that a little later.

Meditation involves simplicity, but it also involves the whole compilation of feelings you've had throughout your life, and all the feelings you are capable of. It involves non-judging and letting go, even though you may want to hold firmly to all your opinions about yourself and about others. It involves oneness and yet a connectedness, confusion and clarity, frustration and peace. It involves patience and a willingness to observe yourself. It involves learning, growing, transforming, becoming, and centering—all achieved through the art of not-doing.

If you might be feeling some confusion and frustration right now, let me also tell you that meditation begins, as do all journeys, with a simple, natural breath. By being fully aware of nothing else, just that breath . . . just that one graceful, calming moment of breath. (Sounds peaceful already, doesn't it?)

As I mentioned in the introduction, this is not a how-to on meditation, exactly. More, it is a bit of a guide, an invitation, really, to explore and experience healing meditation for yourself, using the examples and suggestions in this book. Although I myself meditate regularly, I would no more attempt to teach you how to meditate than I would attempt to teach you how to breathe. There are many topics I've taught over the years, and yet when someone asks, "How should I meditate?" I tell them, "I have no idea." The truth is I do not know how you should or will meditate, I only know the ways I meditate, and what has worked well for people in my life—family, friends, and clients. What the experience will be for you depends on many factors, including your specific desires and goals as they apply to your own emotional and spiritual growth. There are many, many kinds of meditation, and I encourage you to explore them through books, retreats, workshops, and, of course, through your own experimenting. For that is where meditation evolves for the individual: through the experiencing. Meditation is not unlike the smell of bread baking, the yellow of a daisy, the feel of a breeze: it is a rich, personal, and wholly indescribable experience. Words are woefully inadequate.

What I will offer you are the ways to begin your journey, using the affirmations and the very user-friendly meditations in the following chapters. This book deals primarily with "contemplative," "awareness," "empowerment," and "healing" meditations, which are designed to help you be present to your thoughts and feelings, to enrich your internal universe with greater insight and strength, and help you to heal from emotional wounds.

Healing requires being present, being aware of yourself. When we have a physical scar, the body automatically knows how to focus on that scar, and it begins to heal the wound on its own. This provides us with a metaphor: When we have emotional wounds, we must learn how to focus and be present in order to heal those internal scars. Emotional healing does not happen without our conscious participation, our vigilant focus. In order to repair our psychic wounds, we must call upon our emotional, psychological, physical, and spiritual resources. Meditation helps us to do that; to be present, focused, and aware.

At the heart of meditation is a concept called *mindfulness*. In his book, *Wherever You Go, There You Are*, Jon Kabat-Zinn describes mindfulness this way:

Mindfulness means paying attention in a particular way: on purpose, in the present moment, and nonjudgmentally. This kind of attention nurtures greater awareness, clarity, and acceptance of present-moment reality. It wakes us up to the fact that our lives unfold only in moments. If we are not fully present for many of those moments, we may not only miss what is most valuable in our lives but also fail to realize the richness and the depth of our possibilities for growth and transformation.

Being fully present to who we are, accepting and not judging, really knowing about ourselves and being true to that knowledge, can seem to gay men and lesbians a frightening luxury. In a society where the norm is based on numbers, being a minority—particularly a minority that is endowed with strong historical prejudice—can be a harsh slice of reality, a reason to feel like running from the truth as opposed to embracing it. Being "in the closet" means hiding this truth in the darkness; "coming out" of the closet means revealing the truth to light. Coming out, like meditation itself, is an individual, highly personal process.

Just as the sun's rays shine down on all living things, allowing for life itself, so does shining light on inner truth allow for life, an honest and fully integrated life. We cannot be whoever we are capable of becoming without conscious participation in our individual, personal truths. In other words, the question is: Who am I? The answer is found through a commitment to rigorous honesty. If we are to bloom as gay men and lesbians, then genuineness, self-honesty, and self-exploration must be at the core of our efforts. Only then, once personal truths are acknowledged and accepted *for oneself,* do the growth possibilities become rich for nurturance, self-esteem, and transformation. As Ralph Waldo Emerson once said, "Nothing can bring you peace but yourself."

Coming out is not about others. Coming out is about oneself. Like meditation, it is a highly personal process each must come to when ready. Meditation is but one path in this process, one path to enlightenment via the self-exploration of fears, doubts, and inner prejudices that keep us from ourselves. The worst enemy of a gay person is not the homophobia experienced from others. It's not the small-minded people in the small towns we live in; nor the damning preacher at the pulpit who claims to speak God's word while in actuality preaching intolerance; nor the self-aggrandizing politicians we elect; nor our own unenlightened family members. No, the worst enemy is within.

Internalized homophobia is what keeps us from ourselves and from truly connecting with others. It keeps us from knowing our spiritual selves. It is what keeps us from pursuing the better job, moving to the better neighborhood, and developing the healthy relationship. *It keeps us from feeling deserving.* It is the insidious voice that says we do not deserve to be acknowledged, accepted, and loved simply for who we are.

Gay people, fearing exposure, ever aware of the messages, moods, and responses from others, have developed a keen social radar—*gaydar*—which distinguishes acceptance from nonacceptance. It seems in our society that nonacceptance spews out of the biggest, loudest mouths, often couched in the saccharine terms of family values and religious or societal preservation. (As if a family, society, or congregation of gay people are not *of value.*) And so, in an effort to keep from internalizing such cruel invalidities, we shout right back. We parade. We protest. We learned from our Stonewall forefathers and foremothers not to take it anymore!

Each of those public efforts (while affronting to those who wish us not to flaunt our sexual identities in their faces) is earnest and important. It is a way to change laws: with the right to freedom of speech. It is a way to increase AIDS funding: with the right to assemble. It is a way to be heard through the deafening roar of homophobia, bigotry, and status quo. It is a way to rock the boat. It is a way to shine the spotlight on important human injustices, to explain to the world that gays and lesbians remain the one group of human beings who, even now at the doorstep of the twenty-first century, are still denied basic human rights which are granted to all other persons in our country. *Listen up, world!* we shout.

But where is the internal peace of which Emerson speaks?

Where can we find the healthy voice within, to protest and over-take the *internalized* shouting that says we are not okay. There are messages we picked up in childhood starting, perhaps, even before birth, that have influenced our feelings about ourselves. Messages that, even then, contained the condemnation of being gay. Messages that were planted early, watered often, and have had plenty of time to take root. They have taught us not only how to behave, but how to *be,* if we are to be accepted, if we are to reap the rewards that come from being like others, from pleasing others. Messages that said what was right and what was wrong. These messages, carrying with them the lesson that nothing short of the withdrawal of love is the price to pay for disregard, taught gay people to listen very carefully to what is being said on the outside, and disregard instead, what is true on the inside.

So the young child, whose ego is still in the formative years, learns—at school, in the library, on the streets, at the place of worship, at the family dinner table—exactly which path to follow to find the love and acceptance of others. As the child grows, developing and noticing feelings that are different from those of other kids, from those described in books, on television and in conversation, the inner conflict begins.

Most unfortunately, due to the unrelenting barrage of societal messages, this conflict is accompanied by great fear and tremen-dous shame. Gay people learn early on that they are not simply a minority in society, but they are also a minority in their own heterosexual family. A straight person of an ethnic minority likely still has the bosom of his or her family in which to feel some safety, empowerment, and unity . . . to learn that society's preju-diced voice is the wrong voice, the one *not* to internalize. A person of a sexual minority stands alone: a closet within a closet, as their own family feels like a very unsafe place. This is not to say that the family is necessarily unloving. This is to say that the family can feel unsafe. To the gay child who hears, within his own home, the telling of jokes at gays' expense, the love of that family is very clearly and frighteningly conditional. Unless a gay person is born into a family that gives the message, "You're gay! Good for you!" then he or she learns exactly which voice to heed, the inner or the outer. No wonder it can be so difficult to come out of that damn closet!

Through meditation, the inner voice can speak. By being quiet and with ourselves, we can witness internalized shames and fears while we witness the voice of our true nature. We can return to our true selves. Keep in mind: The development of internalized homophobia began its process after birth, as the messages came in and took hold. At birth however, the spark of life that was the new human person was, on its own, one of pure love, and carried with it the developing ability to unconditionally love others and love itself.

To visualize a world without the homophobic messages that become internalized is to visualize a world of people who are able to love themselves, whomever they may be, whomever they may become. A world that embraces, naturally and without reservation, gay men and women with the same acceptance, love, and peace afforded to all others.

This is the world that awaits within.

The Affirmations

Try repeating these to yourself—one at a time, or all together—several times a day, especially first thing in the morning and right before going to sleep at night. Which speak most directly to your own coming-out issues? Which touch your true nature? Are there other affirmations you can create, designed to honor your true self?

In the quiet, I know who I am.

In the quiet, I know I am good, and loving, and lovable.

I breathe, and know I am uniquely, beautifully human.

I breathe, and know I am deserving of love.

There's no shame in my game!

Chapter 3

Everyday Life, Part I: Altered States of Consciousness

I will work in my own way, according to the light that is in me.
—Lydia Maria Child

I was talking to my best friend's mother, Sue, about meditation, hypnosis, guided imagery, and visualization. She is a very kind and gentle spirit, devoting much of her life to helping others and to her spiritual path, which happens to take the form of the Protestant Methodist religion. I believe it is safe to say that she (along with the rest of her family) had very little exposure to gay people, living, as they do, in a modest city surrounded by agriculture in California's central valley region. That is, until her daughter became best friends with a gay man.

I was not aware, until our discussion, that she held some personal beliefs which would be considered quite progressive by others at her church. I was telling her how awareness-enriching techniques, such as those I mentioned above, were often considered New Age, and yet were quite ancient. Self-hypnosis and meditation have been around, in one form or another, for many thousands of years, being received by different societies, alternately, as wise and organic and spiritual, or bewitching and supernatural, depending on where history's pendulum had swung. Ever since my own mother told me, as a young child, stories of ancient Native American tribes exercising their meditative powers for healing and wisdom, as well as in their holy dying processes, I have always believed in meditation as a path for the balance of mind, body, and spirit. Consequently, I've looked upon Western medicine with some degree of trepidation, and some degree of appreciation.

"Really," Sue said, "meditation is simply a form of prayer. And the calmness, the asking for inner strength that comes with praying is a natural part of everyday living, whether people are aware of it or not."

"So you think meditation and prayer are synonymous?" I asked.

"Whenever we are quiet, with thoughts of ourselves or our Maker, or just sitting with peacefulness or love, aren't we in prayer? Aren't we meditating?"

That's when I realized that meditation is a commonality shared by all people, regardless of spiritual or religious orientation, in one form or another. Meditation, however one wishes to think of it, or whatever one calls it, happens all the time, perhaps to all of us, in everyday living.

In a sense, we are engaging in meditation whether we pray formally with an organized religious group, or we stop in the middle of unloading groceries from the car to take a deep breath. Maybe we're "sitting zazen," the formal meditation practice found in Zen meditation, or maybe we're sitting in our car on the freeway, in the middle of stopped traffic, turning inward in thought. Meditation can occur at the beach, in a synagogue, in a bus, park, shower, airport, crowd, garden, living room, or elevator. One can be standing, sitting, walking or lying down, and be meditating, in one form or another. It can happen right smack in the middle of a business meeting. It can be spring, winter, morning, or night. Raining or snowing. It occurs at age two, twenty, or a hundred and twenty. Meditation can just happen, or can be prepared for and engaged thoughtfully.

The reason for this is that what we're really talking about here is an altered state of consciousness. Sometimes we purposely guide ourselves into an altered state, and we call that meditation, or self-hypnosis, or visualization, etc. Sometimes we have another person helping to guide us, as when listening to a meditation tape, or doing a group meditation or guided imagery. And sometimes we spontaneously enter an altered state for reasons of stress, relief, emotions or thoughts we may be having, or simply due to the body's natural internal clock.

When you awaken in the morning, you are actually moving through several altered states, as you arise from deep sleep, to lighter sleep, to partial consciousness, to a fully awakened state. (Some people notice a heightened creativity at one or another of these states; others notice emotional changes. It's a different experience for each person.) Similar shifts occur when you are driving your car along a monotonous road, or when you're listening to a lecture, or having a creative idea, or feeling a strong emotion. You shift, usually subtly, sometimes abruptly, from state to state. It's the most natural thing in the world; and if you're not paying close attention, it happens without your conscious awareness.

Ever notice how sometimes when you're driving, you can cover several blocks or even miles without being mindful of what you're doing? When you re-emerge into awareness, what's known as full beta consciousness, you wonder what happened back there. Where did those miles go? What was I thinking about? Very often when this happens you cannot remember anything— not your thoughts during that time, your feelings, the scenery— nothing. You really seemed to zone out.

While we can consider this the opposite of being mindful (see Chapter 2), I would suggest to you that entering such a state of consciousness, a state whereby you leave, take a break, seemingly withdraw from your life, is most often in response to some primary physiological or psychological need. It's almost as if your body and mind have taken over to give you a break. Your body and mind know better than you that you need a few moments to, on the surface anyway, zone out. What's really happening is that your body needs to relax its systems—for instance, slow down your breathing or adjust your heart rate. Perhaps your mind has been overwhelmed and needs to settle down and clear out; your whole being needs to relax and recharge. You were in a state alert enough to avoid a fender-bender, but you were on automatic pilot for a few minutes there. You were in an altered state.

This is not to say that all altered states, or all meditations, are created equal. For instance, certainly there is a difference in quality and intent between formal meditation that fills the purposeful hour each morning and simply enjoying a quiet moment with a cup of designer coffee. While both may offer undeniable benefits of serenity, energy, and perhaps even mindfulness at times, there are distinct differences to such moments. Depending on the individual's needs, one's meditating may serve to quiet the mind, allow for the nonjudgmental arising of feelings, heighten focus, strengthen awareness, or provide any number of other benefits. Meditation often opens the emotional pathways that allow for the answers to a person's highly personal questions to emerge, as the time is right. Although drinking coffee has seemed lately to be elevated to a near-spiritual status (How many Starbucks do you have on *your* block?), we're usually not quite so evolved because of a good cup of java!

On the other hand, there are similarities between meditation and what we do by rote every day. Whenever we are sitting quietly, perhaps relaxing for a moment after breakfast and listening to the birds singing in the trees, or when we are taking that first big, yawning stretch in bed before beginning the morning routine, on some level we are indeed attempting similar benefits to that of meditation, in a less structured and informal way. Maybe we are organizing our thoughts for the day, shoring up our focus for what lies ahead, taking a final, strengthening breath to gather our energy. We are then clearing our mind and helping the mind-body connection to kick in, giving our physiological systems a chance to start working in harmony, which we'll need for a long, illness-free day.

Again, all of this may be totally outside of our conscious awareness. If someone were to ask what you're doing, you'd probably say, *Oh, nothing. Just sitting here.* But the point remains: Whether we know it or not, on some level of our consciousness where mental and physical health receive priority attention for their importance to our very survival, we are engaged in reaping the benefits of meditation.

So, we see that it's happening all the time, whether we're mindful of it or not. Now, if we want to further our commitment to our mental and physical well-being, if we want to learn to focus our attention in a *conscious* way, if we desire greater awareness of our thought processes and feelings, if we want to better understand ourselves and the world we live in and if we want to heal ourselves emotionally, then we begin to look at meditation as an everyday way of life. We already do it in one form or another. Now we begin to give meditation our conscious attention.

The Meditation

This short meditation is an excellent beginning for people to become more conscious of their own altered states, and to realize their internal ability to shift these states. We can grow more mindful of our day-to-day shifts in consciousness, and learn how to guide them to our advantage, by working on the focus of the breath. Try this meditation daily, or whenever you wish to slow down the pace of your day. It may be read slowly by a friend, or silently to oneself.

Take a deep breath. And exhale. Again, slowly inhale. And exhale.

As you continue to breathe, let your focus come to the relaxing of your body.

Inhale . . . exhale.

Slowly and mindfully, feel the air moving into your lungs, then feel the relaxation as you exhale. Feel your shoulders rise and fall. Feel your chest rise and fall. Take in cool, clean air every time you inhale, and breathe out stress each time you exhale.

Pause.

Let your awareness come to your whole body now. As you breathe, focus on each individual body part and notice how it responds. Head . . . shoulders . . . arms . . . torso . . . stomach . . . buttocks . . . thighs . . . legs . . . feet.

Observe what happens to your body as you breathe.

Pause.

Now let your awareness move to your mind. Watch your mind think as you breathe. Witness your thoughts. Just witness, without trying to control.

Pause.

Return your focus to your breath. What is happening to your breath? Has it slowed down? Become deeper? Lighter?

How do you feel, physically, at this moment? How do you feel, emotionally, at this moment? What is happening with your body? What is happening with your thoughts?

Pause.

Now, let your mind clear. Let it settle like small dust particles falling to the ground. Picture your breath clearing out your thoughts. With each breath, the dust settles more and more. Relax. Settle.

Let your inner voice become quiet. Peaceful. Let yourself enjoy this deep, relaxed feeling, this altered state. Feel the relaxing quality of meditating.

Long pause.

When you are ready, take a very deep, energizing breath.

Chapter 4

Everyday Life, Part II: Self-Esteem Messages

Life teaches us to be less harsh with ourselves and with others.
—Johann Wolfgang von Goethe

We've looked at how meditation and other altered states exist in everyday life. There's something else that happens every day, too, especially for gay people, and it can pose a tremendous challenge: It is the ongoing affront to our self-esteem. Again, whether we are aware of it or not, we are constantly being bombarded by messages that are intended, consciously or unconsciously, to keep us down, alienate us from our true selves, or make clear just how unwelcome we are in certain arenas of life.

Some of these messages are more direct and cruelly motivated than others. Some are simply the result of careless thought or action. These messages come from people we know, and people we don't know. They come from nearly all areas of life at one time or another. Sometimes they are done with malicious forethought and sometimes with regret. Regardless of the motivation involved, the effect can be the same. It can be devastating at a very central, core, primitive level of who we are. It threatens to destroy our innate ability to be happy, successful, productive, uninhibited, free-thinking, creative individuals. It is destructive to our mental, physical, and spiritual health.

Again, if we want to heal ourselves emotionally, if we want to better understand ourselves and the world we live in, if we want to deal more effectively with threats to our self-esteem, then we give these challenges, these obstacles, our conscious attention. Remember: Knowledge *is* power, and ignorance is *not* bliss.

Ignorance is the hallmark of shallowness, a life without free thought and creativity. Without conscious attention, there would have been no movement at all toward women's rights, minority rights, or gay rights. We would not understand the meaning of sexism, racism, homophobia, anti-Semitism, hate crimes, or discrimination.

Without conscious attention, societies around the globe would never have produced a Reverend Martin Luther King, Jr., a John Fitzgerald Kennedy, a Cesar Chavez, a Mahatma Ghandi, a Rosa Parks, or an Oscar Wilde. Or any of the hundreds, perhaps thousands, of others—heroes sung and unsung—who, in their own ways, bravely guided society toward the truth and enlightenment necessary for growth. Such work was often accomplished at the cost of great personal hardship, but collectively, we did produce these people of vision. Because, much like the living organism that is the human being, a living society must progress or die. As a people, we either collectively grow forward or we wither and fail. (Even status quo is a bit like slow death, as other societies continue moving ahead without us.)

So, what is it that happens every day of our lives that keeps gay people from the infinite growth and creative potential of which we are so capable? If we are to put our conscious attention toward these challenges, and face head on what we're up against, what will we find?

We'll find obstacles to healthy self-esteem occurring in a variety of arenas: at home, at school, on the playground, at church or temple, in the workplace, at social events, in the media, and in other examples of day-to-day living.

Let's look more closely at these . . .

At Home

The scenario is a common one. A young gay man or lesbian is not out to his or her family, and the family is not aware of this person's sexual identity. So, for instance, at the dinner table a sibling makes a homophobic joke, a joke that makes fun of and puts down gay people. It's a blatant example of the motivation behind bigotry: the need to feel "better-than" another individual or group. If I laugh at you, I feel better about me. I feel superior. For the time being, you are no longer stirring up threatening feelings for me. I've put you in your place, your position is lower than mine.

The family laughs. Their laughter validates the bigotry. The joke-teller feels vindicated in his humor aimed at homosexuals. At that instant, the message to the gay person becomes clear: Being homosexual is a joke, something that it's okay to make fun of. His or her already considerable anxiety gets cranked up a notch; in that moment is all the evidence needed to confirm that it's far too risky to come out of the closet to the family, that the lies must continue, that the false front must be maintained at all costs. At least that's how it feels.

The costs may be extreme anxiety or depression, drug or alcohol abuse, intense isolation and feelings of shame, or worse. The suicide rate for gay teenagers is thirty percent higher than the national average. It's no wonder: If a gay teen can't even feel safe to be who he is in his own home, then what worse fate might the world at large have in store for him? For some, it's unthinkable.

Another at-home scenario might be a family gathering of some sort—maybe a Fourth of July picnic or holiday party. Some rarely seen relative or family friend starts asking: So, John, seeing anyone special these days? Do you have a *girlfriend*, John? Although the question may be, on the surface anyway, harmless and nothing more than simple curiosity, it projects a message about the expectation that John is heterosexual. It is *assumed* that he's heterosexual. This unspoken assumption is not lost on John.

However, John is gay. So, if he says that yes, he is seeing

someone, he knows that some very personal, previously undisclosed information about himself is about to become a topic of conversation. He may not be ready for that to happen, may feel that his family is not ready for that, and he would be denied the thoughtful, planned approach of coming out to them that he'd prefer. Also, if he says yes, he may be led down a path of further lies, attempting to paint a picture of the *expected*—of heterosexuality—that will at once satisfy curiosity and (he may hope!) squelch any further comments.

If John answers no, then he has colluded with the assumption that he is not seeing anyone special, which we all know is meant to imply a female; that he does *not*—thanks so much for asking—have a girlfriend. So, while that may be a partial truth on one level (he doesn't have a girlfriend), his omission of the actual truth has continued the charade. He's gay, but everyone's left thinking that he is straight. Or, perhaps he *is* seeing someone, another guy, and he has now denied his relationship with this person. He has, in fact, denied the very existence of this other person. Whether he's in a serious or casual relationship with this guy, a denial of the relationship is, in this case, a denial of who John really is. He is undoubtedly left feeling a little worse about himself, a bit anxious and, more than likely, depressed.

So, it's a lose-lose situation for John, at least while he's in the closet, to try and answer that seemingly harmless question. We see, then, that for a gay person, such a question is far from harmless, because each time we have to lie, we lose a little bit of our ethical makeup, our integrity . . . we lose a bit of ourselves. We are taught not to tell lies. Yet, we receive messages that we are not to be homosexual. Talk about being stuck between a rock and a hard place! This is a classic example of what is known as "avoid-avoid" anxiety: feeling the internal need to avoid telling a lie, while feeling the necessity to avoid telling the truth. There's no solution with the situation the way it stands, therefore John's anxiety and/or depression increases tremendously.

It is well known in mental health fields that, aside from a higher suicide rate, there is a higher rate of drug and alcohol abuse among gay teens. The above example illustrates why. If a person does not possess healthy ways to cope, he turns to unhealthy ways to cope. The anxiety feels intolerable; he has to do something to ease it. How unfortunate that such turmoil has to exist at what ought to be a safe haven: home.

In the Classroom

It is certainly a great detriment to a gay person's self-esteem when a teacher allows taunting by other children—homophobic comments, slurs about one's sexuality, maleness or femaleness, etc. To allow for such an atmosphere is to be careless and cruel. In grade school, a person may be too young to be aware of a sexual identity, but memory retains the pain far into the upcoming years. And if a young child *is* aware of his or her differences from other children in terms of what they find interesting or exciting in other people, then being harassed by other kids begins a scarring that could last a lifetime.

Much like the family that laughs at homophobic jokes told at home, when a teacher does nothing to stop verbal or physical taunting, then the behavior receives validation. The message to the child who is different, appears different, or feels different is clear: You are laughable. You are an object of ridicule and shame. You will not find solace or protection in the classroom because I, your teacher, agree.

In the library, the message is similar when a book is pulled from the shelves because it contains gay content. If the teachers and librarians don't protest, then they give their tacit approval. If the parents don't fight it, then they are giving their approval, too. So the young gay boy or girl (or the boy or girl of unknown sexual identity, but who will identify as being gay or lesbian later on in life) is denied any of the validation and self-esteem that comes from seeing one's own story in print.

There is a growing body of literature that teaches children tolerance and acceptance of those who are different from them. For the gay child, there are story books about daddy marrying a man, being raised by two moms, having a gay uncle, and much more. When a school librarian, principal, school board, etc., makes a decision not to supply such books for the children, or to pull these books from the shelves, then they have made a conscious decision to deny gay children the same positive, self-worth–affirming literature that is afforded to all the other children. Whether their short-sightedness keeps them from seeing it this way, or their stance is political, they have chosen to discriminate against gay people, denying them in their formative years the foundation for good mental health. They have taken a stand that may have consequences in the lives of young people for years to come.

On the Playground

The stereotypes are well known. There's the "sensitive" boy who, perhaps gifted in music or art, is uncomfortable and awkward on the playground or when playing sports. He is inevitably the last one chosen on a team. He does not receive the same encouragement from the coach that the other kids do. He is not good at conforming to what boys "should" be like. He is called names.

Then there's the "butch" girl, the tomboy who forgoes dolls and plays softball with the boys. She's aggressive on the playground and excels at physical activities. She can run, she sticks up for herself, doesn't shy away from an arm-wrestling match, and gets her uniform dirty at recess. She, too, is called names.

For that matter, the female physical education teacher is called names, too.

All too often the playground becomes yet another unsafe place, a place where there are negative, harmful messages being sent and received. These messages are destructive to a young person's self-esteem development, and too often go unmonitored, ignored, or in some way, consciously or unconsciously, encouraged by the adults in charge. Recess becomes, then, a very tense, upsetting time of day for the young person who is the object of scorn.

The playground is supposed to be a place where a young person can learn to develop motor skills, participate in the value of teamwork, and understand what healthy competition is about. Imagine having to learn, instead, what it feels like to be anxious about what might happen today. Will I be called names? Will I be beaten up? How can I avoid such situations? These are the questions the child who is different must spend his or her energy on, while the others are having fun.

Whether a child is stereotypical or not (stereotypes of negative connotation evolve, mind you, from those who believe themselves in the majority of the population—the ruling class, if you will, of society), there are damages that occur on both conscious and unconscious levels when it comes to homophobic physical environments. In a few years, the grade school-age student will be in junior high, where the kids hit the showers after gym class. If the verbal abuse of the playground continues unchecked, unreported, unmonitored, into the junior high school gymnasium, the fear and shame also continues. But now, the stakes may be higher.

Recently there was much press coverage about some boys in a Midwestern junior high who tried to rape another boy in the showers. Several of them held their victim down, while others took turns attempting anal penetration. All the studies done on bullies would indicate that the boys who were participating in the junior high attack were the same ones yelling *fag* and *sissy* on the playground a few years prior. The assault and aggression had continued, but took on another, even more dangerous, form.

Like any rape, such an example of gay hatred will contribute to the ego formation of this boy, seriously affecting how he feels about himself as a person, as a male, and especially as a gay man. He will have to incorporate this experience into his identity, until he learns that the attack wasn't his fault, that he did nothing wrong, that he is nothing wrong. There is a saying, *what doesn't kill us, defines us*. He will survive physically. How will he survive psychologically?

The biggest crime is that such hostile, dangerous, emotionally scarring events do not have to happen. Which parents taught their kids that it's okay to abuse another person, verbally or physically? What intolerant, racist, homophobic, or sexist conversations did the bullies hear at home to give them such permission? Because that's the effect of teaching your child intolerance: It gives permission across the board to abuse others, be the victim male, female, of a different race, national origin, or sexual identity. Which teachers allowed these same bullying kids to be derogatory toward others? What coach looked the other way when the sensitive boy was verbally or physically taunted, unconsciously expressing his—the coach's—own homophobic attitude vicariously, by laughing it off. *Well, boys will be boys.* Each and every one of these factors contributed to the eventual attack in the shower. And each could—and should—have been avoided.

How? By teaching tolerance and compassion, by modeling openness to others, by subscribing to the belief that each human being is of worth, and needs to be treated with respect and dignity. By teaching that our differences are part of the fabric that makes for a unique and interesting society. By celebrating what each individual has to offer in the lives of those around him. And by teaching that, if we take the time to notice, we all share in our humanness, and we all have common points of interest. There are endless ways to form a connection with each other, none of them need be violent.

At Places of Worship, Places of Business

If your reverend, pastor, priest, rabbi, alderman, deacon, or other congregational leader makes a comment that reduces a homosexual person to anything less than one of God's loved and valued creations, something's wrong. If your congregation believes that either homosexuals or homosexual behaviors (whatever *those* are) are to be condemned, something's wrong. If your religious leader will not perform same-sex ceremonies and bless the union between you and your significant other, your life partner, in front of your community and loved ones, something's wrong.

What's wrong is that you are worshipping at the altar of bigots. How can it be good for your self-esteem to put money in the collection plate to help an organization which doesn't believe in your right to love another person the way you wish? Which doesn't support your commitment to another human being? Which thinks you are "less-than" in the eyes of God? Let's be honest: Such an organization is one that doesn't accept who you are. (You can read much more about this in Chapter 16, The Religious Right Is Neither.)

It is insidiously harmful to your self-worth to sit and listen to someone preach, directly or indirectly, that there is something wrong or unnatural about you; that you are not good enough to participate in the afterlife of your spiritual beliefs, while being told that the heterosexuals in the crowd will indeed reap such rewards. Do you honestly believe that they are better than you, more deserving of God's love than you? Do you agree with them? If this is the situation at your place of worship, perhaps it's time to reconsider your involvement, your motivations, and your choice of religious practice. Perhaps it's time to make an appointment and have a talk with your pastor. Then, have a talk with a pastor at a church that *welcomes* gays.

Likewise, do you have an accountant who is homophobic, or gay-supportive? Or gay him/herself? And what about your dentist? You pay a lot of money for your teeth . . . is this money going into the pocket of someone who doesn't approve of who you are? Or do you have a gay dentist, and your money (or your insurance money) is going back into the gay community to support causes that are important for our civil rights? How about your mechanic? Does he advertise in the gay magazines in your area? He should, if you're bringing him your business, or you're going to the wrong mechanic.

Are you in school? Have you ever heard your professor make a homophobic remark? If so, maybe it's time to have a little meeting with him or her, and include the dean of studies at that meeting. You're a student at that school, and deserve the respect afforded any other student, regardless of that professor's personal opinions of homosexuality. Are you willing to allow yourself to be the silent target of prejudice throughout your entire education?

Are you a member of an HMO? When it comes time to choose

a medical doctor, do you ask for someone who is gay, lesbian, or gay-sensitive? If you do not, how will you be assured that your physician is well versed on the medical concerns of gay people? How will you deal with safe-sex and HIV questions? How will you feel if this person, in whom you've entrusted nothing less than your very health, is overheard making homophobic (or racist, or sexist, or other bigoted) remarks? Will you feel safe enough and secure enough in your relationship with him to confront him on it? If he is not gay-supportive, then perhaps you are not out to him. To what degree of honest communication can you then engage, with this person with whom good communication is absolutely essential, and may mean the difference between life and death . . . *your* life and death?

If the HMO is not able to offer you someone that they are certain is gay-sensitive, what can you do to help educate them to the importance of this issue? A phone call or letter to the board? You might contact a local chapter of a gay and lesbian legal defense association in your area for guidance. If your health maintenance organization is not prepared to offer a high level of sensitivity to the health needs of gay individuals, then they are certainly out of touch with national health concerns in general.

An important study was done recently that shows that lesbians report a much higher incidence of having no medical doctor whatsoever, due to the fear that they won't receive quality health care if they come out to their physician. This is a travesty. What's missing in medical schools is gay-sensitivity training. As gay-oriented and HIV-related health clinics become more and more sensitized to women's health issues and HIV-related health care, so must the rest of the health care industry. Is your HMO (or other health care service) in touch with your needs? If not, something's wrong.

Your psychotherapist, physician, chiropractor, car salesman, computer dealer, veterinarian, gardener, grocery clerk, druggist, gym owner, and pet groomer need to be gay, lesbian, or gay-supportive. (Gay people, after all, are found in all these professions!) If they are not, then something's wrong with this picture . . . the picture that is your life. What's wrong is that you are bringing benefit—financial benefit, at least—to people who do not accept nor support who you are, your very being. In their eyes, you are less-than, and you are putting your hard-earned money in their pockets. And the ramifications continue . . .

It's okay for them to make a homophobic comment behind your back once you're out of earshot. It's okay for them to vote for politicians that support anti-gay rights legislature. It's okay for them to blatantly or subtly register distaste at having to serve you. What makes all this okay? You bring them your business. Get the point?

Now, understandably, in rural areas this may be much harder to accomplish, and may require some creative inquiry, but you can do your best to get as much of your life, the people in your life, and the businesses with which you regularly interact, to be gay-supportive. If you care enough about your own self-esteem, you'll do just that. It's not usually so very difficult once you've put this goal into your consciousness. After a while, it becomes important to you, as you realize that you're part of a chain reaction, part of a process that either is helpful to you and your community, or is not.

Beyond your own efforts, you can educate your loved ones about the importance of being conscious of where they bring their money, and with whom they interact personally and professionally. A good friend of mine, not being gay himself, never used to think about this issue. Now, because he cares for me and other gay friends of his, he has begun to make careful choices when he opens the Yellow Pages. In fact, he often uses the Community Yellow Pages (the gay directory in the Los Angeles area) when looking for services to help him work on his home, property, and car. Good for him, and good for us. That's the kind of support that says, *you're important to me, your concerns are important to me, and I'll do whatever I can to support you. I care about you. I'm not bringing my business to anyone who thinks less of you or the people I love.* How's that for a positive self-esteem message!

In the Workplace

How professionally damaging might it be for a gay person to be out at your place of employment? Very, somewhat, or not at all? How gay-supportive is your boss, do you think? What can you tell, by the comments heard around the proverbial water cooler (which these days looks a lot like an espresso machine) about the general level of acceptance there for gay and lesbian employees? More specifically, what kind of policy—if any—does your place of employment have in the personnel manual that ensures the safety of—and protects the rights of—gay people? Has any gay man or woman brought a same-sex partner to a company party?

These are the questions worth thinking about when it comes to understanding some important self-esteem issues for gays in the workplace. There are wonderful books out now that list the best companies for gay men and lesbians to work for in America. They provide policy and health care information and more. While they may be invaluable references for people deciding where they want to work, or even which companies they wish to invest in and support, it's a shame that there has to be such a listing. If all employers cared equally about the rights of all their employees, then we would all enjoy the same protections, benefits, and comfort levels at work. Perhaps we need employers worldwide to understand that historically, gays have been grossly and cruelly discriminated against in the workplace. Unfortunately, at some companies, it continues.

Here's a challenge for you, whether you are gay or not: If, after asking yourself the questions about your employer that are suggested above, you find that there's some room for improvement for gays at your job, think about what you can do to help the situation. If you are gay, are you out to your employer? If not, why not? Is it too professionally risky ... and is that the honest truth? Is anyone else out at work? How are they faring? Have you reviewed your personnel policies lately? What about health care? Is your employer keeping up with the ever-growing national trend of large companies to offer domestic partner health benefits? Now ask yourself this: Are you not worth the same level of professional treatment at your place of business as your co-workers? Do you feel professionally less-than because of your sexual identity?

At Social Events

Pretty much everyone, at one time or another, wears their "social face." (Remember when one of your parents would be angry at you for something you did, and then he or she would answer the phone with a pleasant, lilting *hello*, as if nothing was wrong? A friend of mine refers to this as her mother's "company voice"— the voice she'd use when talking with non-family to indicate that everything's happy and fine. This is the vocal equivalent of the social face.) Another way to refer to this is "false front" or "false self." We all have one.

Actually, we all have many. They exist in varying degrees of honesty and openness, or withdrawal and protectiveness. We usually adapt, unconsciously, to our environment by deciding how much of ourselves we can show to others, given any situation. This environmental evaluation usually happens in a split second, without our even being aware of it, and happens subtly many times throughout the course of a day.

There are times, however, when we are very aware of it: We decide what parts of ourselves we feel safe expressing, and what parts we don't, and we proceed accordingly. Then we enter a careful thought process that tells us what degree of, say, professionalism, friendliness, vulnerability, assertiveness, etc., to bring to the fore. This is how we survive in a world that at times feels friendly and nonthreatening, and sometimes feels unknown or hostile. When we are relaxed with a loved one and can feel safe with our vulnerable sides, we show those parts of ourselves freely. We behave quite differently when we meet a competitive old college buddy for lunch and want him to think we're doing quite well in life, thank you very much. Get the idea?

The false self is not necessarily a negative trait, *if* one is aware of it, knows when he/she is using it, and why. It can be seen simply as a part of yourself that you bring to the front of your personality in particular social situations, perhaps to mask the less pleasant, less sociable aspects to your personality, or maybe to help put yourself—superficially, at least—in a happy mood, sort of working on your disposition from the outside in.

Sometimes the false self occurs as the manifestation of shifting from one part of your life to another. You were at work and felt serious, now it's time to relax, laugh a bit, and try to enjoy yourself at the party. Again, if you are aware of when you are engaging your false self, it more than likely doesn't pose you or anyone around you any long-term or significant hardship. Putting on a pleasant front can be seen as a kind of natural defense mechanism, a protection, defending against feelings that you are not comfortable having, at least not at the moment. It may be how you survive through fear. Or certain insecurities. It's a survival choice.

However, when people engage their false selves without ever being aware of what it means for them, or that they are doing so, or when they seem to be *always* wearing a false self, then that's usually indicative of an unaddressed identity problem. Their life becomes one of continual disconnection from who they really are. I don't like who I am inside, I'm deathly afraid to show that person to you, so I project onto you my belief that *you* will not like that person, either—the real me. Instead, I'll show you who I believe you *will* like, and I'll keep this up for as long as I need to.

It's an exhausting, anxiety-ridden, and ungenuine way to live. It is the false self working overtime.

Perhaps the thought of showing any true emotions is frightening or threatening for some perfectly valid reason. In highly dysfunctional or alcoholic families, for instance, children learn very well not to ever show their true selves, lest they risk exposing some fragile part of themselves to a hostile or careless environment. Instead of learning to be true to themselves and to others, they learn that their first priority is to *protect* themselves. So they grow up believing that they have to protect themselves from the people they work with, the people they date, the people they marry . . . everyone with whom they interact. We can see how this can lead to all sorts of intimacy problems, and tremendous anxiety and depression at not feeling truly connected with anyone, including themselves.

Now think of those people who grow up in situations where they have a very big secret they feel they must hide. They are taught to hide it. Unfortunately, such is the case for a great number of gay people. They've learned all too well that there will be a huge price to pay for not being who they are encouraged and expected to be. In order to appear that they are worthy of that encouragement, and that they can indeed live up to these expectations, they may develop a false self that must be maintained. It must be present not just at parties, but *all the time.* At home, play, school, work, gatherings of any kind. Their very survival depends upon it. Until they find a safe place—with other gays, or with people who do not harbor any prejudice against sexual minorities—the stress they feel, full-time, is incredible.

It may be impossible for a person to sustain so much stress, which, when alone, may very well take the form of a severe depression. So a person turns to whatever he or she can in order to cope. Sometimes the coping takes a healthy form, i.e., therapy, and sometimes it doesn't, i.e., alcohol abuse, drug abuse, or even suicide.

I've described what is probably a worst-case scenario, one whereby a gay person has *no* safe venue in which to be his/her true self. (Although, judging from the painful stories that I've had confided to me as a therapist, it is a scenario that nevertheless does exist, and all too often.) Perhaps it happens more in isolated, rural areas; perhaps when someone comes from an oppressive community or highly intolerant family situation. Even when a gay person has a support system and a generally high level of acceptance in their life, they have, at some point, still been exposed to messages of nonacceptance. Maybe when they were a child, maybe when they were in college or at their first job.

To some degree, a false self was learned. It wasn't just a false front to show one's success to an old college buddy. It was one that felt much more urgent, more pervasive. The negative repercussions of one's actions tend to take on worse dimensions in the imagination than they often do in real life, true. But, as we all know, people do get ostracized, they do get rejected, they are made to suffer great emotional pain, and they do get bashed. That's all too real.

The false self, then, can feel pretty damn urgent.

So, instead of looking at that cute guy, a gay man in certain company may stop himself, fearful of repercussions. Instead of saying who she's really dating, a gay woman may refer to "this *person* I'm seeing." Each time it happens, the false front is maintained, because it feels awfully urgent to do so. Each time, the anxiety at the thought of disclosure being tremendous, a little part of that person dies away. A part of him- or herself has been sacrificed at the altar of intolerance.

In the Media

No discussion of the obstacles to healthy self-esteem for gay men and lesbians would be complete without a discussion about the media.

Certainly, the media have come a long way in portraying real, accurate, and honest depictions of gays and different aspects of gay life. To no small degree we have GLAAD (Gay and Lesbian Alliance Against Defamation) to thank for that. GLAAD's vigilance and dedication in consulting with television and film executives have resulted in more gay-positive portrayals in the media than ever before in history. Yet we have so much farther to go.

When I give presentations about gay and lesbian self-esteem, I show all the mainstream commercial ads I can find that have a healthy and honest portrayal of gay life and relationships. Let me tell you, they are few and far between. There's the ad for antique beds, showing several couples on different beds, one of which is a pair of men cuddling. There are eight beds, so the gay image represents fifteen percent of the people in the ad. That's pretty fair, considering that the gay population is generally considered to be ten to fifteen percent of the population on the whole. That's a bed company I can support.

There are a few other examples I use. There's *Life in Hell*, the comic strip by Matt Groening that cleverly and humorously details the neuroses of two creatures, Akbar and Jeff, presumably a male couple. It isn't found in the mainstream press, though; I get that from an alternative L.A. paper.

In the gay newspapers and magazines, there are a plethora of ads that, of course, show same-sex couples. Mind you, these same companies do not use these ads in their mainstream marketing. Same thing goes for billboards along Santa Monica Boulevard in West Hollywood. There, various homoerotic imagery is used. (Sex sells!) Throughout the rest of greater L.A., the same products are portrayed using heterosexual images. I'm glad we at least have our own people depicted on our own turf, if you will, but why can't the same images be used in the mainstream? What's wrong with seeing same-sex couples selling a product? The message is clear: In your own corner(s) of the world, we'll market to you, because, let's face it, it makes good financial sense. But for advertising in the world at large, your kind are unacceptable/bad-for-business/not good enough (take your pick).

Television comedies like *Ellen* and *Will & Grace* have broken ground with leading characters who are gay. Enthusiasm rippled throughout the gay community as we all received a self-esteem shot in the arm during *Ellen's* "coming out" episode. And the character of Will portrays the boy next door as successful, funny, human, intelligent and gay. Now every television-watching person in America can say that they know a gay person or two. Yet these are the only shows in the entire history of network television with leading gay characters. There is also a sprinkling of secondary gay characters being humanely and positively portrayed on other shows (*Spin City* comes to mind), so progress is certainly being made. But are ten to fifteen percent of the television lives we invite into our homes each day representative of gay or lesbian experiences? Of course not. And of the gay characters who are on television, how many can you say have romantic relationships that are multidimensional and genuine, reflective of the relationships in our own homes?

Films are progressing, too, both within mainstream studios and independents. Every year gay and lesbian *auteurs* win Sundance Festival awards for their sensitive and enlightening portrayals of gays from many cultures and of various ethnicities. Some of the mainstream films' portrayals are accurate and well-depicted, too. However some are embarrassing, shameful, and cruel. The next time you go to the movies and there is a gay character in the film, pay close attention to how that character's portrayed. Is it honest or stereotypical? Do the characters have real relationships or two-dimensional, nonthreatening, superficial encounters only? Are the portrayals feeding a bigotry, or expanding perceptions? Even films considered beautifully done and successful often rely on a stereotypical gay character for comic relief. Gays know all too well the pain of having to be the butt of jokes to survive. To continue that kind of abuse, couched in humor for all to see up on the big screen, is damaging to our self-esteem, and is inexcusable. Gay people go to movies, too, or don't these producers care about that?

Day-to-Day Life

I was driving through Orange County recently, just south of Los Angeles, in an area not known for its acceptance of sexual minorities. There was a red, white, and blue bumper sticker on a fence that proclaimed, *Boycott Disney!*

This was right after Disney, owner of the ABC network, had aired the coming-out episode of *Ellen*. Not long before, Disney had wisely and progressively instituted a domestic partnership policy, becoming the largest company to date to offer such a policy to its employees (many of whom are gay). Although the domestic partnership policy benefits both heterosexual and homosexual committed relationships, the homophobes had had it: *Ellen* was the last straw. The Southern Baptists were riled up. The protests were beginning.

Even uglier than the intolerance suggested by not wanting an entertainment company to be fair to all its employees, is the insidiousness of coloring this toxic bumper sticker sentiment in red, white, and blue. As if only those opposed to gay rights are true Americans, or that to be a bigot is the American way. Not only don't the bigots have exclusive rights on being American, if you ask me, they are one of the more embarrassing aspects of modern society. Maybe the bumper sticker should really say, *Boycott Bigotry!*

It is an example of coming across a message in everyday life that's antithetical to healthy self-esteem for gays and lesbians. Such examples abound. What about finding out that the owner of your favorite fast-food chain has contributed money to anti-gay rights bills in congress? Are you still going to buy your meals there, knowing that you're putting money toward anti-gay legislature?

Or you hear a homophobic remark in the music store made by an employee, and the manager just laughs. Or a clerk at the grocery store mutters "fag" under his breath at a customer. Or a night club has a posted sign reading, "No Queers Allowed," and rationalizes it to the press by saying it's meant to be humorous. To whom? Will that club still get your patronage? Will you bury your head in the sand to these types of affronts, or will you empower yourself to realize that this is not okay, and you don't have to sit back and take it?

These are all real-life examples of just some of the kinds of obstacles facing gay men and women every day. They are but a few that have been casually observed in a large, fairly wealthy and educated, fairly liberal, technologically advanced metropolitan area, on the threshold of the twenty-first century. Other smaller, less progressive communities offer, I'm sure, many more blatant examples of prejudice.

If we don't bring these aspects of our society into our individual and collective consciousness, who will? To say, do, or feel nothing is to collude with those of small heart and vast ignorance who do not want gay people to feel good about themselves.

If we, as gay men and lesbians, are to commit to deservingness, health, self-esteem, spirituality, human rights, peace, joy, healthy relationships, loving families, education, fair work environments, and the same freedom afforded to others, then perhaps we must begin by conditioning ourselves to recognize the obstacles in our way.

We can only rise to the challenges of which we are aware. And rise we must.

Knowledge *is* power.

The Meditation

This meditation is particularly helpful when you want to feel better connected to yourself and to others. Sometimes it's easy to feel disoriented or disenfranchised from the world. Confusion, alienation, and feeling as if you don't belong can come more easily than a spiritual or emotional connectedness, especially during times of stress or depression. And that's when we need our center the most. Try this meditation whenever you need to feel centered, or more engaged with the universe—both within and without. It may be read slowly by a friend, or silently to oneself.

Take several deep breaths. As you breathe, focus on your given right to your breath. You are human, you deserve to breathe.
　Pause.
　As you breathe, think about your body. Become aware of how every part of your body is connected to every other part. This body is yours. It is alive. It is a part of all things living. The planet is affected because you are here, breathing and alive.
　Pause.
　As you breathe, think about your mind. Your mind is connected to who you are. With your mind you make choices every day which begin chain reactions throughout humankind. Your choices touch others, directly or indirectly. Your choices matter.
　Pause.
　You breathe, you live, you matter. You occupy space and time.

You interact. Your aliveness is uniquely yours, yet connected to all other things.

Now let yourself focus on a positive, joyous, significant relationship in your life. This may be a relationship from the past or present. Visualize yourself engaging with this person.

Pause.

Now, let yourself experience the rich fabric of feelings that come with a meaningful encounter with this person. Enjoy all the warm and positive feelings attached to this relationship. Let yourself fill up with the goodness, the happiness, the contentment.

Pause.

As you have your feelings, bring this understanding into the picture: I deserve this.

Pause.

Let these words resonate in your mind, loudly and clearly: I am fundamentally as good a person as I can be right now, in this moment of my life. I am deserving of love because I am human. I am deserving of happiness, because I am human. I deserve to be here, side by side, with all other living creatures. This is my home, too.

Pause.

Repeat these thoughts hourly, daily, weekly . . . whenever you desire to feel a spiritual oneness with your world. Whenever you need to feel that you belong.

You belong here. This is your home, too.

You are alive.

You matter.

Chapter 5

Progressive Relaxation

What lies behind us and what lies before us are tiny matters compared to what lies within us.

—Oliver Wendell Holmes

Progressive relaxation is a wonderful and highly effective tool for providing total relaxation of the mind and body. Aside from focusing on relaxing your physical being, it also calms and quiets the mind and generally helps you feel a greater sense of peace. Pretty good, for an easily learned, basic breathing technique!

Clinically speaking however, a great deal occurs. The progressive relaxation exercise elicits what is known as the "relaxation response." This refers to its ability to promote the harmony and healing of your internal systems and organs by slowing the flow of blood, lowering your blood pressure, reducing the output of adrenaline, regulating your breathing and heart rate, relaxing muscles, reducing anxiety, heightening your focus, and producing a calm, centered feeling overall.

See, if the physiological systems in the body are stressed, then there is little or no reserve energy for the process of healing. Relaxing the systems allows the body to return to its natural state of homeostasis, and encourages its natural tendency to self-correct and self-heal. For this reason, progressive relaxation is being used increasingly in hospitals, hospices, clinics, and healing centers nationwide to assist preoperative and postoperative patients. It is very effective with pain control and it's often used in conjunction with various forms of body work, chiropractic techniques, massage, acupressure, acupuncture, and other healing methods.

I like to use progressive relaxation as the first part of any hypnotherapy or meditation session. Aside from the above mentioned benefits, it begins the process of conditioning the mind to accompany and augment the goals of the session. In other words, it fosters a harmony of relaxation which benefits the many types of hypnosis, visualization, creative/guided imagery, and meditation. The deeper a person relaxes, the more potent is the imagery during session. *Any* form of meditation work is greatly heightened by a relaxed, centered mood.

The following progressive relaxation can be used in conjunction with (that is, prior to) meditating, or can stand alone as a body-awareness meditation unto itself. As I mentioned, I like to begin any meditation with some form of relaxation, and any form that you find comfortable for you will be beneficial. The mental focus and physical calmness this particular exercise elicits combine to provide a natural antidote for stress, anxiety, depression, pain, and phobias. It's truly a wonderful way to maximize and fully appreciate the benefits of meditation.

It's called progressive because it relaxes the body progressively, moving from head to toe, or vice versa. I prefer beginning at the top of the body and moving slowly toward the feet, so that the points of tension in the neck and shoulders are targeted early on, giving those areas the full session to grow more and more relaxed. Also, the mind is allowed (and encouraged) to settle down right from the beginning, which I find helpful. A case can be made, however, for starting at the feet and working upward. In this way, saving the head and shoulders for last, these areas are already more relaxed by the time you get to them. It's really a matter of personal preference, there's no one correct way to do this. In fact, that's one of the beauties of relaxation and meditation techniques: There's really no right or wrong; it's simply about what works best for you. I encourage people to experiment and find out which relaxation approach they find more comfortable.

Also, I'm offering in this chapter both a long version and a short version of the progressive relaxation. I recommend the long version to begin with, and you may want to try it several times a week, letting yourself become more and more adept at quieting and focusing the mind. I've noticed that after only a few sessions of using the progressive relaxation with some clients, they begin to go into a deep state of relaxation from the moment they close their eyes; they have become so attuned to and motivated for the process of relaxation. Each person is different, however, and you can see what the experience is like for you.

For the maximum benefit from both versions I suggest that you have a friend read it slowly to you, preferably someone whom you trust, and who can offer a relaxed, soothing way of speaking. Another option is to tape-record it in your own voice, taking your time, using the language to promote a quiet, a calmness. The language of meditation is important, each word chosen carefully to guide, soothe, or provide the most helpful image. You may find, however, that some words or images are especially to your liking, have the most relaxing effect on you, or elicit the more powerful emotions and thoughts. In time, you may want to adjust the language to suit your needs. Nothing is written in stone!

That's true for the meditations throughout *all* of this book. I've chosen the wording because I feel it will be most helpful to you. It's important that you learn to treat the meditations as starting points, discovering your own tastes and preferences as you increase your experience. In time, you can develop your own style, your own verbal preferences, your own ways of relaxing and using meditation for the goals of your specific life issues. What's so interesting is that no two people experience the same meditation in exactly the same way. We all listen through the unique filters of our experience, and the ultimate result of those filters depends on our individual life histories. So, no matter what the wording, you may find that you take away from the experience of meditating exactly what you are ready for.

First, the full version: "Head to Toe." You may want a friend to read this to you, or you could prerecord it yourself. Remember to go very slowly, gently.

The Meditation

Take several, slow deep breaths.

Pause.

When you are ready, close your eyes. There is nothing for you to do or be, other than to allow yourself to relax and listen to the sound of my voice.

As you continue to breathe, imagine that cool, clean, fresh air moves into your body with each inhale, and you exhale any tension or stress. Inhale cool air rich with oxygen and nutrients, exhale stress. Inhale. And exhale.

Pause.

Continue breathing, and start to become aware of what your mind is doing. Is it fluttering with thoughts . . . or quieting down? It's perfectly okay to have your thoughts. Simply acknowledge them and then let them float off like tiny thought-bubbles, blowing away on a breeze. And return your concentration to the sound of my voice.

Now I invite you to imagine that a feeling of relaxation is starting at the top of your head, and slowly spreading down and around your head, moving gently down to your neck, around your temples and ears, and across your forehead.

Let this relaxation float across you and through you, and experience it however you wish. There's no right or wrong. You may be experiencing a relaxed heaviness, or it may feel like a slight tingling sensation. Or something else. However it feels to you is fine.

Now feel the relaxation spreading out across your eyelids, relaxing all the tiny muscles in your eyes, allowing your eyelids to feel heavier. Let it move across your cheeks, over your nose, and around your mouth. Feel it relax your mouth. You may want to leave a little space between your teeth, as your lower jaw feels heavier and heavier.

Pause.

Now your entire head is heavy and relaxed, as the relaxation moves into your throat, and down the back of your neck and into your shoulders. Let the sensation massage your neck and shoulders, easing any tension you may carry there.

Pause.

Feel the relaxation as it now moves down your spine, one vertebra at a time. Relaxing and massaging as it goes. Slowly relaxing your spine and all the muscles around it.

Let the relaxation now spread, slowly, across your back through your shoulder blades, and around your sides to your front torso, relaxing as it goes, massaging as it goes. Your back is strong yet relaxed. Strong yet relaxed.

The relaxation now heals and soothes all your internal organs and systems. You are breathing naturally, without any effort on your part, and your heart is pumping lifeblood throughout your body. All your systems are working in harmony. All your organs are relaxed and healthy and strong.

Pause.

Now the relaxation focuses on your heart area. But instead of a heaviness, you feel a lightness, an openness around your heart. Let your chest breathe. Let your heart breathe.

Pause.

Now imagine the relaxation working outward from your shoulders, moving slowly down your arms, letting your arms feel heavier and more relaxed. Massaging all the muscles as it goes, moving along your upper arms, your elbows, your forearms. Now the relaxation moves into your hands, the tops of your hands, the palms of your hands, and throughout each individual finger. Massaging and relaxing. Massaging and relaxing.

Your arms are heavy. Your head and shoulders are relaxed and heavy. Your entire torso is very relaxed. And you're feeling more and more at peace . . . with yourself, the world, and everyone in it.

And if you hear any outside sounds, let them serve to remind you that it's a busy, fast-paced world out there, but where you are, all you have to do is relax. And then return your concentration to the sound of my voice.

Pause.

Your entire upper body is calm and relaxed now, your mind is quiet and focused, and your powers of concentration are great. You're listening only to my voice, and enjoying the wonderful peace that comes with relaxing.

Pause.

And now we'll continue on, relaxing the rest of your body, so that you can experience a relaxation more fully than ever before. And in fact, each time you do this exercise, you'll experience a deeper and deeper relaxation and sense of calm. Let the relaxation now move around your waist and pelvic area, relaxing as it proceeds. It moves down your backside and into the tops of your thighs, moving through your entire pelvic area, relaxing all the muscles as it goes.

Now through your thighs, your knees, slowly down through your calves and shins . . . relaxing, relaxing. Your legs feel heavy. Very heavy. Now down into your ankles and the tops of your feet. It relaxes your heels, arches, and each individual toe. The relaxation feels like a wonderful, soothing foot massage. So that your legs and feet now feel heavy and relaxed. Heavy and relaxed.

Now your entire body is relaxed and at ease. And you feel calm, safe, and very good about yourself. Take a moment now to mentally scan your entire body for any leftover signs of stress or tension. Go very slowly, up and down and back again. And if any points of stress are found, simply concentrate on breaking up that stress into tiny pieces, and letting the pieces float up and out of your body.

Pause.

And we will continue on now, to a final level of relaxation even deeper, where you will continue to relax, breathe, and feel the most wonderful sense of peace. I invite you to picture yourself at the top of a short flight of stairs. There are five stairs in all, covered in thick, plush carpeting of your favorite color. I will count downward, from five to one. Come with me each step of the way, letting yourself become more and more immersed with each number I say. At the end, I will say "deeply relaxed," at which point you will be in a total and deep state of relaxation. Now, listen to my voice, as we move slowly downward: Number five . . . deeper and deeper. And, four . . . deeper and deeper. Three . . . deeper and deeper. Two . . . deeper and deeper. And one. Deeply relaxed.

Pause.

Very good. Your mind and body have worked together to bring you to this very deep place. This place is where you can relax, recharge, soothe yourself, and heal yourself.

Pause.

This deep relaxation is a gift you can give to yourself any time you please. You now have the power to go to this place whenever you desire. It is always available to you. And it all begins with a breath.

This is your new tool to help you relax, feel healthy, centered, and strong, and help your mind and body work in harmony to reach whatever may be your goals.

Well done.

Long pause here. Continue to breath until you are finished, and are satisfied with the level of relaxation you've achieved. Then, you have three options: you can stay in a relaxed state to allow for any thoughts and feelings to emerge, you can awaken (we use the term, "awaken," although you are not asleep, but relaxed) back to full consciousness, or you can simply drift off to sleep. Whichever you choose, one of the following will help you arise gently when ready, with your newfound ability to relax and powers of concentration intact.

To stay with the relaxation: Now you may wish to stay with yourself, quietly enjoying the peace, allowing for whatever thoughts and feelings may arise. Take your time. Let yourself be. Witness. Observe. Breathe.

To awaken: Now, if you are ready to awaken, I will begin to count again, this time slowly upward from one to five. And as I do so, you will return to full beta consciousness, having remembered this wonderful time of relaxation, having increased your ability to achieve a deeper level of concentration, and knowing you can return to such a calm state any time you wish. After you hear me say "five," I invite you to open your eyes, feeling centered and refreshed, rested, and energized.

Number one . . . slowly coming up. And two . . . coming up a bit more. And three . . . getting ready to awaken. And four . . . nearly there. And five. Welcome back!

And now, the shorter version: "The White Light." I recommend this version for use after you have had several sessions of the longer version, and are finding that you become almost instantly relaxed at the very start. You may also notice by now an increase of sharpness to your mental focus and alertness in and out of session.

Again, speak slowly, gently, allowing the rhythm of the words to guide you.

The Meditation

Begin by taking several slow, deep breaths. When you are ready, close your eyes. As you continue to breathe, your concentration is on the sound of my voice, and on allowing yourself to relax fully and completely.

Pause.

Now I invite you to imagine that a beam of white light is entering your head from above. It is a brilliant light that carries with it healing and relaxing properties. Breathe in this light, welcome it into your being. As it enters your body, it gradually makes its way throughout all of your internal organs and systems, swirling as it goes, healing and relaxing as it goes.

This white light fills your body, every nook and cranny, slowly swirling around and around, till you are almost overflowing with it. It protects you, soothes you, relaxes you. Breathe with the pulse of the light. Breathe with the pulse of the light.

Pause.

And now the light concentrates in your chest, around your heart. It fills your heart area and emerges up and out of your body to surround you, bathe you in the glow of the brilliant light.

A beautiful, white swirling fog, wrapping itself gently and loosely around your body, protecting you. As it swirls, its healing properties comfort your skin, all of your external being. This light calms and relaxes you, keeping you feeling safe and centered, cradled in softness.

Pause.

And now the light begins to concentrate more intensely around your head area. And you notice it further relaxing your head and neck, ever so slowly expanding its coverage to include your shoulders. It deeply massages your neck and shoulders, relieving any tension you may carry in those areas.

Pause.

It moves now, down your spine, relaxing each vertebra, one at a time. And it slowly spreads out across your back, and around to your front torso area. Relaxing as it goes, relaxing as it goes. All parts of you, inside and out, are working beautifully in harmony, mind and body becoming more and more relaxed.

Pause.

It moves now, along your arms, letting all the muscles in your arms relax. Your arms feel heavier and heavier as the light moves through your upper arms, elbows, and forearms, and into your hands and fingers. Heavy and relaxed. Heavy and relaxed.

As the light slowly makes its way along your body, it relaxes you and massages all your muscles. It is giving you a greater and greater sense of peace. Peace with yourself, and all those in your life.

And your mind is quiet and focused. You are listening to the sound of my voice, and letting any stray thoughts drift off like tiny thought-bubbles, blowing on the breeze.

And the beautiful, relaxing, healing light continues into your pelvic area, and slowly moves into the tops of your thighs. Massaging as it goes, it relaxes your thighs, your knees, shins, and calves. It moves into your feet, the balls and arches, the toes. You legs and feet are feeling heavier and heavier.

Your entire body now is relaxed and at ease. And your mind is at peace.

And each time you do this exercise, you will relax more and more.

Pause.

A calm comfort has engulfed you, and you breathe into it. Accepting it.

Welcoming it.

Pause.

This is how you heal. How you relax. How you focus your concentration on the harmony of mind and body.

Breathe. This is how you are wonderfully, uniquely alive.

Breathe. Breathe and know that you are full and complete.

Breathe.

Long pause.

Continue to breathe until you feel finished with this session. Then, you may wish to awaken, or to continue on into sleep. If you desire to awaken, simply let your eyes open when you are ready, feeling rested, refreshed, centered, and whole.

Chapter 6

The Sailboat Visualization

*I do not know whether I was
then a man dreaming I was a butterfly,
Or whether I am now a butterfly
dreaming I am a man.*

—Chuang-Tzu

The Sailboat Visualization is one of the most visually rich images that I regularly use with clients (and with myself!). It combines Nature's beauty with a sense of being a part of all things living. Much of it takes place high up in the sky and on water, but even if one is phobic about these elements, humans have an ability to adjust the scenario to make it more comfortable.

Visualization (also referred to as guided imagery) is another way to promote therapeutic relaxation, and the sailboat visualization is commonly used as either an induction or deepening technique for self-hypnosis. While offering comforting, gentle images, underneath it is really a very practical step-by-step process with an end result of a total relaxation of body and mind. Its relaxation qualities lend itself well to reaching a profoundly deep state of mental calm and peace. If you are already adept at relaxing, it can help you go to a deeper level. If you're just learning how to relax, it can be a gentle, welcoming way to begin.

Like the preceding progressive relaxation, this visualization can be used to relax prior to meditating on a specific issue, or can stand alone as a meditation itself. If you wish to use it as its own meditation, I think you'll find it very enjoyable due to its emphasis on vibrant imagery and its use of all the five senses. This visualization can be highly effective for pain control, heightened creativity, sleep disorders, stress reduction, and much more. With repeated experience, you can discover how it might best serve your particular needs.

One way it can stand alone, and I recommend that you try this, is simply to pause at the end to allow for thoughts and feelings to emerge. Bearing witness to your thoughts and feelings, without judgment or criticism, simply noticing and becoming aware of them, can be highly therapeutic and healing. Doing so while deeply relaxed can be especially powerful. One can learn so much about oneself by releasing the judgments, moving them aside and out of the way of valuable, potential insight, and just watching from a centered place. We get to know better who we are by simply watching.

If you'd like to use this visualization as a deepening tool, try coupling it with the short version of the progressive relaxation. (You'll need to read about the progressive relaxation first; see Chapter 5.) Consider something like this: About halfway through the White Light version, after the fog emerges from within and begins to surround your body, *let it concentrate beneath you, forming a soft, white puffy cloud that begins to cradle and gently rock you, supporting you and lifting you, ever so slowly, upward.* Then proceed with the visualization. (You'll see what I mean in a minute.) I often use this exact combination of relaxation exercise and visualization with clients, to assist them in going more fully into relaxation than they have previously experienced.

For your first time reading the sailboat visualization, I suggest you just sit back, relax, and enjoy the imagery. Remember that it can be used regularly every day, or whenever you desire to take a break from our often fast-paced world. Here's a creative, simple, and convenient way to make regular use of its relaxing qualities: Summon up an image or two from the visualization, and use it in the middle of the workday to slow down and relieve stress. For example, the white sailboat itself can become a trigger of relaxation for you. By closing your eyes, taking a deep breath and picturing the gentle rocking of the sailboat, you can condition your body and mind to *instantly* begin to relax. Even a few minutes a day, while sitting at your desk at work, can be enormously beneficial.

As a meditation, deepening technique, or daily stress-reducer, the sailboat visualization is best experienced with your eyes closed. You may want a friend to slowly read the visualization to you, or you could record it in your own voice.

The Meditation

Take a deep breath, release, and close your eyes. Continue to breathe deeply, focusing only on the breath.

Pause.

Now imagine your body feeling very relaxed, very comfortable. Just let yourself sink into feeling loose, limp, and relaxed. Let go of all tension. Let your muscles rest. Let your entire body be supported by whatever's beneath you. There is nothing for you to do. You can now let go. Relax. Relax.

Pause.

At the moment you release your need to hold yourself up, you notice a wonderful, brilliant white cloud beginning to fill the space beneath your body. It slowly grows and cradles you and you feel overwhelmingly safe and protected.

The cushion of the white cloud begins to gently sway you from side to side, ever so slightly, slowly lifting you upward. It holds and embraces you.

You are being lifted higher now . . . out of this room . . . out of this building . . . higher and higher . . . above the rooftops and trees. You are feeling safe and secure, and can delight in the magic of the experience.

Higher and higher . . . you are above the streets, the cars. You can look down and see people as tiny dots, way below you. The air is cool and clean here, you can feel it on your skin, and you are most comfortable on your carpet of white cloud.

Pause.

And you begin moving now, out away from your neighborhood, toward the countryside . . . you are floating above gentle hills, and endless meadows filled with wild flowers of all your favorite colors. Brilliant expanses of color. You can even smell their intoxicating aromas from your perch high above. Inhale deeply and let the fragrance surround you.

You see small rivers and streams below . . . listening carefully, you can hear the soft babbling of water as it flows over rocks, creating tiny waterfalls.

Off in the distance are high snow-capped mountains, and above are trails of long, wispy clouds.

You are feeling free. You are a part of the universe. A part of all things that are, that ever were, and that ever will be.

Let yourself enjoy, feeling deeply connected and at peace . . . at peace with yourself and all other beings.

Pause.

Now, off in the distance, you notice a small body of water. Very inviting, it calls you closer. And so, with the power of your mind, you direct the cloud to bring you closer and closer to the water. You see that it's brilliantly blue, the most perfect blue you've ever known. Crystal clear and sparkling.

And in the middle of this blue water is a tiny, white sailboat. Sitting there, all by itself, with its gently billowing sail. You guide the cloud downward, toward that little sailboat, so gently rocking in the middle of the blue water. You are drawn to the little boat. It looks peaceful.

Down, down you go. Closer and closer, gently, slowly, until the cloud settles you softly onto the warm, wooden deck of the boat.

You relax and sit back, feeling the warmth beneath you. A gentle breeze blows across you, keeping your skin at just the right temperature. The sun is shining. High above are a few white clouds, an occasional bird flies by. You can hear its wings rustle the air as it passes overhead. And always there is the rocking.

You are at peace, and you somehow know that this boat has been waiting here for you your whole life. And now, finally, here you are. Enjoying the sounds, the air, the comforting warmth, the soothing calmness of this very special place. Relaxed and calm. Relaxed and calm.

Pause.

The slow, gentle rocking of the boat relaxes you. Deeper and deeper. Your eyes are closed. You can hear the soft, little waves gently lapping at the side of the boat. Rocking you.

Relaxing you.

Deeper and deeper.

Relax. Relax.

Pause.

Here you are one with all things. Here you are without judgment. Without worry. You simply exist as the pure, loving creation you are.

You are with yourself.

Quietly, with only yourself.

Listen. Relax. Breathe. Breathe.

Long pause.

At this point, you may wish to simply enjoy the relaxation, and when you feel finished, open your eyes. Or you may want to witness the thoughts and feelings that arise for you, free of distraction, and spend some time with them, noticing, watching, discovering.

You may be here with yourself for as long as you wish. Relaxed and at peace. Enjoy the calm. Enjoy being.

Pause.

If you so desire, you may allow for thoughts and feelings to gently arise. Here you have the quiet for your thoughts . . . here you have the peace and safety for your feelings.

Be witness to them, let yourself have them, for they are part of you, they are yours.

Let yourself learn from them.

What are your thoughts telling you?

Pause.

What are your feelings telling you?

Pause.
Breathe.
Spend as much time with yourself as you desire.
And in your own time, when you are ready, open your eyes.

Chapter 7

The Safe Place Image

Everything in life that we really accept undergoes a change.
So suffering must become love.
That is the mystery.

—Katherine Mansfield

Some people did not have a safe childhood. They were not able to feel safe at home, at school, or with certain adults—authority figures and perhaps even family members. There was no place in their world where they could go to feel comfortable, secure, and unconditionally loved. Therefore, they were not able to feel safe even within themselves. This is certainly—and unfortunately—true for many gay people.

If young people are not taught certain life skills, how to develop confidence and resourcefulness, for instance, or how to trust their own perceptions, then they may lack a healthy inner place where they can feel a sense of safety and self-esteem. A place to go to tap into the quiet that contains their own inner wisdom. We all possess a remarkable inner guide that is waiting in the wings to help us make healthy life choices, but we may not have been taught to trust, and therefore, to trust ourselves. Intuition can grow as finely tuned as any of our other senses, but first we must realize that it exists, it is valid, and it is always available.

Our intuition holds for us the key to our happiness, a life

content with sound judgment, confidence, and direction. First it must be born, and then it must be nurtured.

The Safe Place Image is a tool that helps us learn to trust ourselves. By allowing for the inner wisdom to speak, and indeed, watch over us much like a guardian angel, we can develop a pathway to our own inner abilities. We can re-parent ourselves to include the ability to trust our inner voice. By creating a safe place through meditation, we are creating a safe place within.

The safe place image can be used as an ongoing method of developing that inner wisdom, and it can also be used to help a person make a difficult decision, small or large. It can help you get in touch with an issue that although present, may have been eluding you. It can help you increase awareness about who you are and what you need. It taps into the power of your mind in a way that gently accesses your heart. It helps you feel connected to a spiritual side that you perhaps neglect, or have not discovered. It helps you learn that you have vast inner resources, whether you know it yet or not. It can do all this and more.

Again, depending on where you are in your life and in your personal growth process, and depending on what you need at this particular moment in your life, you will experience this imagery in your own unique way. This is a meditation that you can use at different times throughout your life, to help with whatever issues are alive for you. It is interesting and enjoyable for me to witness people using this meditation for the first time, then again a month later, then six months later, then again after a year. Each time it offers them something different and provides a unique insight, depending on what they're going through, what their life is like. It allows an access to the thoughts or feelings or needs that may be hard to identify during their usual, conscious, busy lives.

I've worked with clients who use the safe place image whenever they are coming up against a particularly anxiety-provoking event or situation. Perhaps they are about to do something that they predict will stir up an old phobia. Or maybe they will be reminded of some childhood trauma, consciously or unconsciously returning to a painful episode of their past. Others use the safe place image regularly, as a sort of psychic tune-up to check in with how well they are generally functioning. Your own experience with the image can guide you as to how it will best serve your particular needs.

Much like the preceding sailboat visualization, it may be helpful to take a specific image from this exercise and use it as a trigger to become instantly calm and centered, especially if you're feeling confused or frightened about something. For example, you could take the safe place itself and, by closing your eyes and taking a deep breath, return to that place, with its accompanying mental clarity and feeling of security. Or, you could work with the image of when the guardian spirit enters, offering you the gift of whatever you may need at that particular moment. (You'll read about the images I refer to shortly.) After you become accustomed to this exercise, you can play with the various ways it can be of help to you in your day-to-day life.

Feeling safe in your world, learning to trust yourself, and coming to rely upon your own intuitive inner wisdom are important abilities to be developed. They are well within your reach, even if you've never tapped into them before.

If you like, the safe place image, like all meditations, may be preceded by one of the two versions of progressive relaxation found in Chapter Five. While the progressive relaxation meditation has as its primary goal a deep, rewarding state of physical and mental calmness, and the sailboat visualization aims to relax you even further as well as provide a nature-filled space conducive to insight, the safe place image focuses on developing certain awarenesses and inner resources.

Becoming deeply relaxed beforehand is now up to you.

If you've already used the preceding meditations, you know that you can begin this one with any relaxation exercise—simple breathing, part or all of the progressive relaxation, part or all of the sailboat visualization—to enhance your potential level of insight. If time does not allow you such a luxury, then I suggest that you use the initial breathing at the start of this image to produce the greatest level of relaxation possible. In other words, take your time and really bathe in the breaths, really help yourself relax, okay? Let's begin.

As before, you may want to have this exercise read to you by a friend, or you could record it in your own voice.

The Meditation

Close your eyes and take several deep breaths. Let your focus come to your breath.

Pause.

Know that the very act of breathing is something you can trust. It is within your power to breathe however you may need to. Let yourself breathe calmness into your body. Let yourself breathe peace into your mind. Let yourself breathe in a wonderful, encompassing sense of safety.

Pause.

Now, let your mind travel back in your life, to those times when you felt most safe. To those places where you felt secure. To those ages when all was well with your world. Try and identify these moments of safety. Bring them up as clearly as you can.

Long pause.

Perhaps you were able to envision several moments of safety from your past.

Perhaps you were unable to recall any. Whether many, some, or none, you are now able to enter into a process whereby you can develop such moments for yourself.

Using the power of your mind, we are going to create safety.

Using the power of your mind, we are going to develop your inner wisdom and strength. We are going to open a pathway of creative mental clarity.

Safety, inner wisdom, and clarity. Let these concepts become real to you.

Safety, inner wisdom, and clarity.

Pause.

I invite you now to create your own safe place. This may be a place from your past, or it can be a place from your present. It may be real or imagined. It's entirely up to you. You can use this same place as a safe haven each time you meditate, or you can change it every time.

There is but one guiding objective to this place: It must be somewhere that you feel safe, secure, and entirely at peace.

Take a few moments now, to decide on your safe place.

Long pause.

Very good. Now let yourself be there totally, completely. Use the power of your mind to make this place real. What is your physical posture . . . standing, sitting, reclining? Are others present, or are you alone? What sounds do you hear? What colors do you see? What is the weather like . . . windy, sunny, cloudy, clear, foggy, rainy? What is the temperature? How does your skin feel? What is against your skin? What is beneath you? Above you? What textures surround you? What do you smell?

Pause.

Emotionally, how do you feel? Are you happy? Ecstatic? Contemplative? Peaceful? Melancholy? Do you feel centered and quiet? Excited and energetic? Whatever feelings you are having, make them real. Own them. Experience them now. Surround yourself with them. Fill up with them.

Pause.

Why did you choose this place? What does this place mean to you?

Pause.

Being in this place enables you to feel safe. You can trust that here, you feel safe. This is something that you can count on. You brought yourself here, and here you are filled with a sense that all is well within, and without. Your inner world as well as your outer world, is safe. You are at peace. You are in harmony mentally, physically, and spiritually. You . . . are . . . safe.

Know this.

Own this.

Feel this.

Pause.

Now I invite you to begin to discover a distinct yet comforting sense that you are not alone. In fact, you are experiencing a greater and greater awareness that there is a wondrous, benevolent being near you, slowly but surely approaching your safe place. Gently coming closer.

And you smile, as if to welcome its presence.

Pause.

This one, spiritual being, coming to you—purposefully and only to you—as if you were meant to meet here all along.

It is as if some all-knowing inner part of you, a part that is connected to the entire universe and all living creatures, has led you to be right here, right now at this very moment of your life, in this very spot. And it is here and now that you will finally meet your Guardian Spirit.

This benevolent entity comes closer to you now, so that you begin to make out a gentle, white fog swirling about. It begins to take shape. It smiles at you. The most radiant and unconditional smile you've ever seen. It welcomes you with an outstretched hand. You reach out.

Hand in hand, you look into each other's eyes. And in the eyes of your Guardian Spirit you see reflected back to you all the pain and sorrow, and all the joy and happiness, of your entire life. This Spirit knows you.

And accepts you.

And loves you.

This Spirit wants for you all the goodness in the world, everything you need. And this Spirit wants to help you, unconditionally, asking nothing in return . . . Your Guardian Spirit wants to be close by your side, and deep within your heart.

Pause.

Now you look down, to see that your Spirit is holding something for you . . . a beautiful wooden box, covered with inlays of your favorite precious stones. Your Spirit is handing you this most enchanting box.

Intuitively you know that this box contains exactly what you need in your life, right now, at this very moment. It contains that which you need more than anything else.

Without any words passing between you, you have the knowledge that this is the gift for which you've been waiting.

Whether this gift is actually small enough to fit in this box, or whether it is an intangible that cannot be contained, seen, or touched . . . this is what you've been missing, and longing for, sometimes without even knowing it.

And your Guardian Spirit has brought it to you now.

You reach out and take the box. You open it. A brilliant white light radiates from within, bathing you in its beauty and comfort. You let it surround you. You feel its power, its grace.

And as the light fades, there it is. There is your gift. Specially and uniquely for you. Here it is at last.

Pause.

Did you know that you needed this gift? Has it been missing in your life for very long? Has your awareness of this gift—and its absence—been foremost on your mind, or has it been buried, deep below your conscious thought?

How do you feel, now that it is with you? Let yourself have this experience. Let yourself have your feelings.

Pause.

And as you look up, you see your Guardian Spirit smiling.

And slowly, as before, you see a swirling fog as your Spirit now gently retreats, leaving your place to once again be only yours, your personal domain of safety. The place of kind-heartedness and tenderness.

Your Spirit leaves as gracefully as it entered.

And you know, intuitively, that your Guardian Spirit will return, will be present any time you desire. You've only to close your eyes and imagine it.

Your connection to this Spirit is strong and unconditional.

You will forever have the presence of your Spirit within you.

Pause.

When you are ready, you may open your eyes.

PART TWO

Challenges to Healthy Self-Esteem

*From all the offspring of the earth and heaven,
love is the most precious.*

—Sappho

CHILDHOOD AND FAMILY

*If you really want to hurt your parents
and you don't have nerve enough
to be homosexual,
the least you can do is
go into the Arts.*

—Kurt Vonnegut

Chapter 8

Why Is My Room Blue?

*He has always had astonishing social radar, and I can see now with
horrified clarity that he absorbed the idea of responsibility for the happiness of his own parents like a sponge. I think that it must have been at
a huge cost to himself that he made it so easy for us to be pleased to be
his parents. He became what he thought he needed to be.*

—Robb Forman Dew,
The Family Heart

Dear Mom and Dad,

Well, here we are, just home from the hospital, and whew!
Some birth, eh? Sorry about the whole delivery thing, Mom.
Didn't mean to take so long, although it was awfully comfort-
able, warm and easy in my room.

And speaking of rooms . . . I noticed you guys painted my
new one blue. It's nice, I like it. Thanks. But I do have one
question for you. Is it blue because you want me to sleep
peacefully at night, as if under a canopy of brilliant stars and
a deep blue background? Or perhaps you want me to feel
like I'm enjoying the beautiful days outdoors, complete with
sunshine, blue skies and breezes, that I may be too young to
experience yet for myself. Maybe, when I look out the window
and see the blue of the horizon, I'll carry that feeling into my

own little world here, where the inside and outside blur into one harmonious work of nature. It's very soothing, I have to admit.

But maybe those things aren't what you had in mind when you painted my room. Maybe you have some conscious or unconscious expectations about what you want me, your little boy, to become in life. Maybe you have a picture already in your mind of me when I'm all grown up. What dreams do you have for me? What are your hopes? I guess what I'm asking is, what are you expecting of me?

I wish I knew. In the hospital I heard you guys daydreaming out loud, saying stuff like, maybe he'll be a lawyer, or a doctor, or a baseball hall-of-famer. You know, some of the other new-borns in the nursery were grumbling about how fathers some-times see their children as extensions of themselves, rather than as individuals. So then naturally, such a father would encourage his son to be a younger, hopeful version of what he had wanted to be himself. I guess it's the whole "living vicariously through the boy" thing. Is that true about you, Dad? Do you intend to pass your own, let's say, unfulfilled fantasies and goals, on to me?

If so, jeez, that's going to be a heavy burden, don't you think? I mean, I'm going to have enough on my hands with the whole puberty thing, then the whole adolescence thing. I can only imagine the kind of troubles and heartache that we'll all experience if I want to go in my own direction, and that direction isn't quite what you had in mind. Maybe you'll expect me to excel in something you once tried ... I don't know, maybe to achieve a certain level of intellect, or shine in a certain sport. Or maybe you'll feel proud if I'm extremely popular or good-looking. Or maybe you'll expect me to date a few girls, then get married to a woman and have a bunch of kids. You'll figure, that's what boys do. And I'll figure, that's what Dad expects. So I might as well do it. But where do *I* factor in here? How much do *my* feelings count?

What will it be like for you if I don't turn out exactly that way, Dad? I know you and Mom were counting my little toes and fingers and then you said that I'm just perfect! I liked that. However, you do realize, don't you, that there are aspects of who I am, and who I will be, that you can't see yet? You can't count my I.Q. the way you can count my toes. And you can't see how popular I'll be . . . with guys or with girls. You cannot know if I'll have your looks, Mom's personality, Granddad's smile, or Aunt Gerry's crazy sense of humor. Hmmm, come to think of it, we don't know much of anything just yet, except for the fact that I have all the external body parts that I'm supposed to have. So let's face it, we don't *who* I'll be!

Which brings me back to the blue room.

Now that I've got the knack for breathing, cooing, sleeping, and crying, I imagine I'll need to get started on some of the other tasks at hand. Tasks like smiling, recognizing, and connecting with you guys whenever I see you. I'll move on to sitting up, then walking, talking, and all the rest in due time. (I hope!) Before long, I'll be running, getting into a bit of mischief, going to school, maybe asking to play the tuba in the school band, or needing money for a uniform for soccer or baseball. Eventually I'll need my own car, of course. And I might want to study abroad for a year. I'll do what I can to avoid needing dental braces, but I can't make any promises. I know I could get rather expensive. Then you'll yearn for the days when all I needed was to have my diaper changed and given a fresh bottle, right?!

Well, Mom and Dad, if I don't want to play hockey, and instead, I want to play the piccolo, will that be okay with you? Or if I don't get all A's, but I do show some exceptional ability in painting and dance, are you going to get nervous about that? If Mom and I agree to piano lessons, you're not going to start with certain macho comments, are you, Dad? I can hear it now, "He's artistic enough, Helen. What the boy needs are some boxing lessons!"

What if I march to my own drummer in other ways as well, ways that are distinctly different from what you had in mind for me? For instance, I might not show any interest at all in girls. I might want to go with a guy friend on weekends to the art house over in the big city, and spend my allowance seeing avant-garde movies. Or instead of football camp in the summer, I might like to try theatre camp. Or I might just like camp, period. If you get what I mean . . . wink, wink, nudge, nudge. I don't know . . . all sorts of things about me could be quite different from what you saw in your imagination when you let yourself daydream about my future, all those years ago, back when you first met me. Maybe I'll become a doctor. But maybe I won't. I might become a teacher, or an architect, or a famous designer. Or I might become a trucker or artist or minister or flight attendant or nurse or comedian or computer programmer or street-sweeper or fireman or mayor!

And, I might be gay. It does happen, you know.

I might be a kind of boy that you didn't expect me to be. I might not bring home any girls. I might want to bring home my boyfriend. Will you set another place at the table for him, Mom and Dad? Will there be a holiday present with his name on it? Will you ask me how he is when you haven't seen him for awhile? Will you consider his parents to be your in-laws? Will you introduce him at parties as who he is: my boyfriend? Will you come to our commitment ceremony? Will you dance with him? Will you accept him? Will you accept me?

I pray that your love for me isn't conditional.

I like the blue room. But I want to know what it means. The athletic skill I'm best at may be throwing you curve balls. I hope you remember something: Nothing I am is intended to disappoint you or hurt you. Who I am is not about you doing something wrong during my formative years. I hope you understand that I am not some disembodied issue of right and wrong, "shoulds" or "should-nots." You don't have to worry about my lifestyle, just be there for me in my *life*. I know you've had to make some adjustments . . . I have, too. Just love me. And wish me happiness.

With all my love,
Your Son

When I speak professionally at gatherings to parents of adult gay and lesbian children, I encounter all sorts of stories, and certainly some of the expected concerns and questions. Some parents ask if, clinically speaking, they have done something to cause their child's homosexuality. Such parents really are yearning for a *reason* that their adult child is gay, even if that reason holds them responsible. As tough as the guilt might be, they are willing to absorb it if it means that they have an answer.

There are more troubled about not knowing than they are about being to blame.

Such thinking presupposes, of course, that there's something wrong with being gay. And that's really the issue parents need to deal with. Whatever it was in their own background that taught them about homosexuality (or bisexuality as well) was clearly in error. Maybe their understanding of what it means to be gay came from cultural or societal misconceptions, or from their religious backgrounds. Maybe they grew up in a time or geographic location that isolated them from gay people, or from *knowing* of the gay people around them. The closet works two ways: It keeps a gay person from being who he/she is, and keeps others from learning about them.

A parent can be totally devoted, loving, and compassionate, and still be absolutely clueless when it comes to an understanding about their gay son or daughter. A mother told me that she didn't love her gay son any less since he came out to her, but she actively struggles within herself to reach an acceptance of him as a gay male. She feels at a loss as to what to do with her own feelings, how to synthesize what she's always believed about gay people with who she now knows her son to be. She loves her son dearly, but she was taught that gays were "bad," bad in the eyes of society, bad in the eyes of God. It's all very confusing and challenging for her.

I tell parents that he's the same person on Tuesday, after his disclosure, as he was on Monday, previous to his coming out. And while that may be true for *him*, that he is the same person (although now a person with the accomplishment of being more honest than the day before), it may not be true to the parents. They now have heard of an aspect of their son that was previously not discussed. As long as it wasn't discussed, it was allowed to be denied. While denied, it didn't have to be dealt with, at least not by them. Their son was furiously dealing with it internally, of course, for years. Now however, the "dealing with it" is throwing them a curve, and they don't feel that they have the skills to sort it out, understand it, and cope with it. Even if this mother had very strong suspicions that her son is gay, saying so makes it real.

On the other hand, I hear stories from parents where the coming-out process went quite well. Although these parents, too, deal with giving up or altering their deeply harbored dreams and hopes for their children—you know the dreams: seeing their child walk down the aisle with a traditional mate, the grandchildren, the holiday gatherings, the white picket fence—they are able to adopt a perspective that brings them much peace. "All I ever wanted for my daughter is her happiness," a mother told me. "And what I see is that she's immensely happy with her life partner. I've come to realize that my real dream was to raise a wonderful human being, and I have. Her being gay doesn't change that. I respect and love her with all my heart."

A father told the group, "I used to be worried that a gay life would be such a difficult life for my son. I didn't want him to suffer that. But I see him respecting himself, and so everyone else in his life respects him, too. His life isn't any more difficult than the lives of the rest of us. And it's no less satisfying, either."

For this father, the coming-out moment with his son was fraught with fear. The son feared his father's rejection, and Dad feared a harsh road ahead, but they've gone to support groups together, read books together, and talked to other families with gay adult children. What they've found is a far more satisfying relationship filled with honesty and mutual respect than they had ever hoped for. They learned, and with their knowledge came a dissolution of the fear. It is said that Nature abhors a vacuum. What these two found was that love came in to fill the void that was left by the fear.

The son, in the meantime, realized that the distance he had previously felt with his father wasn't about being gay. It was about the *secret*—the honesty that was absent from the relationship. "There was something missing," he admits. "Our relationship had a superficiality about it that we weren't able to overcome until I came out. Since then, it's felt like I'd always hoped it would. We're much closer and much more honest with each other, about all sorts of things."

Almost all the parents I talk with admit to having hoped for heterosexual children. We gays know this about our parents and we learn to deal with that knowledge the best we can. It often means living with feeling "less-than," and hoping for parental forgiveness if the truth comes out. Perhaps one of the biggest fears children have regarding their parents is about losing that parental love, or finding their love to be conditional. *I'll get their love as long as I'm who they want me to be,* we think.

We also see the difficulty involved with traditional expectations even when homosexuality *isn't* part of the picture. For instance, in a racial context, when a Caucasian marries an African-American. Or in a religious context, when a Jew marries a Catholic. Parental expectations, when there is a strong emotional investment tied to them, can cause tremendous pressure, feelings of disappointment for all concerned, and much heartache.

Parents, comfortable in their assumption that their child is indeed heterosexual, are poorly prepared by our society, by our religions, often by families and friends, to adjust to the reality, whenever that reality strays from preconceived notions. Beyond being poorly prepared, they may even be purposely discouraged from being supportive of their children's sexual identity. The result is nothing short of an abundance of fear, anger, resentment, and confusion.

A Latina mother spoke to me about the difficulties she's faced in her own tightly knit, very Catholic community because of being perceived as an outspoken advocate for gay rights. She has two gay children and complains not about their sexual orientation, but about the hardships posed to her family because of her being a supportive mother. "I adore my kids and frankly, it's none of my business who they sleep with!" she declared. She is a member of PFLAG and so she understands that being gay is not only about one's bed partners, but she says she has trouble just getting some people to understand a basic principle like, "it's none of *their* business, either." So adamant are they that homosexuality is wrong.

I recently heard a minister speak to a gathering of gay men and lesbians and their families. Most notably he said, "If you remember nothing else from tonight, remember this: We are all created in God's image. All of us. Every last one of us, without exception. No matter what *you* had in mind for your child, what God has in mind is exactly how it's happening. If it were left up to us, our ignorance and prejudices might make the world miss out on some pretty terrific people!"

He received a standing ovation.

Real-Life Story . . . Russ and Joey

When Russell was 14 years old, he developed a crush on another boy in his high school, a boy who readily returned Russ's affections. This other boy, Joey, was 16. Although neither actually identified as being gay at the time ("We told ourselves that we were just practicing to be with girls," says Russ), they nevertheless developed a puppy love with all the romantic accouterments. There were flowers and little gifts shyly offered, late-night whispered phone calls, Saturday afternoon bike rides along deserted paths outside of town, and more. They lived in a small Southern town and knew of no one else like them, meaning, they knew of no gay young men.

Both boys were model students, very bright, very well liked by their teachers, and each had his own set of special talents. Russ was quite musical and excelled in all his arts classes. Joey was a gifted wrestler, having brought some distinction to the small high school wrestling team as they traveled around the state competing with other teams. Despite the boys' popularity as individuals, it felt gravely, enormously important to both of them that they keep their relationship a secret.

Russ felt that he and his mother were very close, and that she was proud of him and his scholastic and artistic accomplishments. His relationship with his father was "a bit more distant, but I respected him very much." He had three siblings, all older brothers, and despite the usual hierarchical torments of childhood, he felt close to them, too, during most of his childhood. It's interesting to note that, later on, all of his brothers would be married by the age of twenty. Although not particularly academic, they were quite popular in town for their athletic accomplishments. All had a reputation of being "all-American guys," according to Russ. Getting good grades was not as highly honored or socially praised in their community, nor in their extended family, as were other extracurricular activities: sports, dating, popularity with peers, etc. "Boys will be boys" was the refrained motto their father used to dismiss the brothers' often mischievous behavior.

The families of both Russ and Joey were very religious, as were most of the families in their community. This was the mid-seventies in a town small enough that the liberal ideas washing over much of the country did not ever take root. There was no evident movement of any sort here: no women's rights protests, no racial uprisings, and no sign of gay tolerance to be found. "If you were even slightly outside of the mainstream, you were targeted," explains Russ. "You were hassled at school, or on the streets, or with threatening phone calls. The townspeople were unbelievably intolerant of anyone who was considered different. Their priorities were work, church, and having babies. That was their life. And that's what was expected of you."

As far as Russ and Joey were concerned, that was plenty of reason for them to keep their romance to themselves. The town's fear of anyone who appeared different translated to the boys' fear of being found out to be different. They certainly didn't want anyone suspecting them of being gay; they didn't even want to acknowledge it themselves. Perhaps they felt that saying it, even to each other, might make it real. And, once made real, their gravest fears of ostracism and shame might be actualized.

Despite their best efforts at secrecy, the rumors began. As Russ describes it, there were mumblings in the school hallways, which, in time, escalated to homophobic graffiti scrawled on his locker, vandalism done to his bicycle, and threatening phone calls made to his home. Where once his bicycle was a source of enjoyment for his Saturday getaways with Joey, he was now afraid to leave it anywhere. Where once he felt excitement when he heard the phone ring, hoping it was his boyfriend on the other end, he now felt only dread. He was being mocked, oppressed, and harassed, all because he wasn't the kind of boy others in his community expected him to be.

It was no better for Joey. An only child, he lived with his mother and father, both of whom were considered staunchly religious people and strict disciplinarians. Joey was well aware of the high expectations his parents placed on him, to be the kind of upstanding, successful, intelligent, God-fearing heterosexual man they believed they were grooming. Until recently, they had not let themselves believe that he was becoming anything different from that hope, that expectation.

However, he had begun to notice a certain tension around the dinner table. His mother finally confronted him, after many months of overhearing the gossip at various places around town: the beauty parlor, the drugstore, the grocery store—it felt to her that she couldn't escape the malicious rumors she was hearing everywhere she went. She couldn't know at the time that her experience was but a fraction of the hostility that her son was going through. She herself secretly thought that his friendship with Russ seemed much more than a normal friendship between two teenage boys, and her anxiety increased with each overheard comment. Her embarrassment was becoming more than she could handle, and she now regarded her son with suspicion and barely suppressed anger. She told him that she and his father were worried about him. She asked him why she was hearing that he was thought to be gay by so many others in town.

Although Joey vehemently denied any truth to the rumors, he couldn't deny the love letter from Russ his mother later found in one of his desk drawers. After a verbal altercation where he, in his teenager's lack of eloquence and abundance of righteous indignation at his privacy being violated (which was true), and his mother's hostile and accusatory tone (protecting the tremendous fear, anxiety, and grief she was really feeling), he stormed out of the house and ran all the way across town to Russ's.

After spending the night and most of the next day talking and crying in each other's arms, Joey realized that he had to return home and try to settle the disruption of the previous encounter with his mother. He intended to calmly speak with her about his relationship with Russ and hope that she'd understand. He himself wasn't sure if he was going through a phase with his feelings for Russ, or if indeed he was "one of those homosexuals" that his own father would refer to upon occasion. No matter what his sexual orientation might be, Joey assumed he would have his mother's understanding along the way, despite their differences.

He was wrong.

He returned home to find his closet empty and several suitcases filled with his clothes and some personal belongings. There was a note attached, from his mother. It read simply,

> You are not the boy I raised.
> You have disappointed us.
> You are no longer welcome here.

It wasn't until after Joey's suicide a few years later that Russ learned what had happened to his high school sweetheart. Joey had run off to a nearby city and begun a life that was high in danger and low in dignity. He lived on the streets. He became involved in drugs. After repeated unsuccessful attempts to phone his mother, hoping always for a reconciliation, he could no longer stand the humiliation and shame of her rejection, and he decided to end his life of pain.

What she had failed to realize was that he was exactly the boy she raised, no more and no less, for better or for worse. But to her, he was something that so assaulted her expectations of him, so violated what she had wanted him to become, that she could no longer acknowledge his existence. To her, he had killed her hopes.

Is there a difference between parents wanting what they feel is best for their child, and burdening that child with layers of expectations and pressure to become what they want him to become? Of course there is. Unfortunately, some parents do not see this difference, and so they rear their children as best as they can, but nonetheless crossing the fine line between guidance and expectation. Joey's parents did just that. As did Russ's. As do countless other parents, some unintentionally, some intentionally, some simply too unconscious regarding their parental influence to differentiate what is healthy and what isn't.

As for the more misguided parents, the ones confused by the conflicting messages of society, or the church, well . . . when their child turns out to be homosexual, it can simply be too much of an assault on their long-held expectations for them to be able to cope with it. There's help and guidance available to them, but first they must be courageous and open-minded enough to reach out for it.

That takes strength; more strength, it seems, than Joey's parents had. And so a promising young life was lost.

It greatly behooves parents (of all sexual orientations) to ask themselves if they, symbolically speaking, are thinking of painting their child's room blue, or pink, and why. Such a simple issue has far-reaching—and as we've seen, possibly life-threatening—implications for a person's life.

It's not simply about the color of the room. It's about parental expectations when the news is "it's a boy!" or "it's a girl!" and what may happen when parents are ill-prepared for a boy or a girl that doesn't fit their ideas of who they want him/her to be. Perhaps parents need to deal with their own sexual orientation agendas, their own unfulfilled fantasies and goals, and their ability to cope with life's disappointments—*before* they start a family. Because whether it's about sexual orientation or another issue altogether, all children, at some time and in some way, will disappoint their parents. (Just as the parents will inevitably disappoint their children.) This disappointment is a part of life, a part of growing up. It's natural, but the child shouldn't have to die because of it.

The Meditation

This meditation encourages you to spend time on words, ideas, and images that may hold a more potent meaning for you than you realize. I invite gays and non-gays, parents and non-parents, to spend time with this meditation, using it to stimulate thoughts and feelings in a free-floating manner.

Allow for plenty of time to meditate on each word. I recommend at least one full minute with each before moving on to the next. Let yourself free-associate. Let your mind wander and your feelings emerge. Simply watch what happens. Everyone has a different response to these words and images. Whatever your response is, it is based upon your own personal history of life experiences.

It is important not to edit or judge your associations to these words. Simply observe.

Take a deep breath and let yourself relax . . . allow your body to release all tension and let your mind find a place of peace. Continue to breathe deeply until you feel calm, centered, and relaxed.

Pause.

Now allow your breath to return to normal, without any effort on your part.

Pause.

With each of the following words, allow yourself to free-associate any thoughts and feelings you may have . . . let them emerge as they will. And as they emerge, take plenty of time to observe them, and simply watch what happens, as if from a safe, comfortable distance. Use the power and focus of your mind to allow for all the space your thoughts and feelings may need.

There is nothing you have to do or be. Simply witness.

Take another deep, cleansing breath.

Here are the words:

Birth . . .
Mother . . .
Father . . .

Family . . .
Childhood . . .
Adolescence . . .
Adulthood . . .
Old age . . .
Grandparents . . .
Siblings . . .
Play . . .
Work . . .
Love . . .
Success . . .
Money . . .
Power . . .
Disability . . .
Need . . .
Want . . .
Hope . . .
Dream . . .
Regret . . .
Guilt . . .
Shame . . .
Anger . . .
Knowledge . . .
Freedom . . .
Peace . . .
Happiness . . .
Life . . .

I encourage you to do this meditation next week, then next month, then next year.

Follow your growth.

When you are ready, take a deep, centering breath.

Chapter 9

Parent-Pleasing/People-Pleasing

Trying to be what others want us to be is a form of slow torture and certain spiritual death.

—Anne Wilson Schaef

Each time we act for the approval of others, we put ourselves in a state of anxiety and dependency. We are dependent on others' acceptance and anxious that we won't get it. For some, this sounds like the very definition of childhood.

It is in childhood that we learn our rights and wrongs by whether we have pleased our parent(s). The routine is well known, being one of the first and most repeated lessons throughout the entirety of childhood: If we get a nod of acceptance or a smile out of our parent, then, we understand, that's good. We've done something good. We *feel* good. And, in our naiveté, we think *we are good* because of it. Conversely, a frown, dismissal or reprimand indicates bad. We've done something bad. Perhaps— and here's where early self-esteem formation hits a snag—even *we* are bad.

This is the basic signaling with which each child, to one degree or another, becomes familiar. Even the best-intentioned parents respond with certain signals and messages—some helpful for a child's self-esteem and some not, some through subtle connotation, some more directly—depending on whether their child's actions and behavior is pleasing them, that often blur the distinction between *doing* something and *being* something.

Parents who are "good enough" in their parenting skills are able to distinguish between their child *doing* something bad, i.e., displeasing them, and *being* something bad. Similarly, good parenting also teaches that there's a difference between doing something good and being good, that the former is not a prerequisite for the latter. Healthy parenting helps the child to understand and differentiate this.

What a vital life lesson this is, absolutely fundamental for the formation of healthy self-esteem! Doing bad is behavioral, and therefore changeable. One can *learn* to not do bad. Being bad is about identity, one's very being. It's about who someone is—and what they understand themselves to be—at their very core. It rings loudly in their psyche: I . . . am . . . bad.

Let's take an example. Little four-year-old Tommy is running in the house, which leads, inevitably, to a broken crystal vase. To the good-enough parent, he is *doing* something bad (i.e., something I do not like him to do), but *he* is not bad. He is still a wonderful, curious, energetic little miracle in his formative years. One of the things he is in the middle of forming at this very moment is an understanding of the rules, which include no running in the house. That is all the broken crystal means: no running in the house. It does not mean anything about Tommy's character, his intelligence, his compassion, or consideration for others. It means nothing about Tommy being unlovable. It means, simply, no running.

To the parent who does not understand the implications of doing bad versus being bad on a child's self-esteem, his/her reaction to this little event communicates to Tommy that he is bad for running and breaking the crystal. Suddenly, in an action that lasted no more than the time it takes to watch a piece of glass fall from the table to the floor, giving echo to his felt surprise and foretelling of sure disaster for this grave little offender, Tommy has a new identity, one that with a little repetition will take hold deeply: He is someone who is bad.

How easily the vulnerable, trusting, clean-slated child internalizes the label his parent has now given him! If I am bad, thinks Tommy subconsciously and before he even has the vocabulary to put this understanding into words, then it follows that I must be worthless. (Well, I'm certainly *worth less* than a vase!) And a worthless person is apparently (based on Mom's reaction toward me) undeserving of love. Therefore—and without knowing it, he has learned the beginnings of the "if A leads to B . . ." math concept he'll be exposed to in about five more years, an idea much less painful when it refers to numbers, and not to the self-concept of a child—I am an unlovable person. Awfully high price to pay for running in the house.

And so the lesson that began in his relationship with his parents, and that will lead Tommy into a series of unfulfilling, emotionally abusive adult relationships, has taken hold: I am unlovable. Tommy will have a new quest now: to attract, date, and sleep with the people he finds who share in his understanding. The only people of interest to him emotionally are those that can confirm for him his Big Truth, his solidly learned, continually reinforced (you didn't think his parents only told him that he was bad that *one* time, did you?) understanding of himself, that he is a worthless human being. Worth less than the respect or kindness of a lover. Worth less than anyone's consideration for his feelings. Worth less than the energy it takes to exercise some impulse-control and not get beaten, psychologically or physically. Worth less, far less, than anyone's love.

Has Tommy become a pretty anxious guy? You bet. A man who also suffers from depression? Almost certainly. How is Tommy's overall self-esteem? Well, that would have to be pretty low, wouldn't it? I mean he now spends his time in relationships that encourage him to continually try to please his partner (just as he tried to please his parents) and failing miserably, feeling, thanks to his self-concept, unable to do anything right (just as he felt with his parents). Well good, he thinks now as an adult, albeit an unconscious thought, *this* I know how to do: Try, and fail, and try, and fail. I know all the rules of this game and I know just what to expect thanks to my childhood training. This is *familiar*. This is *known*. Whereas the known is far less frightening than the unknown, this pattern, on some level, is also *comfortable*. And certainly repeatable. Time and time again. With each new-found expectation. Job after job. Relationship after relationship.

Just how did this destructive pattern start? Where did Tommy get this unhealthy view of himself and the world he inhabits? How on earth did this child, inquisitive, trusting, and naturally joyous at birth, get it into his head that *he is bad* and therefore fundamentally unlovable. It all started the moment (and was reinforced in all the following similar moments over the childhood years to come) he was taught that he was bad, worthless, unlovable. Tommy was not born thinking this way; he was *taught* to have low self-esteem. That little broken vase episode really started something, didn't it?

Now let's throw another factor into the mix: Tommy happens to be gay. When he was a kid, Tommy was different from the other kids. He probably *felt* different very early on, likely as early as grade school or junior high. In terms of Tommy's self-esteem, "different" maybe didn't mean much, but "effeminate" did. (Notice how in a society that doesn't value the feminine in all people, terms of femininity are used as put-downs? Read more about this in Chapter One.) He also understood that "queer," "sissy," and "fag" were about the worst things to be called.

Of course this is only one of countless possible similar scenarios, but let's paint the picture further. Perhaps Tommy's father (or big brother, cousin, or uncle) gave him a hard time about not being good at, or not wanting to play, baseball (or hunting or fishing or whatever the males in the family *did* value). Maybe the kids taunted him on the playground. Maybe his teacher didn't discipline the children who giggled and called him names in class; instead of using that opportunity to teach tolerance, the teacher's silent acceptance presented the most potent lesson for the day, one for which some of the children were all too willing to do homework, in the schoolyard, in the hallways, on the bus: It is permissible and acceptable to be homophobic, to make fun of others. In the process, the teacher taught Tommy something, too: He is *deserving* of such ridicule, that no one will come to his aid (nor likely stand up for tolerance and acceptance in general).

Don't expect anyone to defend you, Tommy—you're different in a way that is far too threatening.

So, here's the math equation again, growing more painful with each year of his young life. I am different. The others degrade me because I seem different to them, too. The adults, whom I am forced to entrust with my fragile, still-forming ego, condone this degradation and humiliation. I must be deserving of this. I must be worth less than the others. I must be unlovable. (Starting to sound familiar?)

So, as he tries to do with his parents, Tommy begins to try anything and everything he can do to please his tormentors. It seems like the only way to ease some of the tension, depression, and negative feelings about himself that overcome him, starting with his morning walk to the school bus and not ending until he falls asleep in bed, his censorious dreams taking the night shift.

He sees that the bullies have friends, so maybe he tries to bully the other, younger kids. He likes how it feels when the others laugh *with* him when he intends to make them laugh, and not *at* him. So, maybe he becomes the class clown. He finally gets a nod of approval from an adult when he turns in a good research paper, so maybe he picks up on the advantages inherent in over-achieving and plants the seed for a life of pleasing his bosses by working fourteen-hour days and becoming better than everyone else in the company. Maybe he eventually turns to alcohol or drugs to ease the internal pain. Maybe he confuses love with sex in his relationships, in all his attempts to feel something— anything—like what he imagines "lovable" to feel like.

Whatever path Tommy takes, it includes, at its core, the goal of *people-pleasing*. To him, it feels like this is the only way to cope. Tommy has grown into someone who lives in that constant state of anxiety and dependence. His low self-worth has led him to be dependent upon the acceptance of others at every turn. He seeks their approval in the vain attempt to fill all the considerable space left inside of him, space that should have been filled with confidence and a belief in his abilities, filled with the knowledge that he is still a wondrous and wonderful being and always will be, no matter what he does. Filled with knowing that, above all, he is undeniably, inherently lovable.

Instead of love, Tommy's life is driven by his constant attempt to relive that fateful moment—albeit, in his fantasy, with a decidedly different outcome!—so many turbulent, unsatisfied, angst- and Prozac-filled years ago, when he ran in the house. He is still trying to repair the vase.

Real-Life Story . . . Mike

Mike is an extremely likable and creative man. He is 28 years old, lives in a big city, and will tell you that, for the most part, he is quite happy with his chosen career in nursing. Everyone at the clinic where Mike works thinks very highly of him. He is professional yet witty with colleagues, adored and trusted by those in his care. In fact, his supervisor tends to rely on Mike when it comes time to assign new patients, which in essence means extra work. Mike's "high level of competence, combined with his extraordinary people skills" (as his last performance report stated), make him, in the eyes of all who know him, an exemplary asset to the clinic.

Ask any of Mike's friends about him and they'll tell you he's a terrific guy, great sense of humor, always there when you need him, a selfless giver. Whenever you call him on the phone, even in the middle of the night, he sounds cheerful and available. "Always glad to hear from you," he'll say. "No problem."

About his personal life, Mike states "I've always had a relationship, one after another," and is in one now, although he is quick to point out that he's not very happy with his current partner, Darryl. What is Mike's chief complaint about Darryl? "I always come second to everything else. Whether it's the TV, his friends, his phone calls, his work . . . no matter how hard I try to get his attention, everything else comes first. I try surprising him with something nice, or I give him the silent treatment, or I scream, or I beg. Nothing works. He's so selfish. I can't get him to prioritize ME!" Mike has expressed similar complaints about past lovers as well.

What most people do not know about Mike is that he has been on a variety of mood stabilizers for the past three years, having a history of panic attacks (overwhelming anxiety usually coupled with a shortness of breath and heart palpitations) and at times suffering from debilitating clinical depression (when he's in the throes of one of these depressions, his misery is so great he feels unable to get out of bed). Although he very much wants to get off these meds, he feels dependent upon them . . . "trapped" is the word he uses. Eight years ago, he attempted suicide with a bottle of his mother's prescription medication (even though he himself has nearly limitless access to medications at the clinic). He has never done recreational drugs, although "I will binge on alcohol about three or four times a year," he admits. "Then I feel horribly guilty about it later." When Mike is home alone, he can sometimes be found lying flat on his living room floor, staring off into space. None of his friends knows this side of Mike. Not even Darryl.

Perhaps one of the most important aspects of Mike's background is that his mother has been addicted to prescription medication his entire life. He has no memory of her *not* suffering from one illness or another. What he does remember, quite painfully, is that the family was completely consumed with his mother's physical complaints.

Even when he was a very small child, he remembers that he and his younger sister had to be as silent as mice when his mother wanted to take a nap, which was often several times a day. A particularly acute malady had everyone getting dressed in the middle of the night to take her to the outpatient ward. Most of her medications kept her home-bound and drowsy for much of her adult life, certainly all of Mike's life. School performances, awards banquets, scouting events, even parent-teacher nights found his mother absent from the crowd. In fact, as Mike grew older and obtained a driver's license, it was he who often missed important school functions and social opportunities, instead coming to the aid of his mother's call whenever she paged him. (Not surprisingly, to this day Mike refuses to wear a pager.) Whether it was in the middle of a final exam, or the middle of a date, when his mother beckoned, he had to go to her. "It was simply expected of me," he says. "It was totally unthinkable in my family that I wouldn't do whatever she wanted, whenever she wanted it."

All other lives in that household—which is to say anyone else's *needs*—played second fiddle to the trumpeting call of his mother. Everyone else, apparently, was *worth less* than his mother. Mike was expected to fully participate in his family's hierarchy of needs.

With her unavailability, can we hope that Mike was able to rely on his father to be present for him, at least during important moments of his childhood? Mike's memories of his father, as you might guess, are centered on providing care to his mother. In fact, if the kids weren't appropriately rallied around her needs, they were displeasing the father. They were told they were selfish and suffered emotional punishment such as Dad's verbal wrath or his silent treatment. (Sound familiar?)

Mike came to my office about two years ago, and it was clear from the beginning that, despite his jovial facade, he was in tremendous psychological pain, and that his pain started many, many years ago and ran very deep. Behind the smile was a profound depression, and behind that, a burning rage.

Mike's therapy has been a gradual and gentle journey, focusing on the strengthening of his self-esteem, taking baby steps in an uncovering and reparative process therapists call "re-parenting." He knows he has a long way to go to be able to surround himself with people who care about him and prioritize him, to have relationships where he is not constantly playing second fiddle to another man's needs, but first he has to know (in his head) and feel (in his heart) that he deserves no less, *that he is not worth less.*

Mike is a very competent individual, and knows he succeeds at whatever he does. But wanting to feel loved unconditionally for *who he is*, rather than *what he does for others*, is a major concern and a therapeutic goal for him. He knows that inside, he has a lot of childhood rage toward his parents that will need to come out, at his own pace, as he's strong enough to experience it. Mike sometimes feels very scared, and sometimes ("on my good days") very brave and centered. Most of the time, with a weary sigh and an honest smile, he'll tell you that he believes he is on the road to a happier, more self-aware, and genuine life ... a life where he feels *worthy*.

An update: Mike continues to work very hard at understanding his feelings about his parents, his lovers, and himself. He is becoming more honest with his feelings, and better able to express his needs constructively to others. Being, for the most part, comfortable with the caretaker role he has adopted his entire life, he nevertheless understands how that has led him "to be a door mat for everyone else's needs." And so he strives for a balance between *helping* others and trying to please them, and being aware of what he *needs* from others. This awareness helps Mike maintain a balance in his relationships and a growing sense of self-worth for himself.

The Meditation

One way Mike is learning to approach his self-esteem issues from a calm, centered, and genuine place is through meditation. He began meditating by simply sitting in a quiet spot and paying attention to his breathing. He did this for a few minutes several times a week, until he eventually grew comfortable sitting for ten, twenty, then thirty minutes almost every day. Meditation has become a safe place for Mike, a place of strength from which he can now allow some of his demons to rise to the surface, a little bit at a time. He says it's "sort of like spotting the Loch Ness monster ... first you see a head, then the head disappears and you see a tail. You know there's a lot more of him down there, but he only shows you small parts, just enough for you to see him and know he's around." This meditation may be read slowly by a friend, or silently to oneself.

Breathe deeply and slowly several times, allowing your mind and body to relax with each breath . . . in with fresh, cool, clean air, and out with stress. Let your focus be on the relaxing quality of each and every breath, so important to the harmony of your body and mind.

Pause.

Let your thoughts arise, and then let them float away on a breeze. You let your feelings arise, filling whatever space they need. You are open to your feelings, feelings which are within you for very good reasons.

These feelings may be understood by you, although perhaps some are not. But they are yours . . . as much a part of you as your breath.

No need to judge them, just have them. There is no right or wrong to your feelings. Simply accept them. Witness them.

Pause.

Open up, both to the feelings you enjoy, and to the ones that make you uncomfortable. What are your feelings telling you now?

Pause.

Take them all in, give them all the space, all the time they deserve. They are yours and no one can take them from you.

Pause.

Now I invite you to see yourself as a small child, with small child feelings. What are these feelings? Which are the ones you enjoy . . . ? When did you first feel them?

Pause.

Which are the ones that make you uncomfortable? . . . When did you first feel them?

Pause.

What would you like to say to this small child?

How would you like to say it?

What gift would you like to give to him/her?

How would you help this child to feel like the most important, worthy, welcomed, loved person in the world?

Pause.

Let your heart open to this child.

Let your heart open to yourself.

Forgiveness.
Let yourself be forgiven.
Let yourself feel adored.
Let yourself be worth everything.
Let yourself be loved.

Note: There is a self-assessment exercise in Chapter 20 of this book to accompany the issues discussed in this chapter. You may wish to go there now to further your understanding of the specific issues involving your own family dynamics, or you may want to consider taking all the assessments after you've completed the book.

Chapter 10

Kids Say the Darndest Things, Revised

The Bible contains six admonishments
to homosexuals and 362 to heterosexuals.
This doesn't mean that God doesn't love heterosexuals,
it's just that they need more supervision.

—Lynn Lavner, comedienne

There are many derogatory terms used to describe people of sexual minorities, as well as people of any kind of minority— ethnic, racial, gender, religious, etc. In fact, sometimes it seems that the need for human beings to degrade others in an attempt to feel superior is practically epidemic. In almost all walks of society, one can easily overhear a proclamation of the likes and dislikes toward some group, to which the speaker is not a member, using slang, abusive, or otherwise discriminatory terms.

Perhaps we'd like to think that, as an oppressed community ourselves, gay people will not oppress others. But it isn't true. In fact, much of the discrimination—covert and overt alike— aimed at members of the gay culture comes directly from the mouths of other gay people. As if we don't have enough to deal with hearing homophobic jabs from intolerant non-gays, members of right-wing fundamentalist groups, and others who have problems accepting gay people!

Yet, in bars and clubs, on the train, in airports, gyms, rest rooms, at parties, the theater, in restaurants, you name it: One can probably find a gay person committing an act of intolerance against his own gay brothers or sisters. There's always the joke involving a "faggot" or "bull dyke." We hear terms like rice queen, lezzie, fruit or troll, or whatever the derogatory slang of the hour happens to be. At the gym, I've heard gay men, pumped and oh-so-pleased with themselves, raucously and laughingly making fun of drag queens, as if they are somehow an affront and embarrassment to the rest of us *normal* gays; as if there isn't room in society—in *our* society—for differences in expression or style. They were deriding a segment of the gay population because of a desire to develop stage presence over biceps, and that fact somehow makes them less-than. If you've been the object of such verbiage, you tend to remember it, and not at all pleasantly. Being gay doesn't make it acceptable to be homophobic, any more than being black condones the use of the "N" word!

Our moments of playing the oppressor are certainly not limited to discrimination against our own people. We are also guilty of referring to honkies, spics, beaners, fish, and breeders. Are these words distasteful to read? I hope so. But then why are they allowed to be a part of our vernacular? As the targets of generations of discrimination ourselves, why do we ever even entertain the thoughts that lead to such words? Don't we know better?

I heard Maya Angelou speak as a guest on a talk show. In her usual warm and elegant manner, she told the audience that she will not tolerate, at gatherings at her house, any disparaging remarks made by her guests. If she overhears a discriminatory slur, be it a racist comment, homophobic joke or whatever, she will confront that guest and challenge him on his use of language and the attitude behind it. She will not allow such comments to be condoned, at least not in her home. Such a policy for one's own environment, so reflective of a commitment to heighten awareness of verbal misuse and abuse, strikes me as creative and progressive and good for everyone's self-esteem. I like that.

However, discrimination, as we well know, is not limited to overt verbal affronts. Again, we in the gay and lesbian community can be guilty of these offenses as well. Whenever and wherever a gay person can be shut out, discrimination is at work. For example, covert discrimination can be found in the gay media, where people of color or older people are underrepresented. Or perhaps a magazine shows no one who is not young, blonde, buffed, tan, or smooth. It can also be found in organizations where everyone is of a certain race or color. (I'm not referring here to a group such as Latin Gay Men United, where the point of the group is to promote the well-being of Latin gay men. I'm referring to, for example, an HIV-support organization, or an educational foundation, that consists almost exclusively of, for instance, white males.) Covert discrimination can also be seen in certain gay clubs or at community events, wherein minority people are isolated and left out. You get the idea.

Discrimination sure can be subtle sometimes. You really have to be paying attention. Someone who would never utter a sexist or homophobic comment socially, might exclaim *Bitch!* alone behind the wheel when cut off in traffic. Or mutter *faggot* under his breath. Or restrict his prejudicial comments to times when talking with close friends only. It doesn't feel good, it doesn't help our self-esteem when we are called names, individually or collectively. There's something wrong when we call others names, too. Philosopher Grenville Kleiser has said, "Every good thought you think is contributing its share to the ultimate result of your life." Likewise, every disparaging thought you think or comment you make is contributing to you being less of a person—less compassionate, less concerned with others, less evolved in your own spiritual and emotional growth—than you can be. Everyone suffers.

Well then, why? If it does no one any real good, and it certainly doesn't do any good for the psychological or social health of our own community, why do we do it? Do you think this is an inborn trait, or do people learn this kind of behavior which represents, at a level underneath the surface, some form of intolerance, fear, or hatred for a group of other human beings? If it's environmental, then where do such attitudes come from? Is it a defense, a way of getting even with our original oppressors? Perhaps that's partially true. But then why would we try to get even with our own kind? It is so destructive to others, certainly, to be the targets of discrimination, but also it's highly destructive to oneself: this perpetual need to be "better-than" via the language and attitudes of racism, homophobia, sexism, and other forms of bigotry. Perhaps most disturbing: What has contributed to such low self-esteem that we would feel the need to be better than others, anyway? These aren't easy questions and the answers aren't simple, either.

Let me tell you this: We were not born intolerant of others nor hateful. We were born perfect little bundles of joy, ready and receptive to be nurtured with love, healthy thoughts, and healthy food. We were vulnerable, and open to having our hearts, minds, souls, and bodies fed by those we would entrust to do so—ready to embrace everything and everyone in our path with excitement, curiosity, and passion.

But we weren't always fed the good stuff. Sometimes what we were fed came from the spiritual and emotional baggage of our parents and others involved in our upbringing; later from our friends, their parents, our teachers, what we read in the papers, and heard around town. Across the paths of probably all children come, at one time or another, messages of prejudice, intolerance, fear, and hatred. Modeled for us are blatant as well as covert examples of putting others down for our own benefit, for our own perceived security. It's usually what is behind gossip. We've all sooner or later heard some gossip, likely participated in it ourselves.

Even if you were raised in a compassionate, secure environment where energy was not put toward hurting others, but toward lifting up the spirits and lives of all beings, eventually, you went to school. Whereas not all of the other kids were raised in such loving homes filled with tolerance and acceptance, you probably ran into some child carrying the parent's emotional baggage, containing at least a dose of discrimination. At least. At the other end of the spectrum, I've heard many stories by gay people in which homophobic slurs were tossed around the playground as easily and as often as a football. To be the target of such verbal assaults is to be fed a lasting, damaging, esteem-mauling experience. Think back: I bet you can remember one (or more) incidents where you were the target of some homophobic (or racist or sexist, etc.) violation. Of course you can. Such memories aren't pleasant or cherished, like the ones involving warmth and acceptance from a friend or family member. (Like the proverbial fishing trip out on the lake, just you and dad.) They last a long time just the same. Sometimes they last forever. I meet gay people all the time who, well into adulthood, are still trying to repair the emotional scars left over from some specific verbal abuse on the playground. Or in the neighborhood. Or in some club or organization. Kids say the darndest things, and sometimes the things they say wound for life.

I want to take a moment here to appreciate the plight of gay teachers, who, for fear of losing their jobs, feel that they must remain in the closet. They also have to hear verbal taunts and rampant homophobia which, even when aimed at others, can hurt deeply. I know of a teacher who is somewhat hesitant to correct a student's homophobic comments, even though he knows how destructive such comments can be, so afraid is he of then becoming the object of hatred himself. He has seen, firsthand, what can happen when a colleague is found out to be gay. Some of his gay peers have resigned, after years of teaching, when the atmosphere became too uncomfortable and hostile. The teacher-student and/or teacher-parent relationship can take an ugly turn, and oftentimes without the support or defense of colleagues.

ABC's *20/20* recently aired a feature story about the hardships faced by some high school educators when their community discovers that they're gay. It was a sensitive though tragic story that highlighted the fatal heart attack of a gay teacher, five months after being forced out of the career he so loved. The leader of the anti-gay church that spearheaded the attempt to torment and discard this teacher had only this to say: "Indulgence in sinful lifestyles brings heartache."

Even though this teacher's students reported saying that they were taught self-esteem, teamwork, and love by their much-admired teacher, it was not enough to halt the discriminatory efforts made against him by his superiors, townspeople, and members of this church. Even other youths, by and large far too young to have embraced bitterness and hatred on their own, echoed the sentiments of their narrow-minded parents, saying that it's wrong to put a gay man in charge of a child's education. Do these parents get the irony here? While educating their own children, they must have forgotten to teach tolerance and compassion for all people, including those who may be of a different sexual orientation from their own. It seems to me that this teacher was doing a far better job with their kids than they were. In closing the piece, Barbara Walters wisely and provokingly asked, "When will we begin to look at people as individuals?"

There is a program in a Los Angeles high school called Project 10 which helps improve the educational situation for gay students and teachers alike at their own schools. Started by a compassionate educator, Project 10 is expanding to many public and private educational institutions and making tremendous headway in the fight against homophobia on campus. Unfortunately, there is not a Project 10 at all schools. It's unfortunate that there even has to be a Project 10. Maybe someday there won't be the need.

I would suggest to you that, however a gay person may have come about making prejudicial comments aimed at others, we can consider such behavior a manifestation of internalized homophobia (more about this in Chapter 1). If it has been heard enough times, it's taken in, internalized. The simple yet painful result: *A person who doesn't like himself.* As is discussed all throughout this book, these homophobic comments heard from others— perhaps heard one's whole life—tear down a person's feelings of self-worth. Then, to add insult to injury, they teach an untrustworthy lesson about increasing a person's self-worth, albeit superficially and at the expense of others: *Use hurtful language.* So, the kid who was derisively called a faggot learned to not only believe he was less-than, but learned something on a behavioral level. That the way to feel better-than (the misperceived antidote) is to call others names. And so this tactic was adopted.

The problem with trying to build up one's own ego by using this behavior (aside from the pain it inflicts!) is that, first, it is usually transparent, and second, it is most definitely short-lived.

Putting down our own brothers and sisters leaves a bad taste in everyone's mouth eventually. It's only logical to think that if this guy is talking badly about *them*, what's he saying about *me* when I'm not around? It doesn't do much good for the trust necessary to sustain any healthy relationship. If he can diminish another gay person with a discriminatory comment, how does he feel— inside, where he can't hide behind the facade of superiority— about being a gay man? Probably pretty diminished himself. Undoubtedly, he's been well trained in feeling less-than.

These feelings of superiority do not last; they are, in fact, extremely transient. As soon as the party's over, as soon as the colluding audience, laughing at the hurtful comments, is gone, then the old feelings come right back up to the fore, leaving one feeling low again, perhaps even worse than before. So, trust is diminished and friendships are left on a superficial level at best. A person has gained the reputation of being a homophobic gossip, and feelings are no more elevated than they've ever been for this person. So, the vicious cycle continues: I feel less-than; I'll put others down (I believe it makes me feel better); I feel miserable again.

If we, as gay people, want to do something about the feelings that lead us to discriminate against each other, and want to change in ourselves any behavioral manifestations that perpetuate the individual and collective pain in our community, pain based in prejudice, then there's much that we can do. And it all begins, like other forms of growth, with awareness.

The first step is to ask ourselves if we might be discriminating against others in *any* way. One needs to answer this question as honestly as possible, after taking into consideration not only acts of homophobia, but also of stereotyping and condoning such behavior in others. It may be important at this step to recognize that the crime is not in falling prey to harmful behavior—because we probably all have some qualities or behavior that we're not too happy about, that we'd like to change. The crime is in being unwilling to identify this behavior in yourself, thus preventing you from working to change it. It begins with rigorous self-honesty.

If you find that yes, you do indeed discriminate against others, then you might ask yourself if this discrimination takes the specific form of homophobia. This can be a difficult characteristic to admit, especially for a gay man or gay woman. However, if you're willing to look at this part of yourself, then you are showing a courage to change, and that's a sign of strength. Ask yourself such questions as, Am I biased against men I consider effeminate? Do I consider older gay men to be predatory? Do I laugh at jokes others make of gay teens, arrogantly calling them "chicken" (even though it's pretty thinly veiled envy)? Do I think stereotypically when it comes to lesbians; they're either butch or femme?

The next step is to ask: To what degree do you, either overtly or subtly, *verbalize* or *take actions* that diminish your gay brothers and sisters? Under what circumstances? Have you always done this? Who modeled such behavior for you, and why are you adopting it? Are you trying to get back at someone? Are you trying to repair some damage you feel inside yourself ... attempting, perhaps, to cover up some feelings of low self-worth? Is it working? Does it feel within your abilities to cease this behavior? Can you put yourself in *their* shoes? How would it feel to *you*? (How *has* it felt to you?)

After honestly identifying all the facets of this issue within yourself, and becoming more aware of your own thoughts and behavior, another way to gain insight and effect change is to listen carefully to the comments of others. Really listening to how people sound when they use homophobic slurs is a way to heighten your specific awareness of the problem. Do I sound like that, too? Is intolerance a common quality among my friends, colleagues, family? In time, you may want to bring this to their attention. Taking a cue from Maya Angelou, you may even eventually adopt a personal principle to deter any further assaults against your own self-esteem, and the esteem of others whom you care about. Perhaps you can be the lighthouse of your group, showing them how destructive language can be when used in a discriminatory or prejudicial fashion, and guiding them toward raising their own consciousness about the issue. Speaking out can be very empowering and can help you clarify and commit to your own principles.

Finally, you can become involved, putting your newfound awareness into action. Help a gay teenager to feel better about him- or herself by offering your mentorship and attentions. Become politically active, work on a race-relations project, volunteer for a community, elderly, or minority organization. Put energy toward the elimination of prejudice, bigotry, and homophobia in your school or church. Or in your own family. Start small: Take your little cousin aside and teach him that hateful comments hurt. Teach him what a hateful comment *is*. Call a friend from high school and apologize for calling him names. Commit to pointing out the very next homophobic joke that's told at work, even if it's told by your boss. Make a promise to get some therapy if you can't satisfactorily lick this problem within yourself.

Perhaps most important, remember one of the more *helpful* things you learned as a child: Do unto others as you would have them do unto you.

Real-Life Story . . . Matthew

In my office, Matthew was relating the story of when he first met his best friend's fiancé:

"The thing I think I like most about him," he began, "is that he doesn't assume heterosexuality in conversation. He knew he was talking with a gay man, so he didn't talk as if the whole world was straight. When someone we talked about was hetero, he described him as a heterosexual person. When someone was gay, he said they were gay. He wasn't hung up on people's sexual identity, he was just clear, I think out of respect for me. In his eyes, I was not a minority, let alone a minority to make fun of. I was a person he respected."

This experience went a long way toward repairing Matthew's inner wounds about feeling less-than. He has many memories of being taunted and verbally abused as a child, both at home and at school. He also has had a very difficult time understanding that, even though he is now an adult in his late twenties, he *deserves* to be respected, gay or not gay. He deserves to be free of insensitive, homophobic comments. He deserves to be taken seriously, not discriminated against.

Matthew is bright and articulate. He is very aware of others' use of language. Many years of being called faggot, sissy, homo, etc., have taken their toll on him, however. He finds himself calling people one or another derogatory term when he's feeling impatient, angry, or defensive. In long lines, say, at the bank or gas station, he has thoughts such as, *When will this stupid sissy move along?* Or, *This bull dyke should learn how to do her job!* He'll be horrified at his own thinking when he catches himself, but he still does it the next time he's upset.

Sometimes, among friends, he'll use the term "queer." Although among gays it's a word that has come to indicate some amount of gay pride in the modern vernacular, in Matthew's youth it was a term used derisively, and when he uses it, he means it hurtfully. All those times he was verbally discriminated against really made an impression on him, didn't it? Unfortunately, although understandably, he was unable to deflect this harm from his youth, and instead not only came to think of himself as an "undeserving homo," but also bought into the use of homophobic slurs as a weapon to be used against others. In this way, he discriminates as strongly as he's been discriminated against himself. He gives as good as he gets.

It's no wonder, then, that his friend's fiancé was like a breath of fresh air. With this person he experienced a sensitivity that is the opposite of bigotry and stereotyping. It was plain, simple respect and understanding for another person, something Matthew isn't used to.

Matthew has a strong tendency to believe that any problems that arise in his relationships are automatically his fault, and they would get resolved "if I could just try harder." Of course he feels he's always at fault: his early life experiences have taught him that he's the problem. What he is, is not good enough. What he is, is reason for discrimination. He must be to blame. As you might imagine, all this heavy responsibility was producing a lot of anxiety for Matthew.

It's difficult for Matthew to stand up for himself in the face of homophobia or other types of discrimination. In fact, it's sometimes difficult for him to even identify when he's being discriminated against. But he had an experience that proved to be a turning point for both his tendency to feel less-than, and also for his previously untried ability to take action in his own defense.

After several months in therapy spent becoming more aware of his thoughts and feelings around discrimination, homophobia, his childhood wounds, and his relationship difficulties, Matthew felt that he and his boyfriend, both busy professionals, could use some time together, maybe go away on a vacation, just the two of them. He wanted to create a low-stress environment where they could talk and act honestly with each other. They went on a trip to a lakeside resort area and found a small gay-owned and -operated bed and breakfast inn.

There were two other couples also staying at that B&B, along with the couple that ran the inn. Although this was the first visit to the inn for Matthew and his boyfriend, the other couples apparently were friends or acquaintances of the owners. Each morning everyone would gather in the dining hall for breakfast and conversation—comparing sightseeing notes, sharing the day's plans.

One morning, while all eight men were having breakfast together, the conversation took a harsh turn. Although some of them were laughing, Matthew noticed that "a certain bitchiness had crept into" the dialogue, and many phrases like "Oh, you're such a prissy queen!" and "What a couple of fags you are!" were bantered about liberally. Matthew reports that he noticed a hostile edge to the cutting remarks, not all of which were well received, judging by the distressed looks on some of the guests' faces. He became more and more uncomfortable and ended up not being able to eat his breakfast, so in touch was he with the mean-spiritedness in the room. What happened next was nothing short of miraculous, according to Matthew.

Matthew stood up from the table (ignoring the shocked look

on his boyfriend's face!) and, although shaking with anger, said very clearly and directly, "Look, you guys. I'm sorry but I can't take you using that language with each other. You may just be kidding around, but I've been called a lot of awful names my whole life, and none of this is okay with me. If you're not going to show each other more respect, I can't come out here and have breakfast with you." And with that, he left the room. Quite a powerful exit, don't you think?

Matthew said that the following discussions he had with his boyfriend were honest, warm, and supportive, and that he, Matthew, felt "almost admired" by him. There were no more uncomfortable conversations at breakfast for the rest of their trip, and in fact one of the other couples thanked him for stepping in. They, too, had been feeling affected by the homophobic remarks, but didn't know what they could do about it. Another couple later apologized for their offensiveness.

What began as a conversation with his friend's fiancé became, for Matthew, the start of a series of empowering acts. With each incident of standing up for himself as a gay man, he was fueling his courage while repairing some old hurts. He entered a process that was self-propelling: each time he "righted a wrong" (as he'd say), he felt better about himself. With better self-esteem, he was emboldened to speak out again. A positive cycle had begun. Perhaps he had not been treated respectfully in the past, but he was learning how to treat *himself* respectfully and inadvertently modeling such behavior for others!

As he had found a way to increase his self-worth as a gay man, so too he was able to find the courage to be more honest in his relationship with his partner. By being more aware of his feelings, Matthew was becoming much better able to distinguish what felt acceptable to him, and what felt hurtful. Although it is no overnight process, he no longer immediately felt to be at fault for problems that would arise between them, nor did he feel that the solution to their problems was all his responsibility. Their communication improved greatly, and Matthew's anxiety about the relationship significantly diminished.

He understood that by defending himself, by respecting and

caring for his own feelings, he was better able to care for the feelings of others. He treated his relationship carefully, with a newfound respect for both of them. He even found ways to be more patient with strangers. Resorting to muffled homophobic slurs or thoughts is a thing of the past for Matthew!

The Meditation

This meditation may be read slowly by a friend, or silently to oneself.

Breathe deeply, and allow yourself to relax completely.

Let your mind relax, too. Let your mind open. See your mind as a vast, welcoming space, pure and innocent, waiting to be filled with empowering thoughts, creative thoughts, loving thoughts.

Pause.

Go back now, to a time of innocence in your life. Imagine yourself as a very young child, laughing, wide-eyed, discovering your fresh new world. Happy with yourself, and everyone around you. Everything feels like a miracle, created especially for your childlike enjoyment.

Pause.

You have no words of prejudice in your vocabulary. No words of hatred or intolerance. You've learned only to delight in people's differences.

Now imagine meeting, for the first time, a playmate whom you've never seen before. This child is of a different ethnicity from you and has skin of a different color from yours.

What are your first thoughts upon meeting this new person?

What are your first words to him/her?

What exciting recent discovery of yours would you like to share with him/her?

In your mind, let yourself become best friends with this child. See yourself having great, childish fun together. Playing for hours. Laughing constantly. Feeling free.

Pause.

Now you are an adult.

Living an adult life, filled with responsibility, engaging in lots of adult situations.

This is your life, presently, just the way it is.

And you meet someone who is different from you. He or she is of a different race, sexual orientation, religion, or gender. Choose one that you have the most prejudicial difficulty with, the one of which you are the least tolerant.

Pause.

Upon meeting this person, what is your first thought?

What is the first thing you say?

What is your next thought? And the next?

Would you like to meet with this person again? Would you like to have lunch with him/her? Why or why not?

Now think about this: What is it about this person that you fear?

What is it about this person that you do not understand?

What is it about this person that reminds you of yourself? What mirror is this person holding up to you?

Pause.

Now let yourself meet this person again, but now you see him or her through the eyes of a child.

With a childlike innocence and adoration of all things new, let yourself meet this person again, yet fresh, as if for the first time.

What are your thoughts?

What are your words?

Is your mind speaking, or is it your heart?

How might you enjoy having this person in your life? Think about this person coming to you in a time of great need. How might you rely upon him/her? How might he/she be able to rely upon you? How far might you go to help this fellow human being?

Pause.

Let your hearts meet.

Know that you are alike in far more ways than you are dissimilar. Know that your differences make each of you a unique, fascinating person. Your individual histories are rich and colorful, and you can teach each other and grow together because of the wisdom gained in your pasts.

And you have both arrived here, on this planet, at this moment in time, to learn something from each other.

Open your mind.

Open your arms.

Open your heart.

Chapter 11

Re-parenting for Parents

The violets in the mountains have broken the rocks.

—Tennessee Williams

Recently I was on a hike high up in the mountains north of Los Angeles with four friends of mine. Heterosexual, all, although I consider them to be extremely gay-supportive, as well as intelligent, sensitive, and fun. These four formed two married couples, one of which had brought along their two children, boys, ages eight and one. The eight-year-old also brought a school friend with him. We were a rambling, laughing, huffing, and puffing group.

One of the nice things about hiking with a group is that you have opportunities to spend time talking with each person, as some members hike faster, some slower, some stop to rest, etc. The relaxed yet fascinating ambiance of nature seems to bring out an easy camaraderie in all. On this day we felt humorous at times, serious at other times, often concerned that the kids were doing okay, alternately feeling adventurous, in awe of nature, cautious (there were bear tracks!), exhilarated, and exhausted. Accordingly, as we made our way up to higher and higher elevations along the winding dirt path, our conversations took many turns as well.

Several times I was in conversation with my friend, John, the dad to the two youngsters. As the topic included talking about his kids, he asked about my desire to have children with my significant other. A relatively straightforward and common question to ask of fellow thirty-somethings, although perhaps more common among heterosexual crowds. That is exactly what struck me as impressive about his question. It was asked with no delusions or restrictions about the ability of gay couples to have children. No moral stance, narrow thinking, or religious upbringing stood in the way of him fully expecting me to want kids of my own someday, and furthermore, to want to have them with my gay male partner.

As an artist and teacher himself, it was not that he was just used to being around gays, nor did he simply possess an acceptance of or tolerance for gay people. He was far too enlightened about the beauty in the diversity of humankind to think in such limited terms. To him, a good parent is found in any sexual orientation, and parenting may be a desire of people in any form of non-traditional family. (Perhaps if more people expressed such openness and progressive thinking toward gays and lesbians, such a question as John's would not have stood out as especially supportive or significant.)

His wife, my friend Pam, is also an educator and one of the kindest and most compassionate people I know. When her older son was in school with the children of a lesbian couple, she saw an opportunity to teach him tolerance. She turned the example of same-sex parenting into a lesson that started him thinking of all people as potential friends, and all humans as valid, gifted contributions to the fabric of humanity. (The parenting skills of these friends give me hope for the future!)

And so it came as a surprise the way Pam spoke about her older son's friend, who was accompanying us on this hike. Given this boy's personality traits, she wondered aloud what kind of girl would make a good match for him someday. This boy, being around eight years old, was not yet showing an attraction to members of the opposite sex. Nor to members of his own sex. Why then was she assuming him to be heterosexual? Why wasn't the question, What kind of girl *or* boy will he marry someday? Or even, What kind of significant other (or life-partner, spouse, etc.) will he marry? Even with her wide-open mind and high level of sensitivity, Pam's thinking assumed the boy to be heterosexual.

Perhaps assuming heterosexuality is what comes naturally to heterosexuals. Being attracted to members of the opposite sex, they project heterosexual desire onto others, sort of as the default, the given. Perhaps that's especially true when they're talking about children. Hope springs eternal, and all that. But then, why do we hear gay people doing the same thing? I've heard plenty of gay men and women make the exact same type of comment— "Does *he* have a *girl*friend," or, "Is *she* dating a nice *guy?*"—as Pam did, without knowing the sexual orientation of the people involved. They assume heterosexuality, when the reality is, they don't know. There's about a ten to fifteen percent chance they would have been correct to assume homosexuality.

Perhaps an argument can be made for the fact that open conversation about homosexuality is still a very new concept, especially in mixed (read: gay and straight) company. Furthermore, the concept of gay couples becoming parents is also quite new, historically speaking. While most people can perhaps claim to know someone who's gay, not everyone can say that they know a set of gay parents.

There are still many aspects of sexuality, homosexuality in particular, that elude the consciousness of even the most enlightened people, gay or straight. Gay people are found in every walk of life, every profession, every faith, every type of neighborhood, every level of education, and every income bracket.

Stereotyping is a way to diminish, categorize, and reduce the threat of a misunderstood group. Gay people defy stereotyping. We are everywhere and look like everyone. Not everyone else. Just everyone. Most people understand this. They are understanding it more and more, as ever greater numbers of gay men, lesbians, and bisexuals come out of the closet.

Even in gay consciousness there is a lack of the type of thinking necessary to preclude the assumption of heterosexuality. Just because the majority of people are straight, *if we assume straightness where it may not exist, we are contributing to the exact fears and apprehensions that keep people in the closet in the first place.* To assume someone is other than who he/she is, is to unwittingly offer a judgment about that person. Human understanding about language carries with it the implication that what is assumed, is assumed for a reason. Usually that reason has something to do with what is considered to be the norm.

For example, when a new situation comedy comes on television that features black actors, we often refer to it as a black show, or a new black comedy, etc. We don't have "white television shows" or "white comedies" in our everyday vernacular. Why not? Because white actors are the majority and are historically what television shows consist of. Because *whiteness* is assumed. (It's even assumed in some countries where Caucasians form the minority of the population!)

Why do we refer to a male flight attendant? Or, a female doctor? Or, a male nurse? Because, perhaps due to conditioning over the ages, we *assume* a certain color, race, age, gender, ethnic group, or sexual orientation depending upon the situation. Until we become exposed to more male flight attendants, female doctors, and male nurses, we may not inherently challenge these assumptions. Our thinking, if you will, is simply used to the world presenting a certain face. One which we understand and, to one degree or another, are therefore comfortable with. Accordingly, until more gay people eschew that proverbial closet, assumptions about sexual orientation will continue as well, even among the most enlightened and sensitive of us.

To go a step further, we must also acknowledge that a judgment accompanies our assumptions. Whether it's meant to be critical or not, or offered consciously or unconsciously, our assumptions carry with them unspoken expectations about the way we want the world to work, perhaps the way we *need* the world to work. Or so we feel. We are more comfortable with what is known, than what is unknown. Doctors are men, flight attendants (remember when they *were* all females, called stewardesses?) are women, almost all situation comedies (until recent years) are about white people, and most people are heterosexual.

To many, that's the way it should be. Maintaining the status quo is the way to understand one's role in the universe. It's known, therefore it's comfortable, and so I know who I am and how to act. All's right with the world, my world.

For the sake of argument, we can go further and further with this kind of thinking, into all sorts of areas that begin to brush up against what we now consider to be racism, sexism, homophobia, etc. The thinking goes something like this: Because it's always been that way, because it's what I'm used to, then . . . most people *should* be straight . . . the best doctors and lawyers *are* men . . . I want to be waited on by a woman . . men don't date other men . . . women shouldn't be aggressive . . . a man shouldn't express feelings . . . a girl shouldn't climb trees or be too athletic (you know what they say about women tennis players!) . . . big boys don't cry.

You can see how this kind of narrow, limited thinking can seem ridiculous when held against a backdrop of modern society. Even more than ridiculous, it can be hurtful and cruel, and lead to ugly beliefs and behaviors when applied to oppressed groups of people. Think about country clubs that prohibit African-Americans and Jews. They still exist in this country, believe it or not. Is this so different from "whites only" water fountains, or having to sit in the back of the bus in pre–Rosa Parks society? (Until a few years ago, a restaurant—*in West Hollywood of all places!*—posted a sign that read, "No Queers." Lovely.)

Now ask yourself this (especially those of you who are parents, or are considering parenting): To what extent do you impose some version of such thinking onto your own children? Where do your own rights and wrongs, shoulds and should-nots come from? Are you taking the development of your own child and piling onto him or her your own narrow and limited, perhaps skewed version of the way the world should be? Have you given any thought to what it might be like around your house if your son or daughter doesn't fit your view of the world?

Let's be more specific: What would happen if you began to sense some disturbing qualities about your child, i.e., effeminacy in your son, masculinity in your daughter? Or, let's go beyond such obvious (and rather stereotypical) clues. What if your son is college-age and has never had a girlfriend? Or your teenage daughter has a very, *very* close relationship with another girl? Might you begin to worry? Might you, in very subtle ways, begin to respond differently toward your child's behavior than you had before? Will you start to encourage some activities and discourage others because you fear your child's sexual orientation is other than what you're used to in your world? Or other than what you understand? Or other than what you want it to be? Because of your own background, and the way you need to have your world operate, do you *need* your child to be of a certain sexual identity? Let's look at what might happen.

If a small child, youngster, or teenager (or even young adult) senses a disquieting distance or change in the parent, the child begins to experience acute anxiety and confusion at this change. He/she behaves, commonly, with rebellion, depression, or withdrawal. Perhaps he/she displays even further examples of the type of behavior that started the change in the parents in the first place. This behavior in turn exacerbates the parents' concern and suspicions. The tension in the family grows, and begins to spiral around the big white elephant in the middle of the room that no one will acknowledge or discuss. Everyone knows it's there (it's hard to miss!), but nobody's talking about it. The big white elephant, in this case, is the set of fears, anxieties, doubts, worries, and confusions about certain behaviors that are going undiscussed.

Whatever the parents are going through at a time such as this is very much the result of how they themselves were raised, particularly with regard to sexual identity stereotypes, gender stereotypes, and male-female roles. The parents' own early conditioning plays an enormous role in the development and mental health of their gay child. The very foundation upon which they've felt secure all their lives may be shaken up as they begin to question the sexual identity of their child and the new, sometimes confusing identity of being the *parents* of a gay child.

There's much for parents to think about. You know that you love your child the way you thought he or she was. How do you love your child when the reality is different from what you believed? Do you feel the same love toward him or her? Or do you feel abandoned, foolish, angry, sad, confused? Does it feel like everything you counted on before has been turned upside down? Sometimes those old, ingrained beliefs are formed with the hardness of diamonds, where not even the surfaces can be scratched. Or at least it feels that way.

When I speak to parents, I tell them that their child is the same person today as he/she was yesterday. But today, you have new knowledge of your child. Some honesty has been introduced into your family and now you have to deal with it. What I've learned over the years, however, is that this is truer for the gay son or daughter than it is for the parent. In other words, it *doesn't* feel like everything's the same to the parent, especially if they weren't noticing any clues. Or were choosing not to.

We know that coming out is a healthy, positive, important, esteem-enhancing, honest, freeing step for a gay person to take. However, one reason that it's the gay people who feel better afterward is because *they* know they're basically the same people as they were yesterday. The parents may not necessarily be experiencing this news the same way. When all goes well, to the gay son or daughter, everything's better. They can finally breathe. The tremendous tension and guilt involved with secret-keeping can be released, and the closet need never hide his/her feelings, thoughts, attractions, and identity again. The gay person has been thinking about this for a long, long time. Now it's the parents' turn.

It is extremely important for the sake of the relationships in the family for the parents to enter into a process of questioning the beliefs with which they were raised. It is only through a rigorous reevaluation of what they were taught as children that they can truly come to terms with such significant issues involved in having a gay son or daughter.

It was a different time back then. There were different attitudes toward homosexuality than there are today. Parents, are some of your beliefs getting in the way of a healthy relationship with your child? Do some of your ways of thinking prove to be unrealistic now, even if they seemed applicable when you were young? Are the beliefs with which you are now grappling a result of your family of origin, your religion, society, your circle of friends? How were you taught to think about gay people? What did your family say about gay people? Did they use derogatory terms? Do you know of any gays in your family history? How were they treated or talked about? What did you learn at school, church, synagogue, or temple about gay people?

Now: Are you ready to challenge these teachings? Are you strong enough to question your past? Are you willing to open your mind, to scratch the surface of those diamonds a bit?

If parents are committed to a healthy relationship with their gay child (or children), one based on understanding, love, and honesty, then they must commit to being understanding, loving, and honest with themselves first. If your new identity as the parent of a gay person is difficult for you, then ask yourself: What's really bothering me about having a gay son/daughter? Am I afraid of what other people will think? Am I afraid of, or perhaps confused by, gay people? What has been my experience with gays thus far? Are gay stereotypes all that I have to go on? How will other members of my family react? Am I worried that my child will be unhappy? Will my child find someone to love? These are common concerns. You're not alone.

Something else to think about: Our attitudes are expressed through our use of language. If your language has been offensive toward gays, then you've been hurting your gay child's feelings without even knowing it. There's a wound there that will need your attention. If you've supported anti-gay legislature, or senators, or governors, or church gospel, or school curriculum; or if you've laughed at homophobic jokes or told them yourself, then you'll need to rethink your priorities, your loyalties, your friends, your faith, and your sensitivity. And if you've always wanted grandchildren, guess what? You may still get them!

When there is a significant change in the dynamics of a family, all members are affected, and it behooves all members to work together toward understanding each other's feelings. It may take strength, it may take the courage to be honest in ways previously untried, altering the dynamics further. It may mean traversing uncharted, frightening waters. Again, you're not the first people to have to deal with this, so you need not go through it alone. This is why PFLAG (Parents and Friends of Lesbians and Gays. See Chapter Twenty-One, a listing of resources) was created. Also, it may be the perfect time to consider talking with a mental health professional.

Remember: Change is good. There is an ancient Chinese character that means, "In adversity lives opportunity." By working together, the love you have for each other can help you find the opportunities for growth, honesty, and a deepened, renewed relationship, one not to be taken for granted. Getting along is easy when no one rocks the boat. How will you cope when change occurs?

After all, he/she *is* still your child.

Real-Life Story . . . Donald

Donald is from a small community, about 100 miles outside of Atlanta. He is thirty years old, an only child, and an intelligent, warm-hearted professional on his way to becoming well-established in a promising career. He came to my office after recently coming out to his parents. "They are," he says with some difficulty, "having a hard time accepting me as a gay man."

For years Donald and his parents did not broach the topic of his sexual orientation. As it became more and more apparent that he wasn't bringing home any girls to meet the folks, and he spent all his spare time with several male friends, his parents' behavior toward him started to change, at first in subtle ways, then more openly, until the tension eventually became unbearable.

Donald tells it like this: "When I was in my mid-twenties, I was still living at home, finishing up grad school. My parents were very happy about my educational successes, and very supportive in that regard, but something started to change. It was as if, whenever I wasn't around, they were discussing something about me, something that bothered or concerned them. They were different, somehow. They started to look at me with worried expressions, but wouldn't say why. I had a pretty strong hunch about what was on their minds, but I was not about to bring it up."

As time went by, as you might imagine, the tension in the family increased greatly. Donald's parents were oddly silent whenever he announced that he'd be going out for the evening. They stopped asking him questions about *any* part of his life, including his schoolwork, as if they didn't want to hear any news that might confirm their fears. They started to shut down toward him, more and more, but with no explanation. They had a big white elephant sitting in the middle of the room, and they weren't talking about it.

Fears and assumptions had crept into this family, replacing honest communication. Although their suspicions were unconfirmed, in the minds of his parents, Donald became unpredictable, and cause for the family to feel precariously balanced on a not-so-sure footing. The young man who had been a great source of pride for his family—his scholastic accomplishments coupled with his genuine care for others was well known, beginning as far back as early high school—now seemed to be causing his parents great consternation. Yet, he hadn't done anything in particular to cause this sudden concern. The change baffled him. He was the same nice guy he'd always been.

In reality, it was his parents who were suddenly unpredictable. Wondering what he may have done to contribute to their standoffishness, he started to fantasize that they'd overheard phone conversations or perhaps some gossip about him around town. Much like his parents' imagination, his own fantasies started to take wild twists and turns. Feeling unsure in his own home, he, too, became more withdrawn. Before long, communication in his household had all but ceased to exist.

Why wasn't Donald comfortable talking about these changes with them? "I had a strong feeling the problem was that I'm gay, although I hadn't told them about that part of me," he said. "I simply knew, based on comments I'd heard them make my whole life about how gay people are bad, that they're going to hell, that they hurt children, that I couldn't discuss this with them." So Donald decided to move out.

He felt that he'd rather disrupt his life, even in the midst of graduate school, than have this particular conversation with his parents. And why weren't the parents opening up communication with their son, the person who'd been the object of such pride their whole lives, the person they'd supported and loved? Because their fear of Donald being homosexual was so great, they couldn't allow any confirmation of what they believed was the worst thing that could happen. Their beliefs were built over many years, strong and ingrained: It was wrong to be gay. They did not understand, however, why their thoughts (their belief systems) and their reality were in such conflict. It was causing them great confusion and pain and so they coped in the best way they could: They shut down and, unfortunately, watched as the bond with their son deteriorated.

The boy they'd always loved was becoming a stranger to them, and they to him. All so unnecessary, really, but because of their fears, and everyone's lack of feeling able to communicate what was going on, the family grew apart. "We stayed in touch, but it wasn't the same. Our conversations were very superficial," says Donald. It wasn't until a few years later, with some distance ' time between them, that they finally had a discussion about ''º sexual identity; it was shortly thereafter that he came

Partway into his therapy, Donald's parents joined him for counseling. After a few sessions spent opening up communication, during which time his parents had an opportunity to express some of their fears, disappointments, and regrets, they agreed to seek their own couples counseling to help them through these murky waters. I recommended that they seek help not with their own pastor, but with an experienced family therapist who can be impartial and fair. They impressed upon me the great love they have for their son—although Donald wasn't feeling their love these days—and wanted to make a concerted effort at regaining his trust and healing the wounds. They'd have a long road ahead of them, but one they were willing to take if it meant "we can be a family again."

Donald's parents entered therapy—an important and brave step for them. They are indeed committed to continuing their counseling sessions and now and then report to me that they feel they are making great progress, not only in their relationship with their son, but also in their relationship with each other. They are facing their pasts, their communication difficulties, and how and what they contributed to the family rift. They are taking bold, often difficult steps. Good for them!

Donald continues his therapy, committed to regaining the trust he once felt for his parents, learning to undo those negative messages he heard from them while growing up, and increasing his self-esteem as a gay man. "I am many things," he states. "I'm a son, a lover, a professional person . . . and I'm gay. People who are in my life need to accept all of who I am, not just parts of me, conditionally. And that includes my parents. And I'll accept all of them, too."

Well said.

The Meditation

This meditation is one in which I invite all readers, gay and non-gay, parents and non-parents, to participate. It is designed to help you get more in touch with your beliefs and feelings around sexual identity, your own and that of others. This meditation may be read by a friend, or silently to oneself.

Breathe deeply and relax completely. As you breathe, feel all the tension from your body melt away. Feel your mind begin to slow down and become quiet. Enjoy the breath, enjoy the relaxation.
Pause.
Let your mind focus, now, on the person you are. On your personality, your physical appearance, your mental acuity, your sexual orientation.
Pause.

Who are you? Are you someone's parent? Someone's lover? Someone's best friend? Are you a sibling? Whose son or daughter are you? Who's grandchild are you? Let your different identities come to you now, in a way that is real and vivid.

Pause.

Focus on your sexual orientation. What is it, specifically, that defines this identity for you?

Pause.

When did you first become aware of this identity? In what context? Who was involved, a part of, your discovery?

Pause.

What messages did you receive around your sexual identity? Were they positive or negative? Does any specific memory come to mind?

What messages did you receive regarding sexual identities that were different from yours? Were they positive or negative? From whom did this learning come?

Pause.

Now imagine that your sexual orientation is other than it is. If you are heterosexual, imagine yourself as a gay person. If you are homosexual, imagine yourself heterosexual. What is your initial reaction to this change? What is your first thought? Your first feeling? Make this real with the power of your mind. Without judgment, without editing, own your thoughts and feelings.

Pause.

How do you feel about yourself in this new sexual identity?

What do you now need in order to adjust? What about your life is different? How do you cope with these differences?

Pause.

Think about your relationships now. What is the feeling, the tenor of these relationships? Would you still get to have them? Would you have more or less of them in your life? Who is important to you? Are these people willing to stay in your life? Whose acceptance do you desire? Whose love do you need?

Pause.

Are there ways that you think of yourself differently? How?

What has happened to your overall self-esteem? Why do you feel about yourself the way you now do?

Pause.

Again, take a deep breath and return to your real-life sexual orientation.

How do you feel . . . Relieved? Content? Happy? Sad? Angry? Confused?

Let yourself fully experience whatever feelings you are having.

And also, let yourself witness your thoughts. What's going on for you now?

Pause.

What have you learned here? Are there any changes you wish to make about yourself, your thought processes, your opinions, your feelings, regarding others? Regarding yourself?

If you could pick, which sexual orientation would you choose? Why?

How do you choose to live fully and lovingly, given your sexual orientation?

What do you need in your life, in order to be a more loving individual toward others?

What do you need in your life, in order to love yourself more?

Can you forgive your parents? Can you forgive yourself?

Can you love yourself?

When you are ready, take a deep, centering breath.

ADULTHOOD AND RELATIONSHIPS

Don't you know what your twenties are for?
They're for having sex with all the wrong people.

—Bette Midler

Chapter 12

What a Difference a Gay Makes

Come out, come out, wherever you are.

—Glinda, the Good Witch

Well, there certainly are the horror stories. Dorothy and her friends getting rejected from the Emerald City resonates with (and indeed parallels) some of the real-life coming-out stories gay people could tell! In contrast, there are plenty of stories that speak of greatly rewarding, life-changing, relationship-enhancing experiences. Coming-out stories are as unique as the individual. Yet, despite all the personal trials and tribulations, they all have something in common: Each denotes a gay person who was motivated to live honestly, to be accepted unconditionally, and to break out of hiding. Some people take those things for granted; gay people cannot.

The time has never been better, historically speaking, for the coming-out process, with benefits both individual and collective. As an example, for the first time in our country's history, four candidates who are openly gay are seeking national congressional positions, and no fewer than seven are seeking high-profile state posts in California alone, including the race for governor. These brave, intelligent, history-making men and women are paving the way for future gay and lesbian leaders nationwide, in political fields ranging from the federal level to small-town government.

In the arts, there are increasingly greater numbers of positive gay and lesbian portrayals making their way into the mainstream. Broadway in particular, owing its very existence—at least in large part—to the gay community of actors, directors, writers, and theatergoers, has a long history of leading the arts in healthy, accurate, and humorous (fairly, wittily so, as opposed to humor at our expense) portrayals of gay lives.

In literature, we find no shortage of phenomenally talented gay authors of fiction, giving us insight into the lives of all types of gay people with a literary style at once sensitive and honest. We cry, we laugh, we read about real characters with real lives, not "lifestyles." (Unfortunately, there are still those heterosexual authors who miss the mark regarding homosexuality. This is particularly disturbing when these—sometimes best-selling—authors are themselves a product of an oppressed minority, and use gay characters for nothing more than comic relief.)

In television and films, slowly but surely, progress is being made. Sitcoms, dramas, and movies are depicting gays as not merely fodder for laughs, but as your next door neighbor, your brother, your sister, having multidimensional relationships, dealing with real issues in real-life situations. Perhaps most encouraging is the number of gay films that fill the art houses of major and minor cities and win awards at prestigious festivals. We are a creative lot!

So, as the world view of homosexuality is in slow transition, with a few steps forward, and an occasional step backward, we are perhaps more able to view the world as a place in which to come out. Not all small communities are hostile toward gays, nor are all religions. Gay life does not have to exist only in the big cities anymore, as progress is being made in smaller communities as well. It's certainly true that large metropolitan areas regularly have more to offer—socially, spiritually, educationally, artistically, and domestically—for gay men and lesbians, but gay people often return to their nonurban roots. Sometimes for health reasons, sometimes to escape the big-city experience that can be fun and exciting, but also exhausting, nerve-wracking, and soul-depleting, to find that change has occurred over the years, and occasionally, for the better.

They find that someone they went to high school with is now an "out" lesbian, and is leading a productive and fulfilling life, accepted and supported by those who know her. Or they find that a new community health center in town has a well-funded HIV program, educating schoolchildren and providing for medical treatment. Or they notice a popular gay student union at the nearby community college that sponsors workshops, socials, and speakers. Not all gay activities in all suburban and rural areas take place at the rest stop along the highway just outside of town. Progress is being made, slowly. There is hope.

Further, as people generally live longer, and become better educated over the generations, we can observe a shift in popular perception about what it means to be gay, or to know someone who is gay. A growing and significant influence in the education of the masses regarding homosexuality is largely due to the very act of coming out. Over and over I hear straight people say that once a gay person came out to them, they had to challenge and discard many previously held beliefs about gays. Gay people in the limelight, as well as in low-profile existences (which is most of us), contribute to the changing clime for gays and lesbians everywhere. It doesn't happen overnight, and non-gays are not magically transformed in their attitudes, verbiage, or behaviors instantly. But it does happen, at one's own pace.

The coming-out process serves not only the individual, but all of us. All of us who are gay, and all those who now know a gay person. On a societal scale, in the big picture—the cosmic view, if you will—coming out helps us heal each other as it includes the potential to foster enlightenment, understanding, and connection between people, while reducing the fears at the heart of homophobia.

Perhaps the most important aspect of coming out, psychologically speaking, is realizing that it is a highly personal process, taken on by each individual in his or her own way, and at his or her own pace. No one can tell you how to come out, when to come out, or to whom to come out. Because the life circumstances for everyone are unique, so too is the coming out process. Not all people challenge and revise their attitudes about gays when someone comes out to them. (The Newt Gingriches, Pat Robertsons, and Jesse Helmses of the world remind us of that.) But one thing most mental health professionals can agree on is the tremendous importance of coming out to a person's self-esteem. Being true to oneself, living a genuine life, is a central ingredient for healthy self-worth. Because coming out not only changes the world's view of gays, it changes one's view of the world and of oneself! Let's look more closely at this.

Secrets around your sexual identity (or sexual *orientation*) are shame-based. In other words, you keep the secret because of feeling shame and you feel shame due to having to live a lie. It's a vicious circle that also includes tremendous fear (a future-based emotion) as well as depression (disguised anger) and anxiety. More about these feelings in a minute.

While you're holding on to a secret, you are living as if the world is a frightening and rejecting place, as opposed to it being a place in which you belong. You're *assuming* rejection and, for as long as you assume rejection, your perception is that the world *is* hostile, that everyone *will* reject you, that you *will* be hurt somehow—emotionally, perhaps physically—by coming out. Your expectation of the world keeps you living in a way that fulfills the expectation. It creates a self-fulfilling prophecy of your own particular design.

Now, I'm not going to try to convince you that you *won't* get hurt. I've heard of cases similar to a young client of mine where, after coming out to a family member, he found religious literature had been left on his bedroom dresser during the night. Literature filled with reasons why homosexuality is an abomination in the eyes of God. (Imagine, they cut down trees to make hate-filled, I-know-God-better-than-you brochures such as this!) Is this an act of support, because someone in your family believes you need to be "saved"? I doubt it felt supportive to the young man. I'd say it felt more like passive hostility and ignorance couched in concern. Again, the reality is that everyone's circumstances are different.

There are times, especially if you are a person who, through awareness and introspection, is able to trust your feelings, fear can serve as a very legitimate warning, guiding you toward certain behaviors while intelligently avoiding others. Not all fears are unhealthy! They can be used to help you decide where to begin and how to proceed, especially with something as important as coming out.

The point is that if you hold to a perception that says your world will reject you, whether based on a past experience or simply a hunch, you will perpetuate the feeding of the fears that you are up against in the first place. *My world is scary and rejecting, so I'm not coming out. There will be negative repercussions both big and small if they know I'm gay. As a big-time television star, I must stay in the closet. As a small-town student, I must stay in the closet. As my parents' only child, I must stay in the closet.* The size of one's career or social standing isn't the real factor here. Nor is one's family, religion, or group of friends. The real internal factor is the fear that's being nurtured by your thinking process and constricting beliefs. The drug is fear and the dealer is your world view. Well, if that kind of thinking doesn't keep you in the closet, what would?

To avoid upsetting the apple cart is psychologically seductive. Everything is going along smoothly, why come out and disrupt all that? But remember: That illusion of harmony is based, however, on your deception. As long as everyone is left to *assume* you to be heterosexual, they're happy. You're colluding with the lie. The real test of love and acceptance in a family (or in any group) comes when the veil of deception is lifted and people are allowed to see the truth. How will they handle that?

So, how can a person *not* feel depressed when—by their choice of remaining silent—they have opted to restrict their personal freedoms. They have limited freedom of speech because they can't tell anyone of their truth. They have limited freedom of movement because they feel unaccepted or unwelcomed in certain places in society. They have a limited comfort level, because they live with a heightened sense of anxiety. After all, at any time they may be found out—with a telling glance, a certain word or gesture—and that is a very dark cloud under which to try and exist in any kind of a psychologically healthy life.

Further, one cannot give up such basic, human needs—the freedom to be who you are, the freedom to talk about who you are, the ability to live comfortably without fear of being exposed—without being angry about it on some level. Whether you are conscious of it or not (and most people are often not in touch with anger—it's uncomfortable, unpleasant, and usually avoided), angry feelings are there. Even when losses are self-imposed, the time-proven bereavement adage is true: Where there is loss, there is anger. When there is no attainable or perceived outlet for the anger, it turns into depression. Think about examples in your own life: It is only human nature to get angry and/or depressed when we feel that our choices are limited, our freedom of expression stifled.

And the anxiety! Living with a secret that affects perhaps every single aspect of your existence means that you can never ever relax, you can never let your guard down. You monitor your every word at the dinner table, your every glance at an attractive person, your every reaction to what's being said around you. The most important duty in your life is not to your God, or your country, or to your loved ones or even to your boss. The most important thing is to maintain the secrecy of your sexual identity. People who claim that being gay is only one small part of who they are, are fooling themselves with a denial-based perspective about their identity. Perhaps by minimizing their sexual orientation, they feel less of a need to deal with it, but the truth is that being gay or lesbian is a central, core part of that person, integral to every aspect of his or her life.

It's a very difficult and emotionally pain-filled existence, being in the closet, and much of the pain comes from the constant constricted feeling of knowing that the life you're living is, to some degree at least, a lie. Living a lie, to an otherwise mentally healthy person, goes against one's innate impulse. The natural propensity for the part of the human psyche that we call the conscience is to encourage us to exist in a way that is congruent, genuine to what we know to be truthful. In sum, to live honestly. Living a life in opposition to one's true nature poses a tremendous amount of inner conflict with which to live. The result is the great difficulty it takes to enjoy any of what life has to offer, an impossible feat if you're anxiously trembling through the world always looking over your shoulder and guarding your every action. Yet, to the closeted individual, that's precisely how life feels.

Again, I stand by my pronouncement that coming out is a process to be undertaken *in your own time and at your own pace.* (I'm going to get a little preachy here . . . bear with me.) This is why I am strongly against the practice of "outing," going public with the news of someone else's sexual orientation. The sexual orientation of another person, no matter how much good you think it does the world for that person to be forced out of the closet, is nobody's business until that person is ready to make it someone else's business. Every process along the mental health journey is personal, and its pace and disclosure is solely up to the individual going through it. It belongs to the person going through it. The coming-out process is no different. Coming out is good for one's mental health and society at large, for all the reasons we've been discussing, but outing someone is an act of misdirected anger, based in the controlling belief that one person's hurt is worth the benefit to others. Says who?

Could well-known and highly regarded public figures now deceased have helped society's attitude toward gays if they had come out before their death? Without a doubt. In fact, we can all probably think of several examples of such figures, and it's angering to think of the progress that they might have accomplished! How much farther along as a society would we be now had we their help?

Could admired CEOs or professionals in the world of politics, for example, have helped gays receive fair treatment on federal or local fronts, winning the same basic rights afforded to others? Most definitely. Politicians are elected with the agreement that they will serve the needs of their constituents, not just some of their constituents at the expense of others. We hire them to find a way to take the needs of *all* of us into account. That's the job they're paid, and paid well, to do. The term, "Americans" must include gay Americans. We work, we vote, we matter. Don't they know this?

Can individuals who are alive and well and closeted today, in the influential worlds of entertainment and fashion and art, be of benefit to great numbers of frightened young gay men and women, simply by publicly coming out of hiding and being who they are? Most certainly. Otherwise, they are missing such a wonderful opportunity to be positive role models. The court of public opinion, tolerance, and acceptance is highly influenced by those in positions of power or in the limelight who are viewed favorably by their public, their followers, their fans. We can likely think of quite a few such public figures who are disappointingly dropping that ball.

But who has the right to control the personal growth process of another human being, to dictate where and at what pace such a journey should proceed? No one but the individual so engaged in that process. And what if that public figure has grown rich and famous and powerful precisely because of their gay following? Doesn't that justify our demanding them to go public with who they really are? In our hearts and minds, of course we want that person to now help us, and the society around us, in the same way we have helped him or her: with enthusiastic and unflinching support. But it doesn't give us the right to lay possession to that person's life. We can stop buying the records, we can boycott the talk show, and we can put our gay dollars toward other products or services, but we don't have the right to *out* another person.

That said *(whew!)*, there are ways in which the closeted individual on some fundamental and personal level, very strongly wants to begin his or her rebirth. Such is the person who is feeling the pain and the shame of living a secret life, and knows that honesty is the antidote; the person who would like to live a life that includes freedoms, especially the freedom to live without having to anxiously, at all cost, keep tight controls on this shame-inducing secret.

If you are such a person, it may be helpful to point out that perhaps you've been overlooking something: Your being gay is not about choice. You're gay. God or the Creator or the Universe or Nature—whatever you believe—in Its infinite wisdom of the beauty of diversity, gave you that gift. You had no more choice in your sexual identity than did the heterosexual choose to be straight. You can choose whom to love, but if human sexual orientation were a choice, then a straight person could be gay if he or she wanted to be. Ask any avowed heterosexual if *they* think their orientation is about choice. Or, we could all be straight on Mondays and gay on Tuesdays. (Hmmm, being allowed to breed only on every other day may certainly help with the world's overpopulation problem!) No, being gay is not where the choice lies. Coming out is the choice. Being honest is the choice. Living congruently is the choice.

I think a brief sidebar is in order here, to acknowledge those who believe that we do indeed choose the life we are reborn into. Such thinking would follow, then, that we chose to come back as a gay or straight individual, based upon the lessons we needed to learn from past lives. This position is offered by some, although not all, who believe in reincarnation. While that belief may indeed be true, this discussion will not encompass the concept of reincarnation *per se*, with its many variations of philosophy or teachings, but will be limited to this life as we know it, from birth onward, and the choices versus the predispositions we all face once we get here.

Why else might you be in the closet? Perhaps your sound judgment, your intuition which you've come to rely on and which serves you well in other areas of your life, precludes you from coming out to your family. Perhaps there would be real danger, not just perceived danger, to your well-being in one way or another if you did so. Be that as it may, does that preclude you from coming out to others who *would* likely accept you? If you're worried about family, what about starting with your friends? Or vice versa? It's really okay to rely upon your own valid, internal voice of judgment and guidance to decide where to begin.

Let me share with you the coming-out story of a friend of mine. Stan is in his early twenties, a physically and mentally healthy young man on the verge of a promising career as an artist. He lives at home with his parents and sister in a comfortable, affluent neighborhood outside of Chicago. By all accounts, his is a close, loving family. He has a few friends, mostly from college, but only a couple of them know that Stan is gay.

Stan has dated a few men for various periods of time, but he'd tell you that those experiences were more about experimentation, learning and coming to terms with being gay, than they were about being in love, or feeling love for another man. He learned about gay sex, although not love, through these experiences.

Now, for the first time, Stan *is* in love, and life feels very different to him. Suddenly, it's important that more of the people close to him know about his sexual orientation. He possesses strong feelings for another man now, and wants to be able to confide in and share his happiness with others. In particular, he wants to experience some familial support for his feelings and this exciting new love relationship he's entered.

So, after much thought and trepidation, Stan has decided to begin his coming out process with his family, starting with his sister, who is younger than he by two years. He hopes that her support will not only give him someone to confide in, but will, in time, give him the courage and strength to come out to his parents. If all goes well, he figures, then he will more easily be able to spend time with his lover without the secrecy and half-truths that are increasingly adding stress to his life.

Stan decided to set the stage for his coming out to Sis in a thoughtful, warm, and loving manner by inviting her to join him at their family's weekend home for a couple of days alone, just the two of them. There they could relax, go dancing at a nearby nightclub, go for walks and drives through the countryside, and have ample opportunity for close brother-sister conversation. He was nervous, but, with the emotional support and encouragement of his lover, was confident of the rightness of his desire to come out. He loves (and likes) his sister very much, and she him. His plan made excellent sense.

Stan's personal/social life (as well as that of his sister's) has always been kept quite private. Their parents, trusting their young adult children's choices of friends, are not the prying types. So theirs is not a household of interrogatory questions or suppositions behind one another's backs. Even between the two siblings, dating experiences—and the whispered stories of intimacy that often accompany them—were rarely shared. Perhaps because of this, Sis was not attuned to the sexual orientation of her big brother; she just assumed, probably without spending much time thinking about it, that he was heterosexual.

Thus far, Stan had not upset the apple cart; he hadn't felt a significant enough motivation to muster the courage it would take to break the deception. His strong feelings for another man had changed all that and living more honestly regarding his sexual orientation was his promise and contribution to their new and loving relationship. (His boyfriend is already out to those in his own circle.)

So, on one of their wilderness walks, "the time felt right," according to Stan, to gently give Sis the news. He explained how he came to know that he is gay, that he is healthy physically (he sensed that this would be one of her primary concerns), and that he loves a terrific man whom he would like her to get to know. He told her that he loved her, that she is the first person to whom he chose to come out, and that he hoped their relationship would remain as close as always, if not more so.

He did everything beautifully!

Well, life isn't perfect, and neither is Sis. She didn't react in the manner Stan had ideally hoped she would. She seemed to internalize the news, taking it personally, and shed quite a few tears. She was very quiet for the rest of their weekend, offering Stan no explanation for her reaction, no communication about his news, no support.

Undoubtedly, a much healthier response on her part would have included some dialogue, some give-and-take for Stan to work with, hopefully involving their feelings—concerns, fears, confusions, joys. Ideally, she would not have made this be about *her*. She instead would have recognized the importance of supporting Stan, even as she struggled to come to terms with his news. As disappointing and painful as her reaction was to him, he understood her need to digest his disclosure at her own pace.

Over the next couple of weeks she slowly began to ask some questions and share her feelings, providing him with the opportunity and communication he was hoping for. He answered her willingly and honestly, and even had some no-nonsense literature handy for her, for those questions that were too uncomfortable for her to ask. The ending of the story, in this case, is a happy one, and I'm glad to report that brother and sister are doing fine, reaching new levels in their personal communication with each other. Their trust has deepened (as is often the case), and Stan is now giving serious and careful thought to how he wants to come out to his parents, with his sister's support close at hand.

You see, coming out doesn't necessarily happen all at once, with a bang and a parade. In fact, announcing one's sexual orientation usually doesn't happen like that at all. It's usually a much more gradual, evolving process, whereby a gay person tells someone, then someone else, then more people. You, as the gay man or woman, are in the driver's seat. Coming out happens as you feel you can allow it, guide it to happen. It's a process, remember.

Perhaps you've never heard firsthand any of the inspirational coming-out stories, the ones that serve to help you gather the strength to be who you are. (As you'll recall, the foursome *were* eventually accepted into the Emerald City!) I hope Stan's story can help. Role models, the experiences of others, guidance from someone who's been there all can provide a shoring up of the determination you may feel you need. Besides those whose coming out *would* help us, there are many who have come out, and they are our modern-day heroes.

They tell their stories, write their books, and make their movies. They run for political office and initiate pro-gay legislature. They are the openly gay cops, ministers, lawyers, judges, doctors, writers, and Academy Award winners. They run bookstores, beauty salons, AIDS organizations and races. They are devoted to finding a cure for AIDS, working on a shoestring budget, because they care, not because they want publicity. They've gone where others have feared to tread and they remind us that we are, indeed, everywhere.

They started important factions of the gay movement, and opened centers for gay youth. They are the late Harvey Milk from San Fransisco and the still-active Morris Kight in Los Angeles. They came out when no one else did, and where no one else dared. Our heroes are our openly gay professional athletes. They are found in the faces of the first out gay kid in your neighborhood, the first person in your family to come out, and the HIV-positive gay man who speaks about safe sex at the town's Baptist high school.

Our heroes are the women who led support groups, fundraisers, and the fight against HIV and its resultant homophobia, even though lesbians were the least-affected demographic. Our heroes open doors for the rest of us: The first lesbians to win custody of their children. The first gay male couple to adopt. They got bashed during the Stonewall riots in New York, and in the San Fransisco protests of the early 80s, all so we could hold hands, dance with a lover, and be who we are. They got fired from their teaching positions by bigoted school boards because they believed in practicing what they preached: honesty.

Our heroes teach us to gather our inner resources for just the kind of rigorous honesty involved in coming out, first to ourselves. That's really where coming out begins: within. With a commitment to be a person *who belongs,* just as much as anyone else. Coming out is not just about words spoken to someone else. It is about first being a person who rates his commitment to honesty higher than fear, and is ready to do whatever it takes to put that notion into practice. Because coming out can't possibly be about telling others until you are able to tell yourself. Until you are clear and committed to the rightness of being who you are.

That is the kind of honesty required to come out and it takes vigilance to *stay* out. Ask anyone who's out about the seduction of being pulled back into the closet, for its perceived, transient feelings of safety. They may tell you about being out in most aspects of life, but being self-pressured into retreat when the temperature became too hot. Even in sometimes very subtle ways, like avoiding certain topics of conversation, or editing some aspect of their personality, in order to avoid any degree of disclosure. Out with friends, closeted at work. Out with family, back in when meeting someone new. Out with everyone except Dad. You get the idea. It's very much a process, and one that requires your sincerity, bravery, and commitment, such as found within those who came before you.

The happy endings? They are those things that no one can ever take away from you. The rewards are found in our honest relationships, our open involvements with whatever group, charity, or friends we choose, without fear or apology. The rewards are found every time someone scoffs or mutters behind our backs, and we don't take on their problem as our own, as some sort of statement that "something must be wrong with me." Because we know: Others can believe what they will. I believe in who I am.

Yes, coming out can be a huge, frightening decision, with nothing short of potential rejection from people whom you love and trust the most—the rejection of your very being is on the line! Sure, there are trials and tribulations, but there are also internal accolades that last the rest of your life. Remember: You come out for yourself, not for others. You come out because you believe that you are worth a happy, genuine, honest life.

Our acclaim in coming out can perhaps best be summed up on a T-shirt I saw recently, worn at a gay pride event: "Gay By Nature, Proud By Choice!"

Real-Life Story . . . Luke and Juan

The phone call came from Luke: "I'm at my wits' end! Now he's talking about being 'just friends,' as if *that* could ever happen!"

Luke and Juan had been coming to couples therapy for a few months in order to work on some difficulties in their relationship.

Many of these difficulties were caused by the fact that Luke is out to his family, friends, and colleagues, but Juan is still very much in the closet. Except for a small handful of their mutual friends and acquaintances, no one knows Juan is gay, or that he is in this relationship with Luke. Both men are in their mid-thirties, both are intelligent, successful in business, and together lead healthy social and sexual lives. Luke is from a politically progressive, open-minded Southern California family. Although reared and educated in the states, Juan is from a prominent political family in Europe, where most of his family and several siblings still reside.

Their five-month relationship has come up against issues unique to gay men and lesbians: What happens when one partner is out of the closet and the other is in? What are the ramifications to their relationship, their relationships with family members, their social or political activities, their choices of friends, jobs, where they choose to live, how they celebrate the holidays, etc., etc.? Even in interracial, intergenerational, or interreligious relationships, there is not the same stigma or burden of secrecy that dictates so much of a couples' life together as there is in a gay relationship where one partner is out, and one is not.

Of course, there are plenty of potential difficulties when *neither* partner is out. Then the couple's support system is undeniably lacking and the stress of secrecy is doubled. Although upon occasion I have known closeted couples who are able to form a bond within their adversity—or perhaps because of it—at least temporarily; forged by both people being aligned and working in unison to protect their sexual identity as individuals and as a couple. So, both partners are, in a way, in the same boat.

However, their life together must necessarily face very discernible limitations and constrictions, as their dual identities permeate any freedoms in the relationship: Not only are they unable to lead fully genuine lives as individuals, but their partnership—perhaps the most important relationship in the lives of each—cannot be acknowledged by others. Such a situation can be very trying and painful in its own right.

However, such is not the case with Luke and Juan.

Luke's phone call comes after an argument between the two men, centering on Juan's pronouncement that he can no longer, in good conscience, "relate to Luke sexually." Because of the tremendous inner conflict with which he lives regarding his sexual orientation, their relationship must now be "just a friendship," says Juan. After several months of great emotional investment in their relationship, this is a difficult moment, and one that is bringing Luke to his wits' end—certainly to the end of his patience.

Their relationship has been marked by much fun and passion, according to both men, but it has also included a kind of back-and-forth indecisiveness on the part of Juan, who recurringly struggles with his identity as a gay man. Over time, we all come to understand that his thinking goes something like this: *This relationship feels good to me, and I know that Luke is a warm, good, and kind man to whom I'm very much attracted, but because I was raised to believe that being gay is wrong, I don't feel I can admit to myself that I'm gay. And I certainly can't admit it to anyone else. But how can something that feels so good be bad? And how can Luke be proud of being homosexual? Why can't I feel that kind of pride? What's wrong with me?*

Juan is dealing with many issues here, and therefore, his relationship with Luke also is facing many issues. He was taught certain beliefs about gay people, but is finding great conflict with those beliefs, which is stirred up due to his feelings for Luke. Further, watching how Luke is dealing with his sexual orientation has shaken up Juan's long-held belief about having to remain closeted: Luke is doing quite well with his self-esteem as a gay man. Juan can't help but wonder about the possibility that he, too, could ever feel okay with being gay.

In a way then, Luke is a role-model for Juan. Seeing how someone he loves and respects is handling "the whole gay thing" is making Juan look at his own level of courage. There are brief times when he feels buoyed in his ability to accept his orientation. At other times, such as now, his fear causes him to backslide so far that he's on the verge of throwing away a potentially wonderful romance. While Luke has tolerated this ebb and flow of emotions since meeting Juan, he is also now at a point of great frustration. Further, he does not feel that a friendship with Juan is at all what he wants, in the context of their romance. What he wants is to continue their love relationship, but without Juan's frequent vacillations.

The healthy thing about Juan's current internal conflict is that he is experiencing the kind of upheaval that precedes change. Twelve-step programs refer to it as "bottoming out," that period of tremendous turmoil—sometimes external, always internal—that comes before enlightenment and growth. The growth representing the calm *after* the storm, so to speak. There's no guarantee that Juan and Luke are going to be able to weather this current storm, but if they are able to, then they'll come out the other side with a renewed commitment for the struggle, and perhaps Juan will be closer to coming out himself.

One of the first steps in tackling an issue in couples therapy is to find a way to move the problem from what I call, "You Versus Me" to "You and Me Versus the Problem." By doing so, both parties are able to be on the same side of the struggle, thereby using their combined talents to work toward a solution. It helps them to move past the *blaming* aspect so often found in couples work, and allows both people to feel aligned, to work as a pair. Most importantly, no matter who has introduced the problem into the relationship, it allows the couple to take mutual responsibility for the solution. *If it's going to work, it'll be because we both made it work.*

This is not to say that Luke's feelings of anger toward Juan and fear about the future of their relationship is unfounded or invalid. Juan is threatening the very fate of a potentially wonderful life together. Fortunately, Luke does an admirable job of getting his anger out in the open without any prodding from me! Their occasional heated discourse is usually quite productive, and, they come to find out, their fears are intensely shared. (More aspects of relationship therapy are discussed in Chapter 14, What Was I Thinking?)

Nor is it to say that Juan may not have justifiable feelings toward Luke, such as resentment (for making Juan face this issue at this time in his life), anger (outwardly aimed at Luke, but perhaps really at himself), guilt (at causing the man he loves such pain), or despair (at having unsuccessfully attempted growth with this issue in the past, and now therefore, feeling somewhat hopeless, perhaps overwhelmed). All of these feelings need to be aired and acknowledged as well.

Once the solution to the problem becomes their focus, once they begin to work *together* toward a resolution via honest and open communication, then they have a shared mission! Luke can offer his best efforts at patience, if Juan can refrain from dooms- day pronouncements. Juan can offer his steady, non-wavering effort, if Luke can remain communicative, even when feeling frustrated. They have agreed to work as a team, and are finding real ways to make that teamwork happen.

As the guilt, anger, and fear begin to lift, they find that the strong feelings they have for each other will help them sustain the coming-out process that Juan knows he must enter. In the safety of their relationship, without the continual threat of break- up, Juan can admit to himself what he needs, in order to come out first *to himself,* and then, eventually, to others. His resolve, with Luke's help, is strengthening. Together, they are committed to aiding Juan in this process, with all the accompanying tears, fears, joys, and pride.

As Juan progresses in leaving the closet, so too can their rela- tionship. Then, and only then, can their partnership be seen and celebrated by others. They can feel the rewards of their hard work. They can feel the level of an uncloseted bond and pride in who they are that comes with public disclosure and acceptance. Will everyone in Juan's life accept them as a couple? That is beyond predictability, but no matter who does or doesn't accept their relationship, *they* have forged an acceptance of who they are, as individuals and as a couple, and they need never go back into hiding or secrecy again.

Reality check: There's no guarantee that these men will stay together after all the effort. But if they do, they will feel closer and more strengthened for having stayed by each other's side during a difficult time. If they don't, they'll be secure in the knowledge that they did not easily give up the fight; they gave it their best shot, and can walk away with perhaps sadness, but few or no regrets.

If they remain committed to their process, however, then their prognosis as a couple is quite good. If they do stay together, they will feel a great sense of esteem and tremendous accomplishment for this commitment and hard work, and the resultant confidence to handle future problems. Regardless of the outcome, what they can assuredly count on to last will be their newly developed relationship skills, which can be used in their relationship should new problems arise, as well as in any other—with lovers, friends, acquaintances, co-workers, etc. These are skills—and rewards—that last a lifetime.

The Meditation

This meditation is similar to the one that helped Luke and Juan discover their underlying feelings, as well as their commitment toward each other. The first time they meditated together was in session, with my guidance. After that, they made time to meditate together at home, using either a recording of that earlier session in my office, or with one of them taking the responsibility to guide it. They reported benefits of not only greater clarity with their issues, but also being able to think from a calmer, more grounded place. Feeling less knee-jerk with their thoughts, opinions, etc., allowed them to become better listeners with each other, and their communication improved greatly.

This may be read slowly by a friend, or silently to oneself. Try having someone read it to you and your partner together.

Sit very comfortably, arms by your side and legs uncrossed. Let cushions or pillows support your body, so you have no work to do in keeping yourself comfortable.

Breathe deeply several times, allowing your mind and body to fully relax.

Focus on the slowing down of your thoughts as you breathe,

letting them become like sand settling on the ocean floor. Quieting, calming, settling.

Pause.

Let your mind be wide open. Let your heart open also.

In feeling relaxed, let yourself feel generous, kind, understanding. Be open to the feelings and thoughts of others. Be willing. Feel willing.

Pause.

Identify for yourself the central relationship issue in your life.

Perhaps it revolves around a love relationship. Perhaps it is a family relationship. Whatever is utmost on your mind, let it emerge now.

Pause.

See this issue clearly and fully. Look at it from all angles. Look at it from other points of view. Let your mind wrap around it completely.

Pause.

Now ask yourself to be open to all solutions and possibilities. What answers emerge for you about this relationship issue? Let them flow, let them come to you fully . . . with heightened sensitivity and awareness.

Pause.

What are you feeling now? What are you feeling toward this relationship, this person? What are you feeling toward yourself?

Breathe deeply. Stay with open heart. Stay with love.

Can you commit to the discovery of answers, repeatedly, until you find the one that is best for you both? Can you come back to this place whenever you desire, being trustful of your increasing ability to find the solutions you need? Can you allow your innate creativity to emerge? Make a commitment to yourself now.

Pause.

Breathe and know you are human. You are a growing, evolving, loving human being. Your possibilities are endless. Your potential is eternal.

Pause.

When you are ready, take a deep, centering breath.

Chapter 13

A Thing of Beauty is a Boy Forever

People living deeply have no fear of death.

—Anais Nin

Nip, tuck, tan the front, pull, push, shave, tweak, trim, pluck, tan the other side, pump, sweat, shave again, trim, push, pull, pump some more, brighten, whiten, bond, time to tan again, time to shave again, more pushing, pulling, lifting, pumping, sweating ... How's my chest? How are my abs? How are my glutes? My arms, my legs, my shoulders? Am I losing my hair? And on and on it goes.

Don't eat that, don't drink that, don't do that ... no thanks, none for me ... I can't, I'm watching my figure. I'm going out to the bars tonight, I don't dare miss my gym appointment, my sauna, my facial, my massage, my tanning bed, my acupuncture, my stylist, and my shrink. (Oh, wait ... the shrink is for the morning *after!*)

Want to meet us after work for some Mexican food? Sorry, I can't, I'm going to the gym. Want to go see a movie? Oh, I'd love to, but I'm working out today with a buddy at the gym. Want to go away this weekend? Nope, not this weekend, I've got to catch up at the gym.

Good grief. What happened to the rest of life?

If this sounds a bit extreme, it's meant to. Unfortunately, it's also quite realistic in the lives of many gay men. There is a tremendous amount of pressure, especially in urban gay communities, for gay men to conform to the specific looks, tastes, styles, and trends of the day. Knowing the *au courant* and the *de rigueur* in just about everything is practically a prerequisite in order to be a card-carrying member of the homosexual party: having the right body (with the right amount of smoothness, of course), the right hairstyle, the right clothing (worn just so, especially at the clubs where it's imperative to get noticed); knowing the best place for Japanese food, the best wines to drink, the best brunch to serve; knowing the hottest vacation spot this year; having the necessary amount of disposable income for the newest summer swimwear, clubwear, loungewear, poolwear, partywear, and, of course, office drag. It's as if there's an unwritten manual that changes with the season, the day of the week, and the time of day.

Although many gay people can have a sense of humor about this never-ending treadmill of superficiality and this keeping-up-with-the-Joneses attitude, for some gay men it's no joke. In fact, it is a matter of utmost urgency for the sake of their sense of self-worth to feel that they are in control of how they look and how they appear to others at all times. Of course, they must always look their best.

It can feel like a life-or-death issue, carrying with it a tremendous amount of pressure and anxiety, and not very much fun. Let a wrinkle appear and they are thrown into existential angst about the imminence of their own mortality. Develop a love handle and they swear off anything other than juice, lettuce, and an extra hour of aerobics each day at the gym. For these people, "fat" and "old" are tantamount to the end of life as they know it. "Looksism" and "ageism" anxiety rule their decisions and behaviors, and even dictate their choices of friends.

Why? Because this is what they believe they need to do in order to be accepted. To be accepted by other men, certainly, but more importantly, to feel some degree of self-acceptance. They believe this, because they are taught this. The lessons are plentiful, coming from both the mainstream as well as the gay media, and they serve to create a narcissistic gay subculture of men who pathologically rely on their looks for their self-worth. The harsh rejection, experienced from within as well as from others, feels like too high a price to pay for nonconformity. Better to keep up those gym fees than to enter into a lifelong and ultimately rewarding growth process of learning to love and accept oneself, flaws and all.

Such tremendous social pressure, whether real or imagined, is akin to the peer pressure felt during childhood and adolescence. It is a revisiting of those old fears and anxieties, but with new stakes. Now, instead of having the right lunchbox, friend, and extracurricular sports involvement, the pressure is on to attend the right parties and gyms, and to be seen at the right restaurants and gay resorts.

What's wrong with growing older? The mere thought of such a thing causes some gay men to run screaming straight to the banks of denial. So perhaps that's part of the problem. If we, as a gay community, actually accept aging, then we are forced to confront our illusory postponements of death. In the age of AIDS, perhaps we have seen far more than our share of death. In our materialistic, Madison Avenue–influenced society, where thin, muscled, hairless boys are the standard of health, and some elusive ideal of what we are supposed to look like is dangled in front of us like a carrot, it takes far more strength and insight to allow ourselves just to *be*. So we are denied the experience of seeing the inherent beauty in, for instance, the natural aging process. We are unable to see beauty in *difference*. Instead, beauty exists only where we're told it exists, and that's usually in hairless pecs and taut tummies. We are grossly conditioned.

What's wrong with being heavy? Or skinny? Or short? Or hairy? Or bald? Or old? Or of an ethnic minority? What does it say about us, as a community that has itself felt the sting of rejection for being different, that we practice a kind of elitist discrimination against those who don't conform to "the look"? The discrimination may be overt, such as found in a gay-oriented clothing chain that does not carry extra-large or extra-small sizes, or whose catalogues portray only the buffed, tanned, and sneering. Or it may be more subtle, to be found only in the minds and conversations of those who conform, and therefore are accepted. Such a hurtful, alienating way to overcompensate, to feel better-than.

What are young gays being taught about acceptance and rejection when they see that all (or the vast majority) of the ads in the gay press feature people who do not represent them? That's been the problem their whole lives: They feel different, they don't fit in. Now here they are, entering the threshold of their gay identity, trying to be prideful about themselves and their tribe of gay brothers and sisters, and once again, they don't fit in. The rejection from one's own kind can be far more ego-damaging than from society at large. How much more difficult it is to repair self-esteem wounds when not feeling acceptance even from one's own family. The elusive and conditional acceptance from the biological families of many gay people makes the need for a *created* family's acceptance all the more important. Perhaps that's one of the real tragedies here: These conformist, esteem-damaging messages are not just coming from the heterosexual world, or the fundamentalists, or the right-wingers; they're coming from within our own community!

Women have struggled for decades with the ego-diminishing messages sent by society about not being good enough—not pretty enough, or thin enough, or sexy enough, or big-breasted enough or tall enough, etc., etc. This is why the cosmetics industry in our country is a multibillion dollar industry. It's why young girls idolize wafer-thin models. It's why Barbie has been such a phenomenal success for over three generations. It's no accident that the overwhelming majority of people suffering from eating disorders in this country are women. Want to guess who the second most-affected population consists of? Gay men.

You'd think we'd learn: Self-esteem isn't about thin, or pretty, or sexy . . . or muscled or ripped or shaved.

Let's be clear here. Is going to the gym, in and of itself, a destructive event for esteem? Of course not! Is eating healthfully and exercising bad for us? Absolutely not. In fact, quite the opposite is true: Exercising and eating smart are major contributors to a long, healthy life and lowered stress. Is it somehow psychologically wrong to want to look good and dress well? To have a nice haircut or a tan? To want bigger biceps or a flatter stomach? Nothing wrong with any of that.

We're not talking here about people who simply possess and experience pride in their accomplishments, including their level of health, physical goals, and attributes. Such pride is perhaps on a par with feeling good about, say, earning a promotion at work, or completing an advanced degree. Or taking up running, or painting, or the piano, as you promised yourself you'd do many years ago. Setting goals for oneself and reaching them is wonderful for one's self-esteem!

What this issue is about is crossing a line with your motivation . . . when the organic, healthy desire toward self-improvement becomes an obsessive, *fear-based* need. When pride infests a person's attitude toward others to a degree where brotherhood is replaced by intolerance, and a fundamental enjoyment of life is supplanted by driving anxiety, fed by feelings of not being good enough. I'm talking about the need to fool oneself into believing oneself immortal. I'm talking about the core, childhood fear of being different and looking different. It's also about being afraid to grow old. It's about the dependence on turning heads, on feeling young and attractive always. It's about the need to be a boy forever.

When such a line is crossed, compulsively working out isn't an activity for health, it's a symptom. As is dieting. As is shaving one's body for the sole purpose of looking more boyish, for example, or going into debt to get face lifts and hairplugs. Each of these techniques, in and of itself, does not necessarily indicate a self-esteem problem, but remember, we're talking about the motivating feelings *behind* the behaviors that are the result of learning to feel bad about yourself; somehow, you're not good enough the way you are.

These feelings are based in anxiety and fear: the fear of being different and not being accepted, and the anxiety about failing in the attempt. These are all too familiar feelings for gay people who've had to spend their lives hiding who they really are. These are the feelings that seem bigger than you, that are out of control. They drive you to work out, but not to *enjoy* your workout. In fact, enjoyment doesn't have much to do with it. It's much more about holding the fear and anxiety in abeyance.

The question for you to ask yourself is, why are you buying into this?

Isn't life anxiety-producing enough already, without adding to the stress of modern-day living? You're already experiencing overpopulation, freeway traffic, smog, noise pollution, bigotry, and taxes. Do you also need to run to the gym every five minutes and go into debt for a new Armani every month? Want to feel healthier? Fine. In fact, great! But if fewer reps on the ab master lead to anxious feelings of low self-esteem, that's a problem.

What kinds of problems can occur? When we don't feel good about ourselves, especially about our physical selves, one way that we may seek comfort is through anonymous sex. Sexual addiction is a rising problem in our country in general, and in our community specifically, precisely because of feelings of low self-esteem. Such feelings are also behind increased suicide rates, alcoholism, drug abuse, gambling, overeating, and spending addictions. They are found, on some level, behind any behavior that feels out of control.

People who display an unhealthy (read: *obsessive*) attention to their physical selves, especially at the sacrifice of insight and awareness about their inner selves, also tend to have more sexual partners. It's no coincidence, and it's not simply because they look good. If feelings of low self-esteem are driving a person toward a pathological reliance on his looks, those same feelings may well drive him toward the continual stream of reassurance that multiple sex partners can provide, at least *temporarily*. Psychologically, however, it's important to see this behavior as a symptom. It's like putting one Band-Aid after another on a wound that's not getting any better, not healing. The reason is that the wound isn't on the outside, it's on the inside.

Some other questions to ask yourself: What would happen to you—within—if you stopped your compulsive behavior? If you stopped the race to work out, look younger, keep up? What would you then be forced to deal with about yourself, without your usual, continual distraction that serves to keep your anxiety at bay? While you look at your body in the mirror, what are you *avoiding* looking at, inside? These can be difficult questions which require honest, soul-searching answers. Psychotherapy is extremely helpful in finding these kinds of answers, as is meditation.

Perhaps the solution lies in the process of finding the balance in life, for your life specifically. It's easy to appreciate a well-developed body. (Our society has conditioned us to do exactly that.) To appreciate the importance of developing one's internal beauty, however, takes insight and a commitment to *overall* health. It is toward an organic, holistic view of the whole person that ancient wisdom teaches. More and more often this view is found in the way Western doctors treat their patients. In our philosophies of health and wellness. In our school curriculums. And, hopefully, in our emerging view of what it takes to develop healthy relationships ... loving each other for what's on the inside, not just on the outside. Don't the heart and mind matter at least as much as external attributes?

Let's face it (even if you usually try not to): The natural progression of life dictates that, if all goes well, we're going to get older. In the end, we're not left with the youthful, media-hyped definition of beauty. We're left with a different kind of beauty, one that's not only found in the well-earned lines around the eyes, or the receding hairline, or the expanding waistband, but is also found in the kindness, compassion, and wisdom that comes from a life of learning lessons.

Beauty is not only in the eye of the beholder; it is also in the heart of one who has learned that lasting acceptance—and self-esteem—comes from within.

Real-Life Story . . . Lee

A friend of mine, Lee, was telling me that the dolls and action figures he and his sisters played with when they were growing up in the Philippines were all modeled after young, thin, blond, white girls and boys.

"Didn't you have any that were, well, Asian-looking?" I asked him. He laughed and said that no, they were all pretty much the same, and all looked Caucasian. "Even the male action-hero stuff," he continued. "They were all white-people dolls. Not a minority in the bunch."

Obviously, this is going to make quite a lasting impression on a young child about what characteristics—literally—are held in high regard in life. His exotic and beautiful almond-shaped eyes were nowhere to be found in the toys with which he played. Dolls are often surrogate role models for children. Who he was, was not represented. In my friend's childlike view of the world, the right thing to be was white. Being of any other descent, possessing any other racial or cultural characteristics, was clearly less desirable. Such a skewed and unfair lesson to impress upon a young mind and still-forming ego.

Until quite recently, the same held true for African-American children, Latino children, other ethnic minorities, and gay people. There were no dolls of color and certainly no gay or lesbian dolls. How were children supposed to learn the lesson that *different* is okay? Even beyond okay, that diversity is what makes life colorful and interesting? That we can all learn from each other precisely because we are all different? Well, the healthy lessons weren't coming from the doll store, but lessons about feeling inferior were.

Even messages on a subtle, unconscious level are picked up by kids regarding what's acceptable and what isn't, what is of value, and what is worth less. So, if almost all dolls (and cartoons, coloring books, games, etc.) are made with figures in a Caucasian likeness (which to a large degree, and in some parts of the world, they still are), then any child who is not light-skinned is getting a very strong message about what is of value when it comes to ethnicity.

Further, how many dolls on the shelves, coloring books, and story books show two Barbies kissing or two Kens holding hands? Why can't Ken have an Asian male lover? Or Caucasian Barbie be with African-American Barbie on a date? And by the way, was there ever a Jewish Barbie with seder accessories? What if you're a young, black, Jewish lesbian? Does Toys 'R' Us have something for you? This may sound ridiculous, and that's exactly the point. Why is it ridiculous? Why do we insist on giving our children antiquated messages about gay people, interracial relationships, interreligious relationships and ethnic minorities?

As part of his path toward personal growth, Lee is consciously working hard to unlearn early taught prejudices and expand his horizons when it comes to the men he dates and the qualities he finds attractive in others. He is entering a process of opening himself up to many different kinds of people, sometimes for friendship, sometimes for romance. In other words, he's trying to appreciate the beauty in a variety of individuals, cultural experiences, and physical types—Asian-Americans included.

It comes as no surprise that, until recently, he's only dated what he calls "pretty, young white guys." He claims that he has always been able to appreciate, to a degree, darker-skinned men, at least in the abstract, but for him, this appreciation still excluded Asians. They also had to look right, with white features and well-built bodies, much like the action heroes of his youth.

"A few years ago, I would never have dated an Asian guy. I just couldn't see them as attractive, not even objectively speaking," he admits.

Couldn't see "them" as attractive? Being Asian himself, didn't he really mean, "us"? Perhaps a bit of deeply rooted, socially sanctioned shame was speaking.

Lately however, due to his conscientious commitment to his emotional and spiritual growth, he has experienced a rise in his own feelings of self-worth. He told me that he has been feeling freer and more generous, more expansive with his view of beauty in the world. He finds himself talking with strangers—men especially—who are of all different physical types, not just the ones he finds to be cute. For the first time, he himself feels like an attractive person, sometimes even more so than he had ever imagined, with an appreciation for his exotic features and unique physical qualities. He can look in the mirror and genuinely like what he sees, not because he conforms to what he was taught is attractive, because he doesn't. But because he likes *himself* more. The ways in which his physical appearance is different from others are no longer sources of shame for Lee. He realizes that he is *not* worth less, and as he learns to feel better about himself, he learns to appreciate and recognize the beauty of his own ancestry.

This is not to say that *appreciating* how someone looks is the same as being *attracted to* the way someone looks. These are two different, although perhaps related, ideas. However, in Lee's case, his lack of ability to appreciate anything other than a certain prescribed set of characteristics was an obstruction to his ability to like himself. Further, it had created a narrow worldview where he was missing out on possible friendships, acquaintances, and even romances because of his early life-conditioning.

As he now puts it, "My husband potential has skyrocketed!"

If we are taught, as children or as adults, that there is a certain ideal to which homage must be paid, in defiance of what occurs naturally, then we are falling prey to a gross disservice to our self-esteem, collectively and individually. (Gay people exist in nature, and to many, we are not the norm. Does that make us unattractive or invalid human beings?)

The world is not made up of only well-defined mesomorphs, nor are the only healthy role models white people. Of course, people have their own types to which they find themselves more physically attracted than to others, but as a person's worldview shifts and grows, from being the result of unhealthy messages to one that is more inclusive and embracing, then bigger-picture issues such as discrimination, exclusion, and prejudice cannot help but fall away. That person's definition of "attractive" is allowed to grow as well. To be welcoming of others is to encourage your own sense of being welcomed.

As Lee learned, the world is much more interesting when one's view of beauty encompasses more, not less, of our fellow creatures.

The Meditation

I recommend that this meditation be done clothing-optional. It can heighten an awareness of your physical being and your feelings around your physicality, if, for this purpose, you see your clothing as a kind of barrier or perhaps a protection. Here are a few suggestions:

If you are comfortable with your nakedness, simply do the meditation from a relaxed sitting or reclining position, unclothed.

Or, you could take yourself through a gentle and gradual process toward increased body comfort by first doing this meditation fully clothed, and then reducing the amount of clothing you wear each successive time. It may be enlightening for you to watch your level of body-comfort progress in this way. Which part(s) do you prefer to keep covered? Which do you feel comfortable enough to uncover? Does this remain constant or change each time you do this meditation?

Another procedure to try would be to disrobe in front of a mirror, slowly and carefully observing yourself as you do so, prior to engaging in the meditation. Once undressed, let your eyes move up and down your body, breathing deeply. Finally, make eye contact with yourself. Once you feel relaxed, begin the meditation from a standing or sitting position in front of the mirror.

This meditation is most effective when done very slowly, allowing for plenty of time to fully experience your thoughts and feelings all along the way.

Breathe deeply and let your body relax. As you breathe, become aware of what is happening to your body. Where does it expand, and where does it contract? Where are you more relaxed in your body, and where might you carry tension?

Continue to breathe, fully letting go of any stress in your being . . . mind and body.

Pause.

Let us now progress through your body, slowly moving from

head to toe, with an awareness of how you think and feel about each part of your body. Let yourself have all your thoughts, your accolades as well as criticisms. Let yourself get in touch with all your feelings . . . from joy and pride through embarrassment or shame. Have this experience fully without editing or judging your internal comments. Simply witness your thoughts, and experience your feelings.

Pause.

Focus now, on the top of your body . . . your head and your hair. Textures, shapes. Your face. Your features. Eyes, nose, mouth, chin. How do you feel about these areas of your body? What are you thinking? Take the time to really get to know, internally, your relationship with these areas. Perhaps it is an uneasy relationship. Perhaps it is a joyful one. Let yourself have the experience.

Pause.

Move to your neck. Slowly out to your shoulders. What are you experiencing? What are your thoughts and what are your feelings? Take your time.

Pause.

Your back . . . the shape and width of your back. This skin. The muscle structure.

Your arms . . . the muscles, the length, the hair, the color.

Move slowly, move through your body with awareness.

Your chest. Focus on every quality about your chest. Breathe.

Your stomach and abdomen. What is happening within these areas? Is there comfort or tension? How do you feel about these areas? What are your thoughts?

Pause.

Your buttocks, your hips, your pelvis, and your genitals. What thoughts do you have about your sex organs? What are your feelings? Has your relationship with this area of your body always been the same, or has it evolved?

Pause.

Your legs . . . thighs, knees, shins, calves, ankles . . . your feet. Move slowly and become aware of your feelings . . . witness your thoughts. Observe.

Breathe.

Pause.

Now return to the part of your body which represents to you your greatest degree of self-esteem.

Pause.

Why did you choose this area? What are you feeling as you focus on this area of your body?

Pause.

Now return to that part of your body representing your lowest self-esteem.

Pause.

What are these difficulties about? When did they begin? What is their history?

Pause.

Ask yourself this question: What do I fear?

Pause.

Now ask: Do I distract myself from my fear? If so, how? Why?

Pause.

Are you willing to learn to accept yourself, just the way you are at this moment, as a work in progress?

How can you be kinder to yourself?

How can you ease any pressures you may put upon yourself?

How can you forgive yourself for your "imperfections"?

Pause.

Welcome yourself into the world, your world, as a place where you belong.

Welcome those around you.

Accept your family, your friends, your neighbors for who they are.

Accept your life as a work in progress, fears and all.

Accept your body. Accept your mind. Accept your uniqueness.

Pause.

You are the only one exactly like you. Revel in the unique creation that is you.

When you feel done, take a deep, cleansing breath.

Chapter 14

What Was I Thinking?

Just remember that one needs all the love one can find.
—Anthony Perkins

Ever find yourself waking up in the morning, maybe with a bit of a headache and cotton-mouth, wondering, *Who the heck is this lying next to me?!*

Or perhaps you pause to take some serious stock of your life . . . oh, say about two or three years into a relationship, and you're baffled as to how your life has become what it is, and why exactly you're in this relationship at all.

Or you're sitting at the bar, enjoying yourself as you watch the muscular, shirtless bartender joke and flirt with the customers. Then you stop, look around, and ponder what in the world you're doing here on a Saturday night, feeling lonely, coughing smoke, and listening to music loud enough to shatter glass.

Such moments of introspection happen, of course, not just around the dating or relationship issues in our lives, but also around our work lives, our choices of friends, the quality of those friendships, where we choose to live, the hobbies and activities in which we engage, etc., etc. Really, every aspect of one's life is fodder for moments of introspection and analysis, if one is so inclined.

Wherever your life is, right now at this very moment, I encourage you to ask yourself this: *How did I get here, what events and choices have led me to this particular place, and how conscious am I of taking responsibility for my life?* These are not simple questions, but rather are questions whose answers lead to the difference between living a conscious and aware life, or one that is passing you by.

Life can be tricky if we're not paying close attention, taking stock each step of the way, moving through with a mindfulness and deliberation. Sure, there are those who believe that sometimes life just happens. However, an argument can be made about the collective unconsciousness of the universe, and that all things happen for very specific reasons and needs. The reasons are not coming from some cosmic force out there, but from the collective force of the members of society itself. If society did not need to learn certain lessons, there would have been no Hitler, no AIDS, cancer, child abuse, pollution, crime, etc.

If you wish to follow Freud's theories, then you'd agree that there are no accidents. Every event is the ultimate result of an unconscious urge or desire. Some unmet need is playing itself out, the unconscious mind being far more vast and powerfully motivating than is conscious thought. Again, the idea is that it is the unconscious of individuals which is at play in creating all events in existence.

But one thing is certain: It is your self-esteem that pays the price for a life that happens without your consent.

If you ever have the experience of asking yourself, *what was I thinking?*, then something is occurring in your life without your full participation. Something for which you now need to take responsibility. Maybe it's something positive and serendipitous, like winning a lottery of pleasant little life-surprises. Or maybe it's something that carries with it consequences you didn't expect, nor do you now desire, thus leaving you confused, overwhelmed, anxious, depressed, or feeling poorly about yourself. *Why didn't I just pay more attention?* you muse. *What am I doing to create such a reality for myself?*

As we face choices in life, both large and small, it is not only healthy, it's of tremendous importance to one's happiness and psychological growth to keep self-esteem in mind, each and every step of the way: Is this decision I'm about to make going to be healthy for my feelings of self-worth, or will this deplete, hurt, or otherwise negatively affect how I think about myself?

We come upon crossroads in life every day where we need to make decisions. Some urgent, some so small they escape our notice. In fact, most of the time we make them without much conscious thought at all, and then we're on our merry way to the next one. Each time we arrive at such a fork in the road, metaphorically speaking, we are presented with an opportunity to increase or decrease some aspect of our self-esteem. Perhaps you tend to follow Thoreau's example and take the road less traveled, or you're more apt to move forward in the wake of the great masses. Regardless, there are repercussions to how you feel about yourself with everything you do.

Too often we find that society rewards a person for not taking responsibility for his or her actions. Would we have so many attorneys in our country if people were more conditioned to take responsibility, and less motivated for litigious revenge? I doubt it. Not many societies support such a need for legal representation as does ours. Perhaps one needs to think about what is the first impulse when something goes wrong. Am I quick to blame another for my life, or is there something going on about life lessons I need to learn? What have I done via my decisions, actions, and everyday behaviors that has resulted in some big cosmic lesson, which I can choose to heed or ignore?

Bottom line: The responsibility for your behavior is yours and yours alone.

With all the decisions we have to make in life, it seems that the ones in which we are most significantly and intimately involved—and are most confused about!—are the ones we make regarding our relationships.

In past generations, the choices seemed simpler. So many more people were in the closet then, much less collective thought was going into knowing about a person's sexual identity, or into discovering one's own sexual identity. For many people of earlier generations, it was not until much later in life that they came to understand and appreciate their gay sexual orientation, and so, most everyone got married. That's simply what one did in those days. You married the person who seemed likely to make the best spouse, and the best parent to your children, whatever "best" meant according to you (and often, to your own parents).

So, these days, are heterosexual choices improving at all throughout the generations? Not according to the statistics. There's now a slightly greater than fifty percent chance of divorce for every couple who marries. That's a lot of broken hearts and a lot of fallout for the children involved. (As marriage is not yet legal for gay people, there are no such statistics available. So, we have to assume that the vast majority of those divorces are taking place between two heterosexual persons; even though a very minor, and statistically diminishing, percentage would likely be about sexual orientation issues.) So, straight people aren't doing so hot, in terms of long-term relationships, and they're the ones with the advantages of role models, familial support, and greater acceptance throughout society.

But now, we are facing the topic of sexual orientation as never before, and so the choices of relationships are far more vast and complicated, as gay men and women realize and actualize their need to discover and indeed *create* that which makes for a healthy relationship, one that acknowledges and respects a person's true nature. We are not merely satisfied with marrying someone of the opposite sex of whom our families approve, just because society tells us to. (Younger generations may not even realize that this used to commonly occur!) We are instead legitimizing the importance of being who we are, with all the basic, human desire for healthy partnerships that comes with *any* sexual orientation.

There are many kinds of unique, healthy, satisfying relationships for us to choose. Not enslaved by any social or familial guidelines to which we must conform, gays and lesbians tend to create as we go. And creative we are!

The heterosexual world has rituals to help shape their love lives and romances: proms and weddings, for example. Even a divorce is a rite of passage that is, thus far, a heterosexuals-only institution. The point is that the world acknowledges your relationship-related passages and stages, if you're straight. How many gay people have parents who have said, "Good for you, honey, you're gay! Let me help you learn about love!" Or, "I have just the man/woman for you! Let me help you plan a commitment ceremony, dear! We'll invite everyone. Your father will be so pleased!"

Instead, with a lack of social sanctions for gays comes the widespread and accepted message that our gay and lesbian relationships can't work, won't last, don't count. When we buy into these base pronouncements, we are internalizing the messages: *My* relationships can't work, they're not heterosexual; *I* don't know how to make them last, no one's ever shown me; *my* relationships don't matter, they are not legally nor socially sanctioned. It's no wonder it becomes so easy, once we hit adulthood, to feel confused and clueless about which relationships are healthy for our self-esteem, and which are not. How can we know?!

Well, the first step toward making healthy relationship choices is to *not* buy into the negative messages about our ability to have loving, lasting, rewarding, healthy relationships if these are what we so choose. We can have whatever kind of relationships we desire, all of which are valid, and no one has the right to judge them, socially, legally, religiously supported, or not. Just as each individual is unique, the kind of relationship each person desires is also specific and unique.

What becomes important is for each person to make conscious, mindful choices regarding the relationships, friendships, and acquaintances one wants in life. Our lives would be so very different if, as youngsters, we were routinely given the message that we are empowered to love whomever we desire: We are in the driver's seat and who we choose to love is up to us. Each choice is valid, and each is our own responsibility. So choose wisely!

However, it is never too late. I encourage you to ask yourself: What kind of relationship do I honestly believe I am ready for?

Also: What do I want in a partner, and what am I able to offer another person?

Such simple questions, really, on the surface, but the answers are too seldom given the kind of thoughtful attention they deserve. Instead of a flurry of unsatisfying encounters, a repetition of unhealthy patterns, an ongoing stream of frustrations as we distract ourselves with the busy-ness of disappointing dates, if we were to become quiet with ourselves so we may become better connected with who we are and what we want, we could begin to break our unhealthy relationship patterns. We would then be able to replace these patterns with behaviors and internalized messages that are supportive of our self-esteem.

You see, we do not necessarily get what we *want*, or feel we *need*. We get what we're *ready for*.

So perhaps the next step toward having healthy relationships is to realize that if we are ready to learn certain lessons, and if we are paying attention, we are presented with ample and repeated opportunity for those lessons. Some may be difficult, some obvious, but all have the potential of being richly rewarding.

A gay male friend of mine spent ten years with a whirlwind variety of sexual partners, having a lot of fun on the one hand, and feeling tremendous frustration and disappointment on the other. He felt locked into a cycle, and for as long as he remained on this merry-go-round, he was filled with distraction. He was missing something that he suspected he could find out there, healthier and happier, waiting for him. In ten years he hadn't gotten any closer.

Then he learned how to look inward. He took stock, took responsibility—took a breath!—and grew more in touch with his true needs and wants. After much personal-growth work and very careful soul-searching, he became *ready* for a relationship of the type he'd been hoping for deep in the private corners of his heart. That's precisely when he met his life-partner. (This happened several years ago, and they're still together.)

Now this is not to say that everyone is seeking a life-mate. Nor am I saying that a monogamous relationship is preferable to having lots of multi-partnered fun. I cannot be the one to tell you that ... it depends on the individual. That's a significant point: Much of society judges gay and lesbian lives plenty without *us* imposing judgment on our choices!

The importance here is that whatever kind of relationship one *is* seeking, it can only be found when one becomes aware of what's going on, internally. If having multiple sexual partners is acting as the Band-Aid that's covering your loneliness and stunting your emotional growth, how can you know that without turning inward and listening to yourself? Or if you're in a long-term monogamous relationship, but you're miserable with that choice, it's only fair to you and your partner to get in touch with what's going on for you, within. Only then can you realistically identify the issues involved, and learn to make healthy life decisions.

I believe that we experience what we are ready to experience. How mindful are you of your walk through life, the choices you are making, and the reasons for your choices? How receptive are you to the lessons that are coming your way? Are you catching them? Are you missing them?

How are you preparing yourself for experiences that will help you to be fully actualized, that will help you to realize your potential as a person who is ready to give and receive love? Are you open to learning what the universe has in store for you? Are you willing? Are you ready?

That's how a healthy life happens: as we become ready for it. In that readiness lies mindfulness, the result of a careful process of thinking and feeling. It's really the opposite of *"What was I thinking?"* It is thinking precisely, willfully, honestly. And it's being self-aware and courageous enough to *feel*—just as honestly.

Whatever type of relationship you as a gay person might be interested in—whether for the moment or the long term, with one special person or more than one—it can be found, somewhere. As the bumper sticker says, *We are everywhere.* At work, at school, at the gas station, in restaurants, in stores, in the personal ads, on the beach, on the Internet (this is the computer age!), but the important question remains: What type of relationship are you *ready* for?

Once we enter a relationship, the task shifts from *finding* to *maintaining*. Again, mindfulness and the willingness to take responsibility are the keys to any relationship's ongoing health. It's important to remember that, much as an individual grows, so too does a relationship grow from one stage to the next. Early on, your relationship may be in the "honeymoon period," that time marked by limerance (also called infatuation) and that certain light-headed feeling that keeps you soaring with exciting thoughts of your boyfriend or girlfriend. Limerance, though, is built on mystery, on seeing the other person infrequently. Therefore, limerance will decline over time and upon greater exposure to one another.

Some people find that they are addicted to limerance itself, and they confuse feeling *in* love with feelings *of* love, and may not know how to go from the honeymoon period to deeper emotional intimacy. Once the limerance fades, which is natural and inevitable, they mistakenly believe that what they're no longer feeling is love itself, and they move on to the next person. They've never felt a deeper level of connectedness with someone else beyond the infatuation stage, and so they have not learned what love is, nor how to make it last. (Another issue for which therapy can be extremely helpful.)

If, however, you find that your feelings deepen as your relationship enters a period of greater emotional intimacy and bondedness, then often a kind of unique and personal fabric develops between you as you get to know each other better, understanding each other's likes and dislikes, personality quirks, moods. Learning more about each other requires honesty and trust, and is also a true test of compatibility: Are you able to find happiness with this person, as you discover more about him/her?

If you continue onward together, you encounter more joys and more obstacles, and you move through increasingly mature stages of life as a couple. Unless you are interested in short-term involvements only, some version of these stages is likely to occur in most relationships that last over time, in both romances and friendships alike.

Difficulties arise, however, when, from a driving need to fill the loneliness void, we bypass the earlier, natural, healthy (and fun!) stages of a relationship, and begin choosing china patterns before either partner is really ready. Many people find themselves cohabiting too soon. What's too soon? Well, no one can tell another couple exactly when it is too soon for them—that's one of those murky intangibles, unique to every individual and each couple. It's more *felt* than intellectualized. Again, we can see the vital importance of paying attention to your own feelings in order to identify what "too soon" may mean for you. Being in the grip of romance can pose quite a challenge to mindfulness, and yet that's precisely when it is most important for a healthy relationship.

As a general guideline however, too soon is when major decisions are being made before the relationship has had a chance to build trust; when choices are based on loneliness and feelings of low self-worth, rather than on the growing closeness and intimacy that can only happen with enough time spent together, learning about each other. Like an infant growing up through the toddler, childhood, and adolescent stages, a relationship needs nurturance, attention, and patience in order to grow healthy and strong. To circumvent the "wonder years" of a relationship, pushing it forward under anxious hope and the delusion of rapid closeness, is like giving a driver's license to a four-year-old. It's too soon.

If we don't feel whole and complete as individuals, then we may look to another person to complete us. In that urge to feel complete, we push and rush our relationships, confusing what we're ready for with what we think we need, like forcing a square peg into a round hole. As the saying goes, nature abhors a vacuum; it's human nature to want to fill the void within, and so we attempt to do just that, with alcohol, drugs, overeating, compulsive behaviors . . . and with other people.

With someone else, we hope to feel the oneness, the wholeness that we believe we lack. The problem is that this puts a tremendous amount of unconscious expectation on the other person, to be all that we can't be on our own. Without his/her consent, your new partner has unknowingly been asked to soothe your wounds and fill in all your missing parts. So, instead of just being able to complement each other and add pleasure to each other's life, there's an urgent, unspoken need being imposed upon the relationship, adding tension, inevitable disappointment, and anger.

Precisely because we as gay people often have such a dearth of guidance and support from our families of origin regarding adult relationships in general, and the fashioning of our gay love lives in particular, I'm often asked for practical suggestions to help nurture our relationships and allow them to flourish. I sometimes write a relationship advice column for local gay papers, and, combined with my clinical practice, I've accumulated some thoughts to help increase the chances for relationship success. So, without further ado, here are several tips that I've found to be helpful for clients, friends, and family alike.

1. **Develop your communication skills.** Even when two people are able to forge a close understanding, a linguistic shorthand with each other, it's still important not to *assume* that the other person knows what you mean. Assumptions lead to miscommunications and hurt feelings. If there's the slightest doubt, talk it out. At least half of the couples that come to my office simply need help developing their communication skills.

2. **"It's never about the towels."** A couple came to me with the primary complaint that one partner just throws the clean laundry into the linen closet, while the other one neatly folds and stacks. The neat one's *surface* complaint is about his partner's messiness, but what's going on underneath is that he's feeling a lack of respect and care, which, once they began to look more closely, showed itself in many aspects of their relationship. The towels are but one manifestation. The question to address becomes: What's really going on here?

3. **Know thyself.** A healthy relationship with another person begins by having a healthy relationship with yourself. Are you vigilantly honest with yourself? Only then can you be honest with someone else. Do you prioritize your self-esteem

needs and take good care of your whole person, mind, spirit, and body? That's how you learn to be kind and take good care of another person. With practice, you can discover how to be your own healthy role model.

4. **Communicate feelings.** Thinking is generally a more immediate process than feeling, i.e., you know what your thought is before you know how you feel about it. Communicating on a feeling level, while more challenging, adds depth, intimacy, and connectedness to your relationship. So before you blurt out something hurtful, take a deep breath, look inward, and identify the feelings you're having. Chances are your partner is having some of those same feelings, and there you can find some common ground for honest discussion.

5. **Fair fighting.** It's okay to argue occasionally. (In fact, heated discussions are one indication of passion.) A constructive argument can bring greater closeness when resolved, a destructive argument tears the relationship apart, if not now, then in the future when your partner comes back for revenge, consciously or unconsciously. So, here are a few pointers to assist the productivity of your arguments:

- Move the issue from *You vs. Me* to *You and Me vs. The Problem*. (See the Real-Life Story in Chapter Eleven for more about this concept.)
- Do your best to be a patient listener. Before you state your opinions, pause to make sure you've really heard what was just said to you.
- Use "I feel" rather than "You make me feel . . ." It's less threatening and allows for non-accusatory communication, while keeping the focus on your feelings.
- Don't go to bed in a *huff!* The more familiar saying is, don't go to bed angry, but I don't think that's realistic. If you're angry, you're angry; and if it's bedtime, guess what? You're going to bed angry. Staying up to fight will just make you more tired and more confused. What's helpful is to acknowledge your feelings, and commit to continue working together on the problem in the morn-

ing, after you've rested a bit. An additional tip: Before you roll over, give your partner a kiss. It's a lot friendlier than a cold shoulder.

6. **Develop a support system other than your lover.** To expect your partner to be your lover, mother, father, brother, sister, minister, teacher, healer, best friend, confidant, etc., is to set the relationship up for failure, set yourself up for disappointment, and set him/her up to feel resentful. Having other people of significance in your life helps you to keep a perspective, feel a sense of balance, and helps to maintain healthy boundaries in your relationship.

7. **You're not perfect, either.** And who'd want perfection? Then there's no room or desire for a partner. We all want to know that there's room for us in the relationship, and that we contribute uniquely to our partner's quality of life. We all make mistakes, we all deserve forgiveness. How forgiving are you of yourself, and therefore, of other people? Remember the 12-step adage: This too shall pass. Another favorite: Don't sweat the small stuff.

I hope these ideas are helpful to you. Again, it's fully up to you to pay attention, no matter what kind of relationship you have. Your self-esteem requires it. Your growth and healing via life's lessons mandate your mindfulness. You *are* in the driver's seat. Who you wake up next to is your choice. Remember: *All* your choices matter, *all* your relationships are valid, *all* your experiences count.

What were you thinking? Hopefully, you're able to answer that you were thinking you deserve to invest in your happiness and to have healthy relationships. That you can commit to a relationship with *yourself* first and foremost. That you are receptive to your life lessons. And that you are able to do whatever it takes to assume responsibility for your readiness.

Helen Keller, who had to begin a relationship with herself from a far more disadvantaged starting point than most of us, succinctly offers encouragement and empowerment for life and all it's lessons: "Life is either a daring adventure, or it is nothing at all." And she would know about daring adventures!

Real-Life Story . . . Jeffrey

Jeffrey came to my office complaining of, in his words, "dating frustrations," and a general sense of being "clueless when it comes to relationships with guys." He stated that he feels "walked all over" and "taken advantage of" by just about everyone he meets, whether they are potential friends, sex partners, or men he'd want to be involved with on a long-term basis. Jeffrey says that he falls in love with one man after another, only to be disappointed with the result: Either they leave, or he falls out of love within a short period of time. He does not seem able to trust his choices. Understandably, he now has become quite guarded around men and sounds rather cynical as he recalls some of his recent experiences. His emotional states tend to swing from depressed and hopeless to angry and bewildered. All this angst, and he's only twenty-three.

Jeffrey has moved to Los Angeles from a small southern town to attend college and graduate school in medicine. He is intelligent, physically fit, well mannered and very motivated to try and "figure out what I'm doing wrong." While he had a few dating experiences in high school, with both girls and guys, he says that L.A. is like a candy store for him, "with cute guys everywhere."

Hmmm, interesting (and common in this city) analogy . . . one gets the feeling that, like candy, the cute guys aren't providing much substance or sustenance in Jeffrey's life.

Not out to his family, Jeffrey's coming-out process is taking a form much like many such young people who've moved to the big city: through social avenues, primarily bars, clubs, parties, etc. He's made a few friends at the gay student union on campus, and together, they hit the town on Friday and Saturday nights. It is in the local gay bars that they feel freest to be who they are: young, gay, and single.

Although experimenting and participating in the plentiful gay night life, Jeffrey is quite confused as to what he really wants. Does he desire to sample all the candy he can, or does he want one special person to be with and treat him as he'd like to be treated: with respect, kindness, and affection? Or perhaps he wants not one *or* the other, but some combination of the two.

So, Jeffrey's first task is to get in touch with himself: what he wants and needs, and what, if anything, he may be ready for, in a relationship. In order to accomplish this, his work is to start looking inward, becoming more aware of his thoughts, and giving fuller attention to his feelings. Perhaps a part of him wants to play and experiment, while another part of him needs some consistency and ongoing affection from someone to whom he can trust his young heart, but he cannot know any of this until he starts to develop some insight.

On the journey toward gaining some clarity with these issues, Jeffrey begins to prioritize his self-esteem: Under what conditions and in what situations does he feel good about himself, empowered, centered, happy? And when does his opinion of himself suffer? When is he emotionally filled up, and when does he feel hollow and empty? He has some important questions to think about and perhaps some important lessons to learn. For the first time in his life, rather than looking outward to others, he is putting his energy *inward*, getting to know himself better.

What Jeffrey comes to realize is that he wants to "slow things down a bit." He learns that perhaps he can enjoy his sexual experimentation and continue his playful weekends with not just anyone who gives him some attention at the bar, but someone with whom he feels a degree of comfort and trust, someone *he* chooses. If going with many partners is leaving him frustrated and "walked on," perhaps he and these men (thus far) have incompatible agendas. Maybe they just want to have fun, while Jeffrey secretly hopes for more.

As he gains insight into his issues, Jeffrey becomes interested in developing a relationship with someone that includes a playful and continued exploration of his sexuality, while providing the companionship of a good friend. But friendship takes time. So, by investing the energy and patience to carefully get to know someone (and paying attention to his feelings around his choices of friends), he would be giving himself and a potential partner an opportunity to discover how compatible they really are.

It might not work perfectly the first time out, and so Jeffrey may be faced with lessons about patience. It may not turn into a long-term experience, or it might, depending on what they both want, and if their feelings for each other grow. The point is that the chances would improve for Jeffrey to not feel so used and tossed aside—and therefore so hurt, angry, and frustrated—if he stays more attuned to his feelings and more receptive to the lessons that may be awaiting him along the way.

So, for this process of listening inward, he gets to become more familiar with himself, as he becomes more familiar with a new friend. He may even find unexpected, welcomed points of compatibility along the way, a much healthier prescription for Jeffrey's self-esteem.

Another issue that was causing Jeffrey's difficulties is one that is common among young people, but certainly found in the dating and relationship struggles of people of all ages. Jeffrey was confusing sex with love. It's easy to do when one is at the dawn of both: the discovery of one's sexual identity, with all the accompanying thoughts and feelings which can be exciting yet overwhelming; and the promise of a love different from the forms of love previously known.

How it happens is that the physical intimacy of sex gets confused with the emotional intimacy of love. A person may believe that the presence of one indicates the presence of the other, which is not true. They *may* co-exist, and often do, as in a love relationship that is also sexual, but they are, in fact, independent of each other. If you love your best friend, but you're not sleeping with him/her, then you have emotional closeness without sexual intimacy. Likewise, if you're having physical relations with, say, a "sex buddy," but you don't feel love for this person, then what you have is a relationship of physical, but not emotional, intimacy. Get it?

Clearly, Jeffrey was desirous of an intimacy that is both emotional and sexual. In fact, this is the combination that many people are looking for when they are ready for a significant, long-term, and/or life-partner type of relationship: someone to trust and love and with whom they can feel emotionally intimate, as well as someone with whom they can enjoy a mutual physical attraction and sexual expression.

However, the confusion of the two may be about: 1) some relationship lessons that have not yet been learned, or 2) it could very well be indicative of an area of low self-esteem. If a person suffers from low self-esteem, then where there is an emotional void that needs attention, the physical connection is misperceived as the solution. In the quest for emotional closeness, a person goes looking for sexual closeness, and while sex may *temporarily* address the loneliness problem, it doesn't address the real issue of the ongoing emptiness within.

In such a scenario, physical intimacy—sex—does not provide the type of connection that's needed. *But,* one may think, *it's something* . . . and meanwhile, it's providing a distraction from the inner pain. In reality, however, it's really just a Band-Aid and, in the long run, it's awfully hard on the self-esteem.

Further difficulties ensue when this behavior becomes a pattern. If Jeffrey, for instance, were to continue to think that each time a man has sex with him it means that he loves Jeffrey, then undoubtedly Jeffrey would be having all the sex he could find! As humans, we all want to be loved. If a person mistakenly thinks that the way to acquire love is through sex, then their focus becomes the pursuit of sex, rather than the pursuit of love. The square peg/round hole problem. As Jeffrey was confusing the two, it's no wonder that he felt used by men. He was thinking they were feeling love for him, and so he *expected* a love relationship where there was none. Time and time again his misunderstanding set him up for disappointment. It was only after he learned to look inward, to identify, acknowledge, and validate his needs, did he see the difference between physical intimacy and emotional intimacy. And so, he could begin to take some responsibility for his participation in all that angst he'd been feeling.

We can see that in order to begin such a process, however, a person has to realize that they are *worth* the effort, the soul-searching, the time and attention required to gain insight. The world is not necessarily set up to validate all your experiences as a human being, especially if you're a member of a sexual minority. So it becomes important for you yourself to validate who you are.

It bears repeating: Your thoughts are real, your feelings are valid, and all your experiences matter. If you weren't taught this as a child, and if you don't get the message from society at large, then now is the time to give that message to yourself. Then and only then can you move through your world making the choices that are esteem-enhancing, having experiences that bring self-respect and joy to your life, and for which you gladly and proudly take responsibility.

The Meditation

This exercise may be read slowly by a friend or silently to oneself.

Take several deep breaths and allow your mind and body to relax fully.
Pause.
I invite you to think of a significant relationship, one that is currently in your life.
Who is this person to you? Who are you to this person?
Is this relationship one of willful choice, or cosmic chance?
What are the positive aspects to this relationship? What qualities do you bring to the relationship yourself?
Pause.
Now I want you to think of a significant relationship from the past. Why is this person no longer in your life? Your choice? His/her choice? Chance?
What was positive about that relationship? What was negative?
Do you miss this person? Why or why not?
Pause.

Now picture yourself in the context of your family. Think of a recent family event, the first one that comes to mind.

Pause.

How did you feel about yourself that day? How did you feel about your body? Your intellect? Your personality? Your sexual orientation?

Pause.

See yourself now in the context of friendships. Go, in your mind, to a recent time you spent with a good friend or friends.

Pause.

How did you feel about yourself then? Your body? Your mind? Your personality? Your sexual orientation?

Pause.

Take a deep breath, and spend a few moments flipping through the pages of your history, your own personal scrapbook, and identify all the healthy relationships in your life, past and present.

Pause.

Why have these, in particular, come to mind? What is positive about them? Are there any similarities among them?

Pause.

Take another deep breath. Now create, in your mind, a list of characteristics that you very much desire in a love relationship.

Pause.

Why are they so important to you? Which of these qualities are present in your current relationships and friendships? Are they rare to you, or found in abundance in your life? Are they qualities that you, yourself, possess?

You desire these characteristics in a relationship, so ask yourself now: Am I ready for such a relationship? How will I contribute to it? How will I participate in the nurturing of it? What are your answers?

Pause.

What are you willing to do in order to bring such a relationship into your life . . . or, to create room for these qualities in your present relationship?

Pause.

When you are ready, take a deep, centering breath.

* * *

Note: There is a self-assessment exercise in Chapter 20 of this book to accompany the issues discussed in this chapter. You may wish to go there now to further your understanding of your specific relationship issues, or you may want to consider taking all the assessments after you've completed the book.

Chapter 15

Surviving Grief

If instead of a gem or even a flower,
we could cast the gift of a lovely thought
into the heart of a friend,
that would be giving as angels give.

—George Macdonald

When someone we love dies, what do we really lose? We lose our "other half," we lose our "best friend," we lose our "heart." Perhaps most of all, we lose our mirror . . . that face into which we could look and see, looking back at us, all the love and goodness that a deep, often hidden part of us always hoped we were capable of. We lose how we want to be known. We lose the proof that we are lovable.

The grieving process includes so much. Where there is death, there is loss. And where there is loss, there is anger. The healing work, therapeutically speaking, involves an uprising of childhood issues, adult-relationship issues, feelings of rage, sorrow, hopelessness, helplessness, depression, despondency, relief, existential angst, forgiveness . . . any and all of the above in combinations as unique as the individual who is going through the grieving process.

I have led many bereavement groups over the years. One particular group was a kind of grief circle, which I facilitated while I was the bereavement counselor at the first AIDS hospice in the country, the Chris Brownlie Hospice, set high in the hills of Los Angeles. In this circle, there were many real-life stories almost too painful to hear: There was a mother who had lost her husband a few years back, who was attending the group because her only child had just died of AIDS. She told us, "Losing my husband was like losing an arm." She continued, her hand on her chest. "Losing my son was like losing a lung."

Another participant was a young man who was grieving for the loss of his lover. This was his third lover he'd lost to AIDS. On the first night of group, he told us that he, himself, had just tested positive for the virus.

A young woman in the group had lost her lover, another woman, to AIDS. Because they were a lesbian couple, she found that there was very little support for her in the community. Even in a city as populated, progressive, and filled with nonprofit agencies as Los Angeles, she was at a loss as to where to find the help she needed, where to be among others like herself. The statistics back her up: Lesbians constitute the smallest segment of the HIV-infected population. In our group, however, there was enough diversity among members that she could feel comfortable and welcomed. The group was not just for men, or parents, or lovers, or women. It was for all of them. All united in grief.

In group, participants learned that each and every feeling they were experiencing was a feeling to be acknowledged and accepted, not judged. Every feeling or thought was okay, no matter how ugly or painful. We were not there to edit ourselves, we were there to share of ourselves, and in that room of confidentiality, we could say anything. Because anything we could say or even think, had been experienced at one time or another, by someone else in that room. The common threads of that group were not always pretty, but they were indeed heartfelt.

We learned that other people may mean well, but are often misguided: "Shouldn't you be dating by now? It's been a year already." Or, "Are you dating again already? It's only been a year." Such comments are likely to send an already grieving person into an even more fragile emotional state, screaming with confusion or burrowing under the covers in despair. These comments really have very little to do with the needs of the grieving individual, and much more to do with how comfortable the speaker is with the grieving process, their own and that of others. So, in group, we would not give advice. It was one of the few rules.

As we'd go around the circle, sharing our stories, heads would nod in understanding. Gradually, where once people felt utterly alone, disenfranchised from their family due to the horrible and unfounded, yet still widespread, stigma of AIDS, or too depressed to partake of any social contact with their friends, they began to feel connected.

When children suffer a loss, their first thought is one of self-blame: Did he/she die because of me? Because of something I said? Something I did or didn't do? As adults, we oftentimes need the same kind of reassurance that we are not the cause of painful losses, and, just as importantly, that we are not alone in the experiencing of losses. Until one accepts this understanding at the gut level, not just on an intellectual level, a person's self-esteem can really take a beating around loss. Gathering with others who, again, really *know* at their core what painful, close loss feels like, can be self-esteem healing. Grief groups of all kinds can therefore be almost medicinal in their ability to lift guilt and ease depression.

Among the kinds of guilt that can be found in the landscape of HIV and AIDS is what's commonly called by the descriptive name of "survivor's guilt." People who have lost friends and other loved ones to the disease, especially when they know that they themselves partake of the same or similar sexual behaviors that led to their friends contracting the virus, can wonder, "How come them, and not me?" It's a guilt that can so permeate the HIV-negative members of a community that support groups have cropped up in urban areas to help address this issue.

As more and more friends find out they have the virus, or as more and more friends die, HIV-negative people can begin to feel left out of the very community that offered them refuge from the hostile world at large. No sooner have they come out of one closet than there's a new closet for the "negatives." Now, there exists a community within a community, this one defined by a microscopic virus. The perceived (or real) ostracism that can be acutely felt by someone whose friends are now numbering more "positive" than "negative" carries a very real danger: the desire, be it conscious or unconscious, to sero-convert (meaning, to go from a diagnosis of HIV-negative to HIV-positive).

Overlying this guilt is another, just as insidious in its ability to wreak havoc on those who are already suffering loss. It comes from certain factions of society and is often found cloaked in the name of religious righteousness. This is the form of blame that gays have had to fight since the first discoveries of HIV. "It's their own fault ... It's God's punishment on gays ... They're only getting what they deserve." These are the more obvious statements that, when pronounced enough, can be difficult to *not* believe, especially for those whose newly emerging sexual identity is a dubious and worrisome achievement at best. Accepting these damnations is, of course, exactly what the pronouncers are counting on.

At the hospice, we held monthly services (called Life Celebrations) for the residents who had died. More accurately, the services were *in honor of* the residents; they were *for* those of us left behind. In attendance were parents, lovers, friends, relatives, and hospice staff. This was the late 80s and the idea of an AIDS hospice was, at the time, controversial. How could we create a place that actually accepts the idea that AIDS is killing us, asked some members of the activist gay and HIV communities. How can we run an agency where people—mostly gay men—can go to die? Shouldn't that energy be spent on fostering *living*? Finding a cure? Fighting the inevitable? What was *not* controversial was the overwhelming need for those of us somehow surviving this diabolical pandemic to get together and cry. The city was getting increasingly numb from the losses sweeping through every corner of the gay community, cranking up the volume on mass anxiety and depression. The widespread fears were well described in comments from some Celebration participants: "There's nowhere to hide. It's hitting everyone I know. All my friends are dying. I feel overwhelmingly helpless."

The Celebrations included several of what I call "stimulants to crying." We would play music that, if someone was having trouble letting the tears out, these songs would do the trick! Sometimes recorded, sometimes played live on the old, donated piano, "Wind Beneath My Wings" or "Goodbye My Friend" would get the tissue boxes passed around every time. We would also pass around pictures of the deceased, showing us how beautiful and robust they were in healthier days. We'd recite poetry, share personal, happier moments, plant seeds in pots which, the next spring, would be transplanted to the grounds of the hospice. We would write loving notes on tiny strips of paper, then roll them up and place them inside balloons which were released at the end of the service, a powerful gesture of letting go and saying goodbye. We would sit in a big circle holding hands or we'd stand outside on the patio, overlooking the city's skyline. We would share. We would laugh. We would remember. We would cry. And the healing would begin.

Real-Life Story . . . Grief Healing Circle

Grief groups (also called bereavement groups, grieving circles, etc.) have been around since the first cluster of loss survivors got together to share in a good cry. These groups are perhaps more known for their use among people who have lost loved ones to cancer and other well-known diseases. When AIDS became something to be dealt with, it was the very early 80s. There were more and more memorial services to attend each weekend, there was more individual and collective loss in the air, and more urgent became the need of survivors to join together in a sharing of emotions. The majority of these survivors were gay men and lesbians.

As a therapist who at the time was working almost exclusively in the HIV community, I began facilitating a group that brought together a number of men who felt a strong need to not only share, but to experience in some tangible way a degree of collective healing. We weren't sure what that might look like, or how it might feel, but we began by calling the group a Grief Healing

Circle and we met weekly for the better part of two years. The 12-person membership remained largely the same, although a few people left during the life of the Circle and some new folks joined in. There were several aspects to the group, which, on paper are more clearly delineated than they may have appeared in actuality, but they gave us some focus and provided us with a kind of blueprint for the healing process we came to envision.

As is typical of support groups, the first part of the group's time was spent on introductions. During this time each member would briefly tell of their reason for being at the Circle, sort of a thumbnail sketch of the experience of their loss. This began the connecting (and remembering) process where people instantly, naturally, began identifying with each other.

After the first go-around, we would see if anyone was in a particularly difficult or vulnerable space, and needed a bit more time to talk about his pain. If so, those individuals were allowed the extra time to share and feel the support of the others. In this way, they were rewarded for asking for what they needed. Then, the discussion would be opened up to whatever topic was on anyone's mind: dating vs. not dating, family issues, financial worries, personality changes, guilt, anger, depression, troubling behaviors, health care concerns and much, much more were all given discussion over the months.

After the break, we would then settle in for the guided meditation. This aspect, I think more than any other, distinguished our Grief Healing Circle from other types of grief groups. While I was seen as the one providing guidance and facilitation during the previous discussion (as any counselor, therapist, or facilitator would be; although I happily admit that the group developed such a natural, self-sustaining energy of its own, that I really, over time, needed only to assume the duties of what I came to think of as "facilitator lite"), it was the meditation that really became my primary duty. I was always excited and honored by this opportunity and the level of trust from the others.

Our meditations were unscripted, based instead on the concerns, fears, topics expressed that evening during the shares. They arose spontaneously, meandered freely, and brought the participants to a place where their healing could come home. So far, the group had been talking and thinking and feeling. Now the meditation added the consciousness of breathing, centering and being. In this way, an important healing element was added to the therapeutic talk of earlier. In the words of a Circle member, "this is how what's outside comes in."

The meditation was more than a punctuation mark to the evening, although it certainly was that. It was closure that allowed for all the words, thoughts, and feelings that live inside each individual, that had been all stirred up from the evening's events, to scramble around in there until they had exhausted themselves and could float away, leaving in their wake a healed space more filled with peace than noise. Through the meditation, each person's body and mind could begin working in harmony, and in the process (and, as some would put it, add a most fortuitous side effect) stimulating both mental and physical well-being! It was the light at the end of the tunnel. The calm after the storm. The point at which we were all one—connected, as we were, through grief, and now also through peace.

The Meditation

This meditation may be read slowly by a friend, or silently to oneself.

> Let your attention come to the breath. Let your breath calm you and relax your body and mind as you concentrate on the flow, the natural tide of your breaths.
>
> With each breath you take, your body relaxes more fully and your mind begins to settle and clear. Your body and mind are working as one . . . flowing together in harmony, grateful for the calm relaxation, and open to growth, to healing.
>
> Pause.

In your mind's eye, see your breath as it fogs up a small mirror. You continue to gently breathe and notice that every time you inhale, the mirror clears up a bit, and with each exhale the mirror gets foggy again.

Pause.

This is like grief. Sometimes your vision, your mind is foggy . . . cloudy and confused. And at other times, you can see clearly . . . your feelings and thoughts are in harmony, more at peace, and you get a break from the confusion. Sometimes even your spirits lift a bit.

Now when you look into the mirror, you see the fog disappear, and in its place is the face of your loved one. Looking back at you . . . smiling, accepting, loving you. Loving you unconditionally. You breathe in this unconditional love. Taking it into your very being, your very core. And you feel whole. You feel loved. You feel loved.

Pause.

There is relief in knowing that your loved one is now okay. No more pain. No more difficulties. Only pure being, pure light, pure joy. You can relax about him/her now.

Pause.

Your heart is open to all of your feelings. You share them with your loved one through your unspoken, spiritual connection. Your feelings float gently within you, and you share them, from heart to heart. Back and forth. Together. And always, you feel loved.

Pause.

Forgiveness. With the sharing of your feelings, through the love that connects you now and forever, you forgive. You can be hurt and forgive. You can be angry and forgive. You can cry and forgive. And you are forgiven, too.

All of your thoughts and feelings belong to you . . . they are within you as part of your healing process. They are not to be judged. They are all okay. They are a part of you. And you have them, because you have loved.

You've felt joy and you've felt pain. And now, when you feel joy or pain, you know it's okay. You are yourself. You are slowly becoming whole again. You are forgiven. You are loved. You will always and forever be loved.

Let yourself begin to heal.

Let your heart begin to heal.

You are loved.

SOCIETY

*For a community to be whole and healthy,
it must be based on people's love
and concern for each other.*

—Millard Fuller

Chapter 16

The Religious Right Is Neither

*Lord, make me an instrument of your peace.
Where there is hatred, let me sow love.
Where there is darkness, light.*

—St. Francis of Assisi

Ah, religion. As that famous *Saturday Night Live!* character,
Linda Richman, might have said, "I'll give you a topic: The
religious right is neither. Discuss."

The Bible, that ancient, poetic tome filled with wisdom, gran-
deur, and flourish has been used for centuries to guide people
through the murky right-and-wrongs of life. Unfortunately, in
the wrong hands, it has also been used—and continues to be
used—as a club to bash those who are seen as different—different
from the ways of the Bible, according to certain interpreters.
Different from the rest of the flock. Different from the way God
meant.

In a small, conservative New England town is a small Roman
Catholic church. It is made of brick, solid and trustworthy. It's
on a main thoroughfare, so everyone in town who doesn't attend
the only other house of worship, a Protestant church, can easily
get to it. It's largely a Catholic town with many Portuguese
immigrants. The Portuguese in that area have a reputation for
being hard-working, kind, extremely devout people, with

extended families often all living under one roof. It is not uncommon to find three or even four generations of Portuguese living in the same house in this town. They save their money, take care of each other, believe in the importance of family, and devoutly attend church.

This Catholic church puts on a three-day festival—called a *fashta* in Portuguese—once a year and everyone in town attends. The parents and grandparents spend their days preparing the aromatic ethnic food that will fill the booths set up in the junior high school field across the street. During the festival, the young kids will play games during the days, and the teens will go at night to dance and hide in the shadows for a few stolen kisses. Most people know each other. For many of these families, the church is the center of their lives. The *fashta*, one of the biggest celebrations of the year.

This church is the home of Sunday services, holiday services, catechisms, baptisms, confirmations, weddings, funerals, elders' meetings, big dinners set up on folding tables in the basement, and bingo on weekends. In this community, the church is a very important place.

This was my home town, and this was my church. The priest (or father) in charge, the monsignor, was an elderly, cantankerous, harsh man with a booming voice, who believed that to spare the rod was to spoil the child. He elicited fear in children and adults alike. His was the voice of Elderly and Wise Authority. He was called Father. He knew everyone's family and had baptized entire generations. I don't know who presided over the community's circumcisions, but it wouldn't surprise me if he had a hand in those, too. So to speak.

As a child, whenever I heard this head priest speak to us, his flock, about the wrath of God, it made a lasting impression. One sermon made a stronger impression than the others. It was the one where I heard him (this man of God) orating in his angry, heavy accent and dogmatic style, fist pounding on the lectern, refer to God's hatred of those who are murderers, prostitutes, drug addicts, liars, criminals, rapists . . . and homosexuals. The congregation just sat there, nodding away, too afraid to utter a word, lest they incite the wrath of God *or* this man.

I was young at the time, too young to identify yet with the words "homosexual" or "gay." But what I did realize, even as a child, was how harshly judgmental it all sounded. I was raised to believe that God loved all His children, even if they got into trouble, even if they were different. God *hated* some of His children? I didn't even know of any human parents who hated their kids. Why would God hate? And what was that list, again? One thing was made perfectly clear: I'd better not be on it, or it will be the fiery pits of hell for me!

Now, from an adult perspective and with information gained over the years, I can think of several other people sitting there in church that day who must have been shrinking in their pews. What about the young adolescent girl who was falling in love with her object of desire, her very first crush? Perhaps her love was inflamed by a recent first kiss, and for once in her life she didn't feel like she was the only one. There was someone else on the planet—even if just one other person—who had the same confusing kinds of feelings she'd been experiencing for several years now. There was someone who loved her back (with all the swooning love of a first infatuation) just as she loved. Her world started to make a little more sense as the painful isolation and life-or-death fear of being different started to melt away. Confusion, for the first time, was being replaced by joy; fear of being found out was giving way to relief. She had been, as the song says, waiting to exhale. Now she could finally breathe.

Except for one problem: The monsignor says, if she understands him correctly, that God hates her.

Then there was the boy who was still in grade school. He was, in fact, a classmate of mine. He wasn't walking around *saying* that he's a young homosexual-in-the-making, but some felt that they had his number. There was certainly some tauntings, mutterings behind his back, clicking of tongues and shaking of heads, by the other children and adults alike. At a young age when other children can be especially cruel over things like athleticism, competitiveness, and other hyper-hetero standards of behavior, this boy was losing face fast. He loved art class, was a bright, usually happy boy, quiet, very much an overachiever, never gave his teachers any trouble. He didn't do too well on the playground, however. Stereotypical as it may sound, he was one of the last to be chosen for teams in physical education classes and often the object of scorn from the other boys (as, perhaps, the coach looked in the other direction) when he fumbled or performed poorly on the field. His youthful and fragile self-esteem certainly suffered in such situations.

Now, let's imagine, for a moment, that several years down the road this boy did indeed identify as being gay. Well, there's an awfully powerful memory rattling around in his mind about a Sunday sermon when he was a little kid and was told directly by God's messenger himself that, if he understood correctly, God now hates him. This little boy who never gave anyone a moment of trouble, is supposedly hated by his God.

Remember, this was just one Sunday, in one congregation, in one church, in one small town. After being taught to follow, respect, and fear this monsignor—for he speaks for God Himself; after weekly doses of a doctrine that excludes them from their God's love; after years of confusing feelings, hiding in shame, having their young hearts burdened with keeping a secret . . . and not just any secret, *the* secret . . . what can we suppose was done to these two youngsters emotionally? How deep did those early scars go, after the first cut on that Sunday so many years before? What seeds were planted during that sermon that were taken to heart, and eventually contributed to all sorts of unhealthy life choices later on because they felt so unworthy of anyone's love? If their own God doesn't love them, how could anyone else? How can they possibly ever love themselves?

The priest interpreted the Bible as saying that gay people should be hated. There are sections in the Bible that condone slavery and the oppression of women, too. Thankfully, those sections have been amended or reinterpreted by most of those who preach the word, but many, many congregations, all across the country, are still being taught that gay people should be hated.

Or, even more insidious, as when it is couched in a facade of "love thy neighbor," is when it is taught that it's okay to hate the action, if not the person. This allows people to love *conditionally*, to be quietly self-congratulatory for being nice to a gay person's face, all the while smugly believing that come judgment day, *they'll* be the ones who prosper, not that sinful gay couple who lives down the street.

Such a damaging, soul-depleting stance to preach from the pulpit and adopt in the pews in order for certain people to feel better-than. The priest is saying, *I'll* get to heaven, *you* won't, and all the people listening think that they, too, will arrive at the pearly gates, like some heterosexuals-only country club for the blessed.

The priest spoke in church that day and said that God hates homosexuals and the good, God-fearing people of his congregation nodded. But the priest wasn't around when several of his drunken young male parishioners hid in the shadows with clubs one night, and beat the daylights out of the boy who was different. *(If God hates him, surely we should, too.)* He didn't hear the repeated death-threat phone calls to the teenage girl's family when some of her classmates and their parents began to suspect her of being a lesbian. *(God doesn't want those types around, and neither do we!)* And he wasn't present when, several years after that sermon, the young boy so filled with self-hatred tried to take his own life. The girl learned that her kind of love was wrong, and the boy wasn't such a happy kid after that. The priest used the Bible as a club and his devoted followers used whatever they had handy.

As we all know, still today there are those orators with very big voices and very small hearts misusing the pulpit, preaching to congregations large and small, on radio broadcasts and Sunday morning televangelist shows, the same message that was told to the people in this small church in this small town so many years ago. The Bible-babble of hatred.

Real-Life Story . . . "The Religion Within"

A young woman came to my office extremely distraught over a verbal altercation she recently had with her father. Her father is a doctor of theology minister with a large congregation in a major U.S. city. Theirs is a devout family that follows a fairly conservative, orthodox religion. This woman, Maria, has many siblings, aunts and uncles, nieces, nephews, and cousins. Holidays, especially religious holidays are, as you might imagine, a very big deal with this family.

An extremely bright woman in her late twenties, Maria was feeling some family pressure to get married. She suffered many stereotypical family comments around the dinner table, such as, "So, Maria, do you have a special man in your life yet?" And, "When will you be giving us some grandchildren?" and the like. With most of her siblings married with children or pregnant, she was becoming the standout in her family for being, as far as their heterosexually restrictive ways of thinking would suggest, single and without prospects. Internally, Maria was suffering a great deal of conflict because of being (as you might have guessed by now) a lesbian who was not out to her family.

The recent argument with her father was around her defense of the lesbian couple in the church that had come to him to perform their commitment ceremony. Occasional church-goers, this couple had come to the reverend out of a sense of tradition: They were both from the city, their families had attended this church, and they had both attended Sunday school there as children. Although they harbored some concerns with regard to this man's possible homophobia, he was nevertheless their first choice. After shoring up their courage, they met with him.

He turned them down.

These women were good friends of Maria's, and she was unwavering in her support of their "marriage," much to the consternation of her father. Maria was taking a brave and unpopular stand, if not yet for herself, then for her friends. Further, stirred by the wrongness of his decision, she was now questioning her entire faith—faith in her father, her family, her church, her God—faith in her own ability to ever break free of her family's beliefs and become her own person, someone she could feel good about.

This is precisely what we, as human beings, tend to do when faced with what feels like a lack of options: We think in the extreme. Our perceived solutions take the form of black-and-white, all-or-nothing thinking. *If I can't have my way with "A," then I'll go to the other extreme of "Z."* When we feel backed into a corner, choked, constricted, angry, and without choices, we often have a strong tendency to run off in the opposite direction.

In Maria's case, her tremendous frustration with her father led to her feeling that she was up against a brick wall. The only way to ease the frustration was, she mistakenly thought, to give up everything associated with her father: family, faith, church, and God. Otherwise, she'd simply have to shut her mouth, nod her head, and forever be in denial about who she is. Neither seemed a very satisfying nor healthy solution. All-or-nothing thinking rarely is. And so her internal stress was mounting.

What Maria and I discussed came to be known as "the religion within." It was not that she wanted to abandon her love of church or God really, but she was seriously and justifiably wrestling with following a religion that, according to her father's teachings, was against her being a lesbian or being in a loving commitment with another woman. Although it was awfully tempting to succumb to that all-or-nothing thinking, i.e., "I'll leave the church and this family and never speak to them again!" or, "I'll just stay in the closet and they can stay in denial," she knew these were not the answers. As is usually the case in life, the answer would lie somewhere in the middle, somewhere in the gray area. The answer was found in the religion *within* her.

In referring to "the religion within," what I am really referring to is *spirituality*. As opposed to those religious beliefs that originate outside of oneself, spirituality originates within. A friend of mine discovered Buddhism this way. When she first came across Buddhist philosophy, she felt an *"aha!,"* that feeling which rises up from inside to let you know that you've found something compatible and congruent with your true, genuine self. As she puts it, "When I discovered Buddhism, I felt as though I had found a spirituality that perfectly matched how I've always felt inside."

How she'd always felt inside. Thus began a spiritual path where she learned more about the issues, concepts, ways, and beliefs that Buddhists follow. Far from feeling that these were alien or unfamiliar concepts, or that they were things to which she had to conform in order to be accepted, they felt right at home within her, and gave her much peace, awareness, and inner satisfaction. She had put a spiritual definition on her internal feelings.

Religion, on the other hand, begins with *others*—a preacher, congregation, place of worship, etc.—and is adopted by the individual. Religious organizations are, in fact, reliant upon the group in order to exist. Rather than being solely focused on the individual's growth, many organized religions are often more concerned with the setting up of dogmatic rights and wrongs, what is condoned and what is not ... what is in the best interest of the group's mission, and the rules of conformity required to satisfy that mission. There are a lot of shoulds and should-nots. (I had a wonderful psychology teacher years ago who told her classes, "Don't should on yourself and don't let others should on you, either!")

Now if this definition of religion sounds somewhat harsh, it is not to say that some gay people have not found happiness within organized religion. Nor is it to say that a person cannot experience *aha's,* or feel a genuine, internal compatibility with an organized religion.

On the contrary, some venues of religion can be a healthy, insightful, prejudice-free experience, as well as helpful in the fight against bigotry, largely depending on the minister, priest, or rabbi in charge of the congregation. Some maverick heterosexual ministers perform commitment ceremonies for their gay worshippers because they feel it is the right thing to do, the God-like thing to do, even though they suffer reprimands from their superiors for such defiance. They teach and model tolerance. They talk about forgiveness without the unspoken belief that gay people need forgiveness for who they are. They are truly concerned with the individual's spiritual growth, and the journey that is congruent and beneficial to each person. These spiritual leaders continually re-evaluate their beliefs, because they understand that a belief which does not allow itself to be questioned is not a belief that aids spiritual growth.

Can spirituality and religion coexist? Absolutely. In fact, some people even feel that they awaken their spirituality precisely through the offerings and teachings of their organized religion.

Of course, a lot of blood has been shed during battles throughout history in the name of religion. (Not to mention the present-day religious zealots who bomb and burn abortion clinics, taking the lives of medical professionals and volunteers in the process. Do they not see the irony in that?) While religions have helped, so have they hurt. The sting of rejection from religious groups because gay people have come out to their families, priests or congregations has led to nothing short of professional and personal devastation, and even murder and suicide.

Here's the core of the problem: As long as a religion can exclude some, it can exclude any. No one is free from ostracism. No one is accepted unconditionally. The security one might be lulled into feeling, believing themselves and their actions justified by the Bible, is actually based in exclusion, not inclusion. They're in *because* others are out. It's *us versus them* thinking. Although the message may be couched in love, organized religion can too often really be about rejection, intolerance, fear, and hatred.

So what happens when a person runs into a snag with his religion? What happens when he cannot conform to the rules? What happens when that religious group decides to banish that person? What is to become of such a person? Perhaps he or she has felt, like Maria, that who she is is cause for shame. The rejected individual, far from feeling love and acceptance, is left with pain, humiliation, anger, discouragement and feelings of inadequacy. Such is the result of false prophets who wield the Bible like a club at the gay and lesbian community, preaching that there's no room for homosexuals in God's church. With erroneous accusations about the "homosexual agenda," they deliver a message so hate-filled, it's amazing that anyone is fooled, but many are, and they sit there, week after week, nodding their heads and filling the collection plate.

Is that what a religion is supposed to do? Invoke shame? Reject some while accepting others? Divide its followers into good and bad, right and wrong, the haves and the have-nots? Did Christ, Buddha, or Allah pass judgment on their followers? According to the Bible, Mary Magdalene was a prostitute. Did Jesus tell her that God hated her, or that there was no room in God's heart for her? No, He loved and accepted her—unconditionally.

So how can any human being, simply because he is unquestioningly assumed by a certain religion to be a messenger of God, make the claim that some people are more worthy than others? That some are loved by God and others are not? That only certain ones are to be accepted into the folds of the group? That only certain "marriages" are allowable? If a preacher is claiming to be a follower of Christianity, for example, what right has he to decide who is worthy and who is not, if Christ Himself accepted all people? Isn't that the very definition of Christianity: the attempt to be Christ-like? To follow the teachings of Jesus Christ?

Well, if a person has religion within, spirituality, a sense of what a relationship with his or her Creator really means, then no hate-filled, hot-aired individual or bigoted group can take her spirituality away from her. Fortunately for Maria, she realized that she had a deep and grounded connection with her spirituality. In fact, the argument with her father served as a kind of springboard whereby she could get more in touch with the religion within her—her beliefs about what she feels is important in life, how she wants to live her life, and the love she feels for her Creator. She discovered that, while she may be at odds with her father and church regarding the religious acceptance or rejection of gays and lesbians, she is still a deeply spiritual person and very much in touch with a love for something greater than herself. She feels not at all rejected by the God in her mind and heart. Her faith, for this internal upheaval, has become stronger rather than weaker. She feels assured now, more than ever, that her spirituality is an important, central and vital part of who she is.

When a person is truly grounded in his spirituality, he could not be less concerned with exclusion or intolerance or being better-than. They are far more focused on becoming as loving and open a human being as is possible for them. Their rights and wrongs emerge from a deep soul-searching and introspection that leads them to develop a respect and love toward *all* their brothers and sisters. Far from being concerned with who gets to evolve and who doesn't (whether it is to a heaven or some other concept of an afterlife), they work toward *all* beings ascending toward the next, higher plane.

In fact, in certain Eastern philosophies, the very point of spiritual growth isn't to ascend first, but to ascend last, after everyone else gets to evolve—with your help! As opposed to interpretations of holy writings where the focus is on sins and rewards, these teachings emphasize instead the unity and wholeness achieved through inner contemplation, spiritual lessons, and the welcoming of all beings. Quite a different approach to evolution from what we here in the West are used to!

In time, Maria and her father "agreed to disagree" on the topic of religion, and Maria found that her spirituality was well-served at another church, the Metropolitan Community Church in her city. (Founded by the Reverend Troy Perry, the Universal Fellowship of Metropolitan Community Churches is the world's largest religious denomination for gays and lesbians, with 314 congregations in 16 countries. See the Resources section in Chapter 21 for more information about MCC.) She had heard about MCC but had never explored it for herself. She found this church to be more about *how she'd always felt inside* than was her father's church. Rather than her sexual orientation and spirituality being in conflict, they were quite harmonious within her, and this harmony was encouraged at MCC. Here, she felt accepted for all of who she is, not just the parts of herself that conform to a certain group's agenda. She felt loved *unconditionally*. Here, her religion within found acceptance.

Here, she felt at home.

The Meditation

Meditation is much like prayer to some people. Meditation is a quiet, introspective, gentle, and personal type of energy that helps one discover and connect with the universe within. To some, like prayer, this means a connection with a Creator larger than oneself.

This meditation offers an opportunity to awaken and connect with your own spirituality, your internal universe, and to witness what this connection means to you. It may be read slowly by a friend, or silently to oneself.

Begin by taking several deep, relaxing breaths, and allow your mind and body to slow down, become more centered, more relaxed.

Pause.

And as you breathe, let yourself become aware of the connection between your mind, body, and spirit. With each breath, let yourself feel more and more a oneness, a unity within yourself. Breathe into your heart. Breathe within your whole being.

You are a person made of intelligence, physicality, and spirituality. Your mind, body and spirit are inseparable. Together they form the beautiful creation that is you.

Pause.

Look inward now and find where your spiritual center resides. Is it what you call your "soul"? Is it tangible or intangible? Is it within you, or all around you? Wherever it is, it is real and valid. It is yours. Discover it now.

Pause.

Breathe into your spiritual center. Breathe nurturance, light, and love into it and around it. Hold it within your most precious space, keeping it safe, cradling it with love.

Pause.

How does this part of you show itself in your daily life?

When does it feel most alive to you? When does it feel hidden and quiet?

Has your spiritual center been asleep, or is it teeming with energy, reaching out to everyone around you with gentle compassion, grace, and warmth?

Pause.

Now think about the creation of your very being. Who or what is responsible for your existence in this life? A Higher Power? A Creator? God? The Universe? Do you have a relationship with any force, any energy, or being larger than yourself?

If so, what is this relationship like? How do you experience it? How important is this relationship to you?

Pause.

I invite you to breathe this life force into you now. Inhale, and welcome the abundance of healing life energy into your being. Your mind, body, and soul are open to receiving this gift of life. It has been waiting for you. And with your breath, it is within you now. You are not alone. You are never alone.

Pause.

You are life itself. You are love itself.

And you are loved.

Chapter 17

Slum-Thinking

*The greatest evil that can befall man is that he should come to think
ill of himself.*

—Johann Wolfgang von Goethe

A major, national furniture retailer tried airing several television commercials depicting, among others, what appeared
to be a gay male couple shopping for home furnishings together.
In reality, a very common sight. In the world of advertising, such
a backlash was stirred up that the ads were pulled.

"Don't ask, don't tell," is our nation's current Armed Services
policy that allows lesbians and gay men to die for their country,
as long as they don't admit to being homosexual. It would be
bad for morale, we're told.

Gay men and lesbians cannot be legally married in this country. (Accordingly, we cannot be divorced, either.) While many
people expect this situation to improve somewhat, perhaps in
the near future and at least on the state level, we currently have
no national legislature in the works. Therefore, we cannot enjoy
the same tax, inheritance, or medical benefits as married couples.

While right-wing, conservative politicians and religious leaders continue to accuse homosexuals of being promiscuous and a
threat to the American family, they simultaneously deny us this
right to marry, to form legally and religiously recognized long-

term, monogamous partnerships. (Even those gay people who don't wish to conform to the heterosexual tradition of marriage can see the hypocrisy of this.)

There is no iron-clad, court-sanctioned legal policy automatically available to same-sex couples, as there is to married couples, which provides for hospital and hospice treatment decisions, life insurance benefits, and power-of-attorney status to be carried out according to the wishes of the insured, and not overruled in a court of law by the insured's homophobic parents or other family members. This, even after more than twenty years of early deaths due to AIDS.

I hear frequently from gay men and women who complain of the "lavender ceiling" at their jobs. Unable to prove it, but with a strong intuition that they are being passed over for promotions because of their sexual orientation, they are held back creatively, professionally, and personally. They watch their heterosexual counterparts receive the better positions and all the social and economic advantages that come with them.

There exists in our vernacular the well-known, slang, reductive term, "gay ghetto." Historically it refers to a low-rent district with a predominance of gay urban dwellers—gay folks living where no one else wanted to. The term has evolved, however, to mean just about any area with a significant population of gays, as so many previously depressed areas have become rehabilitated into charming neighborhoods because of the creativity and talents of the gay folks who invest their time, energy, and money into creating an improved community. For example: In San Diego, gay homeowners of the Hillcrest area, having beautified their neighborhood as perhaps only gays can (I'm a bit biased!), have been courted by the surrounding communities in the hope that they will expand their geographic circle of good taste and move into those neighboring areas as well, thus improving the real estate market there too.

Perhaps you've had some similar experiences happen in your life. In your place of employment, for instance, there's some intangible, unspoken dynamic at play—you can feel it, even if you can't exactly put your finger on it, but you know it's real and you know it has something to do with the way(s) that you may be different from your co-workers—you're not married, or you attend office functions solo, or you're not included in certain conversations. Nothing overt, but it's there.

Or maybe you've felt the frustration of not being able to use your partner's health insurance through his/her employer, even though the heterosexual colleagues at that company are freely allowed to do so.

How about when you wanted to go to that cozy bed and breakfast you read about in the paper, a romantic weekend getaway to celebrate your lover's birthday or an anniversary, but when you got there, the innkeeper frowned and told you that no, they would not provide a room with only one bed for two men (or women).

Perhaps you've seen your lover through a long, difficult AIDS-related illness. You've been by his side for months or years, but your voice was overridden when it came time to make legal medical decisions and then you were excluded from mention at his memorial service. (These very incidents happened to an acquaintance of mine just recently.)

Why does there exist a collective thought process in our supposedly modern society, whereby acts of injustice against sexual minorities are not illegal, but are acceptable phenomena? Why is there derogatory, reductive terminology? While there are corners of society that are recognizing and slowly improving upon such injustice, we still are able to find many such examples both locally—in jobs, housing, and health care—and nationally, throughout most government policy.

Well, in regard to our mental health and self-esteem issues, I would suggest to you that the most important question might be: How are we, as gay men and lesbians, possibly participating in this collective unconscious of discrimination?

Let's look more closely at this. This is the exact kind of self-discrimination in which we participate when we pay rent to a slumlord. Or when we begrudgingly work for an incompetent boss, knowing full well that we can do the job so much better ourselves. Or when we accept, without giving the matter another thought, our national, state, and local laws that display blatant disregard for the rights of gay men and lesbian women. The messages are plentiful, and so we buy into the type of thinking which asserts that something is wrong with being gay.

In fact, there's something so wrong with who we are that we deny that we deserve better treatment. Our deeply ingrained belief systems very often exist on a powerful level well below conscious thought. On that unconscious level, we think that we *do not* deserve any better at all! Herein lies the roots of firmly embedded opinions about ourselves and about our deservingness. These are the unconscious, internalized thoughts that guide our choices and decisions every day, decisions both large and small.

We are used to keeping quiet so that we don't become noticed. In living inconspicuously, we find safety. But in the esteem-reducing belief system that accepts mistreatment, we sell ourselves short when we keep quiet. It is this thinking which says that it's okay to discriminate against ourselves; that we in fact do not deserve the better job, house, neighborhood, car, friends, relationships, etc. We do not deserve a better quality of life.

When we *do* feel deserving, our esteem is abundant, but when we internalize messages that tell us we are not deserving, then we are poor. Our esteem, both collectively and individually, is poor. I call this "slum-thinking." We think of ourselves as unworthy. Abundance? Forget it. We think we are no better than the low-rent slums we may inhabit, literally and figuratively, externally and within.

Slum-thinking goes something like this: If the majority of voters want to keep from me the sanctioning of marriage with all the rights, responsibilities, and benefits therein, well, I'll have to accept that, I suppose. The majority has spoken. If my boss treats me differently from my heterosexual colleagues in ways that are subtle yet distinct, well, I'm gay. I'll just have to put up with it. Besides, *it's probably all in my head.* (Now, *there's* an invalidating self-statement!) If, as a high school or college student, I am denied the experience of hearing an out, gay speaker talk about safe sex because the school administrators won't allow it, I'll just have to do without. My education simply doesn't matter as much as the education of others, those who comprise the majority.

You get the idea. Slum-thinking.

Remember that "majority" is just a concept based upon a number that, unfortunately, is used to describe something called the norm. Let's turn the tables for a moment. What if the majority of the United States population consisted of gay and lesbian persons, say around eighty-five percent. And what if only ten to fifteen percent of the population was known to be heterosexual? Then the norm would be to be gay. Gay would be considered *normal*. Anything else, deviant. We'd have a gay President and his or her life partner would be the First Man or Woman. Perhaps we'd have an openly bisexual Vice President.

Straight people, on the other hand, couldn't even begin to dream of being fairly represented in Congress. They could not admit their sexual orientation if they were in the army. They could not marry, and they'd need to march in parades—in cities that would allow them to, although not in the Boston St. Patrick's Day parade—just to raise the social consciousness of society. They'd have to open their own bars. They'd need a Straight Pride month every year throughout the country, and would be backed by PFOSP, Parents and Friends of Straight People.

In unenlightened suburban and rural areas, they'd have to keep the objects of their desires secret, because most people would feel that it's just wrong to love someone of the opposite sex. In the Bible Belt, they'd be going against God's plan. In some areas, they may feel in physical danger of being straight-bashed. Their homes might get graffiti'd and they'd suffer anonymous threatening phone calls.

In some families they'd be forever worried about parental rejection because of who they are. They'd spend their teenage years living a lie, pretending to enjoy dating someone of the same sex and asking a same-sex person to the prom. When asked at family gatherings if there's someone special in their life, they'd use a neutral phrase instead of a pronoun: "Well, there's *this person* I like . . ." All the while suffering alone the confusion and isolation they feel inside.

They wouldn't know who to talk to, and would feel that they must move to a big city in order to find acceptance. Their suicide rates would be higher, as would their alcohol use, drug problems, and other addictions. There would be very little support or guidance to teach them about healthy, loving, heterosexual relationships or even about purely sexual relationships. (It certainly would not be taught in Health Ed at school.) They would struggle with self-esteem issues based on familial and societal abandonment. People would say things like, "I don't care what you do behind closed doors, but don't flaunt it in my face."

There would be a plethora of psychological studies trying to decide if they were born straight, or if society made them that way. Concepts such as "family values" would be quite different (if such a misused concept would exist at all). Same-sex parents would blame themselves. Boys would be forced to take clarinet lessons when all they really wanted to do was play ball. The girls would be forced to play ball. Disneyland would hold Straight Night once a year so these people could go on rides holding hands and dance with opposite-sex partners without ridicule.

When a ground-breaking television show wanted to show a woman kiss a man and declare her heterosexuality, advertisers would pull out and gay Baptist churches would boycott.

G.I. Joe would be packaged with Ken (we all suspected, didn't we?), and Barbie would date Midge. From children's programming to soap operas, commercials, movies, billboards, even the packaging on everyday products one buys at the store . . . all would be aimed at the homosexual consumer and heterosexual society members would be hard-pressed to find themselves and their lives represented in a gay world.

Heterosexuals would find it painfully easy to feel less-than, given this world around them. They'd need specialized support groups. There'd be stories of cruel, misguided experiences with conversion therapy.

(Of course, all of this assumes that the homosexuals would, by virtue of the intoxication of power, adopt the same kind of narrow-minded bigotry, patriarchy, elitism, and fear that is found in some aspects of straight society, the way it is now. We wouldn't. Would we?)

So, what good is a majority when it comes to the self-esteem of all people? Not much, really. If it's okay to exclude some, then in reality it's okay to exclude anyone, once they are perceived, for whatever reason, to be outside of the majority, or the norm. Such thinking is therefore inherently flawed, and results in oppression, discrimination, judgmental attitudes, exclusivity, ignorance, and hatred. We, as gay people, are all too aware of the disadvantages of being a minority in one or another unenlightened area of modern society. While some generations have had it easier than others, and although progress is being made, the phenomenon remains: We are prone to absorbing and internalizing the messages that lead to slum-thinking.

It behooves us to examine our lives from this perspective. Earlier in this book, we learned to see the different parts of our lives as they relate to healthy or poor self-esteem. We also looked at the different identities within us, to begin to learn what about ourselves suffers with esteem issues. Now, let's look at a few areas of life and identify where slum-thinking may be rearing its head, contributing to unhappiness or dissatisfaction in our lives. Where and how do we buy into thinking that we deserve less? Where do our belief systems need reevaluation and repair?

Relationships

Ask yourself: Am I happy in my relationship? Why or why not? Some people feel that it's better to be in an unhealthy relationship than to have no relationship at all. This, life experience teaches us, is simply not true. I would suggest to you that such thinking is based in fear: the fear of being alone, the fear of never finding anyone else again. Perhaps it is the fear of adopting the identity of a single person, with all the social discomforts and stigma therein. Fear of being isolated, left out, discarded, excluded. Fear of not knowing how to find someone, dating in the age of AIDS.

Being in an unhappy relationship could be the result of something else, too, believing oneself undeserving of happiness, of anything better than one's present life situation. If you buy into the negative societal judgments and pronouncements about gay relationships—they don't last, they can't work, their partners are all unfaithful—you may very well feel that you should be grateful for having someone at all. If you've internalized the negativity to the extent that what you've been told has become your own belief system and is therefore contributing to low self-esteem in the relationship department, then you don't dare turn someone down who will be with you. No matter what he/she is like. It is what keeps people feeling miserable and empty in their unhealthy relationships. It's what keeps battered partners staying with the batterers. It's what leads some people to suicide, believing that they deserve no better.

Employment

Again, ask yourself: Am I happy in my present position or job? If not, does it have anything to do with feeling undeserving? Do I believe myself unworthy of happiness here in this place that I spend at least one-third of my life, the office? Break it down: Can you feel comfortable bringing a same-sex partner to office parties or events? What might happen if you do? What about your sense of humor ... can you really be yourself, say what you wish, tell a gay joke, among those with whom you work? Can you point out to your boss a policy, comment, or attitude that you find offensive *precisely* because you are a gay man or woman? Do you feel harassed or even unfairly judged at work? Left out, maybe?

If you can identify with any of the above perhaps you'd benefit from asking yourself why it is that you've accepted this certain level of treatment. What exactly are you putting up with day in and day out that, if you stop to examine it, you don't feel good about at all? And why is that? Can you get in touch with the type of thinking you are employing that leads you to accept being less than who you are, to absorb offenses, to suffer in silence? Can you challenge that thinking with, *I deserve better*?

Where You Live

It happens in urban as well as rural areas: Slum-thinking takes a literal turn. What is your living situation like and are you happy with it? Do you live in a dangerous environment because you feel undeserving of movin' on up? Are you unable to move up because you've kept yourself in a low-paying job? Are you an adult living with your parents in an atmosphere that feels unsupportive? Stifling? Homophobic? Do you have roommates with whom you feel unable to be yourself? If your home environment is uncomfortable, the discomfort usually spreads to other areas of your life. It can be enormously stressful to be afraid to go home, or, to simply be unhappy when you are home.

Friendships

One of the most challenging concepts facing people involved in a 12-step program is that of learning to walk away from unhealthy friendships, and to replace them with healthy ones. If someone is trying to abstain from drinking, it doesn't make sense to continue to socialize with the drinking buddies. If one is in detox from cocaine, one doesn't need to have a dealer as a best friend.

We can borrow that philosophy here. Are your friendships supportive of you being yourself? Is it okay to be gay when you're out with the guys/the girls? (Whether they are gay or straight.) Do your friends understand what a homophobic comment is, or why gay oppression in the workplace is wrong, or that gays and lesbians deserve all the rights of anyone else, and it has nothing to do with wanting preferential treatment?

Certainly, the solution may not necessarily be to jettison your friendships (or your relationship, job, or living arrangement.) However, we arrive at any solution via an honest evaluation of the problem. Such an examination into the areas and relationships of your life may be a difficult and sometimes painful process, and yet one to which you must be committed, if you are to emerge with stronger, healthier self-esteem and awareness.

It can be hard at first to trust your own feelings. So familiar are we with injustice that it begins to feel comfortable! We hardly notice when something is being done to us out of discrimination or some other form of unfairness. If we unconsciously embrace society's definition of normal, then we may think that it's normal to be treated as second class citizens. This is the exactly the type of thinking to challenge.

A heterosexual female friend of mine, Nina, is married with two children, and is herself the daughter of an open-minded, highly educated minister who performs gay ceremonies as willingly as he does heterosexual marriages. When I am in the company of this friend, she never fails to ask after my lover, just as she asks after the husbands or wives of the other people in the room. She's always interested in my experiences and relationships and unhesitatingly brings them into our conversation—not because as *gay* experiences and relationships they are curiosities to her, but just because she's interested in my life, including who I'm involved with, to the same degree and level as she is in the lives of others. To her, a couple is a couple, whether it consists of two men, two women or a man and a woman. Refreshingly, the godparents of her children include both gay friends and straight friends.

Perhaps any change in your life first begins, as do many things we wish to improve, with your ability to envision a better situation for yourself. The effects of visualization, formal or informal, can be profound! We can move most easily and effectively toward those changes which we can most clearly imagine.

Once your vision is alive and well detailed, made real with the power of your mind, then it's helpful to get in touch with the kind of thinking you regularly employ, and whether or not the messages you give yourself will enable your dream to become a reality. How do you support and encourage yourself with your internal dialogue? Where do you get in your own way, throwing up sabotaging roadblocks based upon what society has taught you about being gay? How firmly do you believe in yourself . . . in your deservingness?

I would never presume to encourage anyone to quit a job, or

end a relationship, or move out of an apartment. I believe that such outward change is the result of *internal* shifts. And that's precisely where progress and growth begins: within.

What we're talking about here is the very opposite of rash decisions or behaviors. This is about becoming more aware of what you're feeling and thinking, on the inside, from the inside. Becoming clear about any injustice being done to you and any injustice you are doing to yourself (and to your gay brothers and sisters). This is about learning to trust yourself—your intuition and your feelings.

This is about becoming aware of your thinking, the most minute aspects to your belief systems, and where in life your thinking has led you. An honest and rigorous evaluation of your beliefs and everyday thought processes will unveil for you the type of encouragement versus sabotaging you engage in with yourself. Taking this kind of determined responsibility for your own growth is an important first step.

Making the move from slum-thinking to abundance-thinking is a process, and one that will show itself in all aspects of your life. In other words, if you think more positively about yourself and of what you deserve, as a human being, as a first-class citizen, then you'll find that your thinking will in turn spill over into other areas of your life. For example, if you feel better about yourself in your relationship, firmly and rightly believing that you deserve a healthy partnership that is mutually rewarding, then you'll be able to start making choices about your employment that leave you feeling similarly deserving. And about your home. And about your health, your friendships, your income, your parental relationships, and perhaps many, if not all, of your other life choices. The benefits will spill from one part of your life into other parts, because you've challenged the negative internalized messages that were keeping you from growth.

Deservingness and quality-of-life begins with you. You have the ability to replace any of your slum-thinking with healthy belief systems. Remember: You are worth all that you make up your mind to be worth.

Real-Life Story . . . Julia

When Julia first met her good friend, Elizabeth, she felt that the two of them had much in common. They enjoyed the arts, travel, flea markets on weekends, and discovering new restaurants. Both retired educators, they also found similarities in their personalities. They'd tease each other about being "rather compulsive and anal," but enjoyed the positive aspects of trustworthiness and reliability that often accompany those traits. For the most part, they had great fun together.

When Julia called my office to set up an appointment for couples therapy, she surprised me by coming to her first session alone. Soon, it became clear that the other part of this couple that Julia was discussing wasn't a lover, but was her good friend, Elizabeth.

"Every once in a while, I hear her make a derogatory comment to me, or a put-down of some sort. It hurts my feelings, but I don't say anything to her about it. I just take it," she told me.

It seemed that Julia was very afraid of hurting or angering or alienating her friend, to such an extent that she was allowing herself to absorb Elizabeth's disparaging remarks, and to keep silent about the hurt they caused her. It was a positive sign that Julia's level of unhappiness around this issue was such that she was willing to talk with a professional about it. She was becoming less and less able to suffer in silence.

Part of the problem was that Julia was a lesbian and Elizabeth was straight. Although this did not overtly get in the way of the friendship (both women have friends of both sexual orientations), it affected Julia in that she had been accepting various forms of oppression and discrimination all her life. She accepted this to be "the way things are in a heterosexual world." So her problem was about more than the fear of angering her friend. It was also about what she had been accepting unquestioningly about her (straight) friend. Being conditioned by society to believe herself less worthy of respect and fair treatment than are heterosexuals, disrespect, however subtle, felt normal to her. What we are familiar with, for better or for worse, has a tendency to become comfortable. What is comfortable, we accept as normal, even if only in our own minds.

Retirement found Julia becoming more interested in the world of self-help and personal growth. She had begun reading some pertinent literature and attending a few workshops and seminars. With her emerging awareness, for the first time in her life, she was becoming increasingly uncomfortable with comments that hurt her. Perhaps especially because these comments were coming from such a good friend, the sting was especially strong.

Upon further examination, she discovered that she has a pattern of being nice and friendly with people who are insensitive to others, or insensitive to the differences in others. She realized with dismay that many of her friends—past and present—could be classified as bigots, homophobes, sexists, and racists. She began to question why she settled for friendships that hurt.

In Julia's family of origin, she remembered being treated "not very well" as a child. Although she is unable to report any overt abuse, the lack of support for her school efforts and accomplishments, accompanied by family member's tendency to use sarcasm and put-downs in their humor, led Julia to become comfortable around people who act disparagingly toward her. It felt natural. This is behavior that is known, that is familiar to her. So of course, her choice of friends would include people who engage in similar ways of communicating.

Existentialists believe that in order to live an authentic life, one must take responsibility for his or her choices. In fact, they have a saying, "We are our choices." While Julia certainly could not be blamed for the comments made by others, she did need to accept responsibility for her choices of friends and for playing by their rules. She could take responsibility for these choices once she gained insight into her past and the kinds of examples and role models she had as a child.

It began to make perfect sense to her: If in her youth she learned how people are supposed to act with one another by watching the family's behavior, then she was simply continuing a pattern that was deeply ingrained in her. In Elizabeth she found a friend with whom she not only had much in common, but someone who was familiar and therefore comfortable to be around, *even if the familiarity was unhealthy*. She picked someone that she understood, the same way she understood the relationships in her family. Furthermore, being hurt was a role she learned how to play as a child, and so it was a role she was familiar with now. This was known. This she accepted.

However, at this point in her life, her increasing self-esteem was not allowing her to be comfortable with these patterns any longer. So began the unfolding and liberating process of Julia gaining insight and accepting responsibility for her choices of friends.

As I mentioned earlier, once someone begins a growth process in one area of life, growth tends to occur in other areas as well. Julia began to identify the obstacles to her being able to even *think* about herself in positive, supportive terms. She was getting in touch with the ways in which she thought of herself as less-than, and less-*deserving*-than. This was her slum-thinking.

She also began to acknowledge and respect her feelings as a prelude to requiring respect from others. If she wanted to commit to changing her patterns, she realized that she needed to look at *all* her life choices and develop a way of making choices that was healthy for her self-esteem, not destructive. She began a process that challenged the way she thought about friendships, love relationships, her family dynamics, and her connection with other people, both gay and straight. She was scouring her life-long belief systems, the positive as well as destructive beliefs that comprised her old ways of thinking.

In time, Julia was able to find ways to talk to Elizabeth about the parts of their friendship that were working well and the parts that were not. They continue to be good friends; in fact, according to Julia, they have grown even closer as their communication has grown more honest.

And honest communication is something that Julia has come to value in her relationships, her day-to-day dealings with others, and most importantly, within herself.

The Meditation

One of the ways Julia was able to find the strength and confidence necessary to make such important changes in her life was through the use of meditation, similar to the one here. Like an infant discovering the world for the first time, Julia felt a renewed excitement over the fact that she had within her the power to make healthy changes. Through a process that involved visualizing both the healthy and unhealthy aspects to her life, especially around her relationships, she was able to observe the thoughts and feelings that were destructive to her self-esteem and replace them with a positive, affirming sense of deservingness.

If deservingness is an issue in your own life, I recommend you do this meditation several times a week at first, and then occasionally, whenever you feel the need, as a kind of self-esteem maintenance program. This meditation may be read slowly by a friend, or silently to oneself.

Breathe relaxation into every ounce of your being. Let your mind and body settle into an easy, relaxed calm. Breathe and let go of tension, worry, fear, and doubt.

Pause.

Bring your focus to your childhood . . . specifically, the rights and wrongs you learned as a youngster. From whom did you learn your value system? Who taught you the do's and don'ts in life?

Pause.

What did you learn about "deservingness"? Did you ever think of yourself as deserving? Was deserving a positive or negative idea to you? What childhood incident comes to mind when you think of deservingness?

Pause.

Looking back, how were you treated as a child . . . by your family? By your friends?

What message did you receive, what did you learn from this treatment?

Pause.

Now let your focus come forward, to adulthood. Think again of deservingness. What is your relationship now to deservingness? Do you ever think of yourself as deserving? What incident comes to mind?

Pause.

How do your friends treat you? How does your family treat you? How do you treat yourself?

Pause.

What messages are you receiving from others about your deservingness?

What messages are you giving yourself about deservingness?

Pause.

Take a deep breath.

Let your awareness come to how you feel about yourself, right at this very moment.

In what ways do you nurture your sense of self-worth?

What changes would you like to make in order to feel better about yourself?

Can you see yourself as a deserving human being?

Can you see yourself as deserving of love?

You were born deserving love.

You still deserve love.

You . . . deserve . . . love.

Chapter 18

The Road to Wholeness: A Path, Not a Pill

Every good thought you think
is contributing its share
to the ultimate result of your life.

—Grenville Kleiser

What is the most effective treatment for healthy self-esteem? Unlike remedies that can be found in a bottle of pills or a jar of salve, the reclaiming, recovery, and enhancement of self-esteem is not found over the counter at the pharmacy; it is found in a journey.

Unfortunately, our society does not tend to encourage its members to take the road less traveled. Stepping off the path of the norm, in order to pursue the wisdom of one's own inner voice—the beat of a different drum, if you will—requires great acts of courage, original thought, and vision.

You see, in Western civilization we are taught and encouraged to follow the traditional roads to achieve financial success, to be respected and liked by our peers, to earn tenures in our chosen fields, and to achieve material wealth. Likewise, we are well conditioned, both by messages received from society as well as through the examples set by our own well-meaning families, in the best ways to maintain physical, spiritual, and mental health. We tend to follow the ways we are taught, in a kind of inertia of lesson-learning, and this often includes how to care for our minds, bodies, and souls. But is this inertia really the best we can do?

Under the unspoken laws and guidance of Western culture, rewards for following protocol can come in odd packages. It may show itself in the form of a pay raise and promotion for being a workaholic, for instance. For a man, the approval and camaraderie of friends is the reward for being sexually compulsive and then bragging about it. If you're tough enough (as a man *should* be) and can cause bodily harm to your fellow human beings, you might even be rewarded with a multimillion dollar contract as a boxer or a pro football player!

If all that pressure to behave according to plan causes you to have too much to drink sometimes, and you take your repressed frustrations out on your spouse, you're just "blowing off steam." By going to church every Sunday, just like you're supposed to, you'll likely be considered a good Christian, no matter what activities occupy your time Monday through Saturday.

Odd what we'll deny, mislabel, or turn a blind eye toward, if we're behaving in expected and socially sanctioned ways. External rewards for thinking on your own, however, for being different, creative, taking a unique path, are generally far and few between. That's much too threatening to society at large.

When it comes to physical and psychological health, we have been trained to run quickly to a physician or at least to the medicine chest. With everything from a simple, passing headache to chronic depression or anxiety we tend to put our blind trust in doctors and nurses in sterile rooms, wearing white lab coats, sometimes making us wait an hour or two in discomfort and misery. We visit our HMOs with the urgent hope that they'll know us there, and actually treat us like individuals with specific needs and not like just another patient with an ID number. Collectively, we spend billions for these people to give us a quick fix.

The simple irony is that a medical doctor cannot know your body as you do. He or she may know it well, but not in the same way as you do, living inside it. You've spent your whole life in your body. The textbooks may offer guidance to the physician, and experience offers wisdom, but nothing offers the specifics of what makes you you.

Proper and complete care happens with your earnest participation and opinions, with the manner and methods of healing that work best for you taken into full account. That requires a great deal of clear thinking, communication, awareness, and self-trust. Too often we just follow what someone else tell us to do, going in whatever direction we think will offer the fastest, easiest balm for our ills. We trust them, but we don't trust ourselves.

With a take-a-pill mentality, we've allowed ourselves to be brainwashed into thinking that faster and easier is always better. We'll readily use our minds to make shopping lists, calculate taxes, and to figure out how much tip to leave the waiter, but not to heal our diseases, soothe our anxieties, or fight our phobias.

Why use your own mind to help your body—through the practice of meditation or breathing techniques, or by entering into a process of insight-enriching psychotherapy, or by taking the time to learn from the wise masters of ancient civilizations—when you can just pop a pill? Insight be damned, just write me out a prescription, doc! (I've actually received such a short-sighted request from an acquaintance of mine.) We're so busy doing, acquiring, striving, and looking *outward* that we seem to forget, or not bother to learn, about the limitless powers *within*.

The irony is that we can achieve whatever we set our minds to achieve, but this belief, this type of thinking is *different*—it isn't covered by insurance.

What is the price we pay for taking the road *more* traveled? Well, all along the journey we'll find endless opportunities to distract ourselves from the stress of the realities we create, but we don't necessarily know how to focus on our internal reality. So we pop antacids instead of finding ways to lower the pressure of our lives. We pop pills for headaches instead of setting aside ten minutes to meditate. We self-medicate with alcohol or recreational drugs instead of doing some deep-breathing exercises to feel centered again. We reach for a cigarette rather than go for a walk to take in some fresh air and clear the mind. What we need to do is address the stress, and a pill is not always the best way.

Thousands of years ago, the ancient *rishis*, or seers, of India took the mind-body position that we can make ourselves ill, we can make ourselves well, and we can watch ourselves doing both. They understood that the boundaries of the mind are human-set, not society-set. Unfortunately, we tend to ignore the strength, courage, and lessons about health and healing offered to us by the wise masters of those ancient times. Here in the West, in modern society, we fall far short of realizing our healing potential by accepting what others tell us are our limitations.

It is within the power of each individual to decide to think outside the box. We must first realize, however, that there are many seductive, manipulative messages that disapprove of such creative thought, messages that have gained strength over the years, and are passed down to us, generation by generation.

You can't possibly take care of that chronic headache just by breathing and meditating, so come and see me for a pill.

You cannot heal (many forms of) cancer through nutrition, lifestyle and attitude, you need my prescriptions for such a daunting task.

It's impossible to have a happier, healthier, more bliss-filled life without this little magic vial of medicine.

These messages all carry with them the same, basic doctrine: I know what's best for you, you don't. Trust me, I have the solutions for your problems. The answers await, but they are outside of yourself.

We suffer greatly when we buy into these manipulations, instead of learning to trust ourselves.

This is how the choices one makes around self-care affects self-esteem: Whenever someone tells us, either directly or indirectly, that we are incapable of self-care, and we accept this notion, then we are submitting to their false superiority and denying ourselves. First, we deny ourselves the sense of worth that comes from using our own intuition. Second, we deny ourselves the confidence that grows by using the inner wisdom which leads us, each in a unique way, on the path to self-healing.

Last, we deny ourselves the wholeness and wellness we experience based on our body's innate propensity to heal.

Self-worth, confidence, and wholeness. That's a lot to give up. They are key ingredients for healthy self-esteem and it's up to each of us to safeguard them. If we do not trust ourselves in the realm of our own healing, we are denying ourselves a vital and fundamental growth process. It simply isn't true that our answers lie outside of ourselves. Self-trust leads to our answers within.

Ultimately, a physician's greatest good is to teach people to learn about their own health, and empower them in the ways to stay healthy, especially as a person ages and acquires ever greater knowledge (as well as concerns) about their own body. A psychotherapist's greatest good is to teach someone how to eventually continue the psychological and emotional growth process on his/her own, to whatever degree is possible for that individual. A spiritual leader's greatest good is to encourage an independence of thought that may lead to a person's most rewarding relationship with his or her higher self, whatever highly personal, unique, and intimate form that may take.

Many philosophers, ancient, certainly, as well as more and more modern sages and healers, agree that the overall health of an individual is more reliant on an inward journey than on a prescription. So, one might wonder, do we need Western medicines and healers at all? Of course, we do! There are many devoted researchers who toil unceasingly to make tremendous headway with the very real and devastating ills of modern society. We are still at war with certain types of cancer, and we are most certainly still on the long road to effective, life-saving treatments for HIV, just to name a couple. With each year of new discoveries of diseases comes a need to rise to new heights medically. Western medicine saves lives, there's no doubt about it. To sweepingly discard Western health care as anything other than necessary, and sometimes vital, is folly.

Modern wise healers—physicians, chiropractors, nurses, therapists, nutritionists, hands-on healers, midwives, spiritualists, and clergy—are at the forefront of an important and growing movement whereby holistic healing is married with traditional medicine. Much like the yin-yang within us all, the two routes to health, Eastern and Western, can absolutely coexist in harmony. What's important is for a person to listen to what his/her body is saying and to become familiar and comfortable with whatever approach, or combination of approaches, feels most beneficial. What we *believe* will work has the greatest opportunity for success, as a person aligns the mind to augment the goals of the body. In fact, the most beneficial healing occurs when the mind-body connection is fully appreciated and utilized, each helping the other.

For example, I have a friend who, like me, is very holistic in his approach to mental and physical well-being. He puts most of his faith, however, in natural vitamin supplements, organic teas and herbs, meditation, yoga, and massage. He is comfortable with these concepts and believes that the vast majority of his health concerns are well treated using these approaches.

There are some instances, however, when he wants to address a physical problem via a consultation with his Western-skilled physician. In conjunction with his usual daily health routines and, indeed, his very philosophies around wellness, he will follow the advice of his medical doctor and supplement his self-care with Western medication. He feels very positive about taking the prescribed medicine because he has brought it into his usual, natural lifestyle only after careful consideration and thorough communication with his doctor. Because of his thoughtful approach, he *believes* in what he's doing, and is therefore wisely giving his combination treatment every chance for success. His mind and body are on the same team, working in harmony toward health.

The point is, he trusts himself and possesses the awareness to be able to have a strong sense of what is best for his whole being, mind and body. He doesn't blindly accept any healer's suggestion, Western or Eastern, without first listening to his needs from within, educating himself when necessary, and then arriving at a decision that he can support wholeheartedly. Nor does he foolishly deny outright the benefit of *any* type of treatment, without first considering whether it would be an empowering tool, a good match, for him. He uses his inner wisdom: If he can intelligently and intuitively give a program of treatment his endorsement, he'll synthesize and incorporate just about anything for his health. I believe him to be a role model for conscious and mindful wellness!

Perhaps one of the most important concepts to understand, when it comes to our self-care, is that human beings have a strong, determined propensity to be well. The body is ready and willing to repair itself, whether we watch, participate, or hinder. The body, in fact, is repairing damaged cells continuously, stopping the formation of detectable cancerous states before they can gain strength. Old cells are constantly being discarded for new, healthy ones. This process goes on twenty-four hours a day, seven days a week, for our entire lives under usual conditions, all without our conscious awareness. The body knows what it's doing. To align whatever powers we possess within is to give the body all that much more opportunity for healing. It provides an opportunity for us to be aware and involved in ourselves, participating in the art of being human.

Mentally and emotionally, we have the same drive and desire for health. Ask anyone with, for example, a disabling mental disorder, or who may be suffering from crippling anxiety, if they'd like to be well. Again, under usual conditions, the direction the mind wants to move in is toward health. When we're anxious, we desire to relax; when depressed, we miss feeling joy in our lives. When our self-esteem suffers, we'd give just about anything to feel worthy again, to feel that we're *enough*.

Perhaps what we must realize is that our powers for healing and repair are much greater than we've been taught. If, as the *rishis* believe, we participate in our illness, then we can participate in our wellness. Let's be clear here: this is not to say that we are to *blame* for our illnesses. There is a tremendous difference in quality and healing potential between anger-based blame and the empowerment that comes from taking responsibility for our own healing.

Take the HIV pandemic for example. Are gay men, initially the hardest hit segment of the population, to be blamed for engaging in acts of sexual expression that, we've come to learn, transmit the disease from one person to another? Of course not! Gay men have every right to embrace sexuality and fulfill their sexual needs as does anyone, gay or straight. However, can we learn how to protect ourselves and adopt safer sexual practices in the interest of saving our own lives? That is taking responsibility for our health.

Let's look at cancer. It is widely believed that there are several ways to develop cancer. Exposure to carcinogenic elements in the environment and heredity are but two of these ways. Less understood is how we might participate in developing cancer through difficulties found in certain personality types, the unhealthy coping mechanisms we may regularly rely on (such as repression of emotions), tremendous levels of prolonged stress, etc. Is heredity one's fault? Is exposure to unknown toxic elements one's fault? Can we be blamed for coping in the only ways we've been taught? Certainly not, on all counts. Even more pertinent, perhaps, is that blaming oneself, a condition filled with shame as well as anger, is probably as lethal as any disease in the first place.

However, do we have the ability to educate ourselves about toxic environments and develop appropriate legislature so that our children are not unnecessarily exposed to danger? Can we learn about healthy nutrition and about utilizing the anti-carcinogens that are found in nature to help in the battle against inherited problems? Can we learn healthy ways of expressing our feelings and dealing with stress so that we don't become cancerous time bombs waiting to happen? These are ways of taking responsibility for healing.

Self-worth, confidence, and a sense of wholeness.

Gay men and lesbians, considered healers and sages in many ancient tribal civilizations, are once again, I believe, in the fore-front of a unique exploration of spirituality and healing. Through necessity and creativity we set the pace, knowing full well what it's like to be wounded and receive messages which lead us to lack self-esteem. We understand the inherent wrongness of being treated as second-class.

In a collective manifestation of the life-wish, we are propelled by our desires to improve what daunts us, and heal what causes pain. Our drums indeed beat differently, and that, perhaps, has always been our saving grace.

For we have tremendous power if we choose to look inward and utilize it. Literally and figuratively, we heal one another through community. We save each other *vis-à-vis* everything from funding research centers to taking up the frontline care in the fight against HIV/AIDS. We form healing circles, rap groups, therapy groups, and medical practices. We open gay centers, youth centers, and low-cost pharmacies. We try New Age spiritualities as well as traditional religion. We take herbs, and we go to doctors at HMOs. We try passivity and gentleness, and we try activism and protests. Despite obstacles, we have a natural propensity for life. We must remember: It is by removing the self-blame and the shame that we can move toward creative approaches for our well-being, individually and collectively. Then we can be mindful and conscious and *engaged* in whatever healing process we choose.

It's when we fall away from our journeys that we suffer. When we believe what is said about us and what is told to us, unquestioningly, we deny our innate creativity and highly tuned intuition. We've overcome a tremendous lot in the past, socially and collectively, as well as in uniquely personal ways. Which of us doesn't ponder how much further we have to go, be it regarding AIDS funding, social acceptance, legal rights, educational equalities, bigotry, or ignorance? We don't succeed by ignoring what we inherently know to be right or true or honest. We succeed by questioning authority whenever that authority preaches what we know to be false or unfair. With self-trust we can lead each other and we can follow each other. When we are firmly on our paths is when we flourish.

How do we determine where our healthiest options lie when choosing our road to wholeness? By listening to ourselves. By celebrating our uniqueness, our creativity. By embracing the free thinker in each of us.

Everything we need awaits within.

Real-Life Story . . . Duane

A client of mine, Duane, has been dealing with his HIV-positive status for the better part of this past decade. He first came to see me shortly after his diagnosis, and has been in therapy, on and off, since then.

What works well for him is to engage in psychotherapy and/or hypnotherapy and past-life regression work for a period of time, anywhere from several months to a couple of years, then go off and "try life on my own," as he puts it. He has a talent for applying what he learns about himself. So, he'll come to my office in order to deal with new issues or recurring old ones, to gain insight, discover more about his personality strengths, weaknesses, and coping skills, uncover some hidden inner resources, or to increase his abilities to use meditation and creative imagery. Then he endeavors to apply out in the real world what he's learned about himself in therapy. He is committed to being mindful about his growth process and making the most of his life experiences.

Being from a lower socioeconomic background, Duane has worked very hard to put himself through school, find rewarding employment and a nice home, and build a satisfying life for himself. He is now in his late thirties and has been happily dating a twenty-six-year-old man, also HIV-positive, for about two years.

I believe a new relationship can give rise to many wonderful aspects of one's personality. Even after the early period of being "on one's best behavior," the sheer concentration required to learn about the other person, and having that person often occupy our thoughts and attention, can lead us to flex and sharpen our interpersonal abilities. These abilities may include communication skills, increased self-awareness and insights, patience, kindness, humor, esteem, even how to romance another person.

A new relationship does something else, too. It stirs up childhood issues, mother and father issues in particular, past-relationship issues, insecurities, fears and anxieties, existential angst . . . you name it. If the payoff of love, companionship, physical affection, etc., is worth it—i.e., helps soothe rather than increase the hurt and angst found in our psychic closet—then we continue on, growing together as a couple and providing each other with the self-esteem that comes from feeling loved. With a commitment to the healing and growth process, we work through past wounds and neuroses and find ourselves in the company of a partner whose love helps fill the void and adds to our sense of self-worth.

In Duane's family of origin, there were too many siblings for the parents to pay much attention to any one child. They were often left to fend for themselves, or to be taken under the wing of an older brother or sister. Being one of the oldest of the brood, Duane often cared for his younger sibs, the positive result of which has been the development of his resourcefulness, problem-solving abilities and self-confidence. He is a good, trustworthy, and reliable friend. The downside is that he never learned to prioritize his own well-being. Instead, he is quick to make sure that everyone else is taken care of before any of his own needs are met. The responsibility he felt to his brothers and sisters when they were all growing up together has continued in his relationships as an adult.

It's no accident that Duane's choice of partner (Leon) is younger than he, and is also dealing with his own health issues. Although both men are physically fit and in very good health, the specter of AIDS is with them, often in their thoughts and conversations, and in conversations with friends and family.

Duane's childhood learning as an older sibling shows itself strongly in this relationship. With Leon he has found someone he feels a need to look after and take care of, much like a younger brother. This is a role he knows well. While an argument can be made for any two lovers to care for and tend to each other, Duane's attentions sometimes seem burdensome to Leon, over-bearing and often unnecessary. In effect, Duane robs Leon of the opportunity to take care of himself, and the feelings of accomplishment and pride that come from learning self-reliance. This care-giving issue is out of balance.

Wisely, a major part of Duane's efforts in therapy has been to learn how to take care of his own mental and physical health, and not just through the satisfaction he feels when everyone else has received his tending. In other words, he's come to realize that he gets his emotional strokes by playing nursemaid, but that's not always what is desired or needed by the other person. Nor is it particularly healthy if it comes at the expense of his own needs. There has to be a way to balance his need to be a caregiver with the healthy attention his own life—particularly his physical health—requires.

When Duane was young, he had to be in charge of the other children, he had to be in control of them, providing guidance, protection, and looking out for their safety. That's precisely what is being stirred up in his relationship with Leon. His need to suffocate Leon with mothering is a control issue, and one that comes from having to be extra responsible as a child. (Readers who were highly responsible as children, and those who were firstborn, can probably relate to this.)

At the expense of his own childhood, including being able to just be a kid—which means not always being responsible, careful or protective of others—Duane learned how to be a little adult at a very young age. Unfair as it may have been to him, he needed those skills in order to help with the parenting duties in his family. He's paying a high price for it now, trying to have an adult relationship that contains balance and mutual independence, as opposed to one that is controlling and overbearing on his part.

Duane's process includes learning to trust himself enough to have a relationship without trying to secure his place in it through mothering/smothering his partner. He can make himself indispensable to another person, at least in his own eyes, but the irony is that he runs the risk of losing the other person in a fury of resentment precisely because of his efforts. Doing for others, if done to an unwanted degree, throws the power in the relationship to the giver, with the receiver left impotent and angry. This makes for a highly unbalanced and, in time, stressful relationship. While Duane and Leon's situation has not yet reached this extreme, it's well on its way, and they both know it.

Now is the time for Duane to get in touch with his control

issues and how his childhood conditioning affects his adulthood relationships, both positively and negatively. It isn't that Leon wants none of Duane's attentions, but he wants them to a healthy degree of give-and-take, a degree that permits a balance of power and love between them. With greater balance and sharing, there is more room for Leon in the relationship, and he can then have opportunity to show his care for Duane, too.

Duane realizes that learning to prioritize his own health and well-being may, at first, go against the grain for him. It may feel unnatural, perhaps selfish, for him to consider his own needs. He's not used to doing that, but even if he were HIV-negative, a healthy and balanced outlook on life would require him to pay better attention to himself, to *listen* to himself and what he needs. The fact that he is dealing with a health concern only heightens that need.

His prognosis for making such a shift regarding his own care is quite good, for his commitment to therapy displays an awareness of this issue. In other words, coming to therapy *is* an effort to take good care of himself. The part of Duane that believes in the benefits of therapy, that desires emotional and psychological growth and maintenance, as well as the learning of new skills, is a healthy part of him, one that appreciates good self-care.

Given Duane's long-term exposure to the medical world of HIV, he has been quite well versed in the treatment options that are available to him, both traditional and alternative, but he's devoted little energy to really becoming involved with his medical treatment. While he would be the first to advocate others becoming enthusiastically and intimately involved in their health care, he himself has taken a rather passive role, following his doctor's orders unquestioningly. He almost feels guilty if his doctor spends "too much" time with him, or shows too much concern for his health. Since becoming HIV-positive, there have been advances in treatments that may work for him as well as, if not better than, the protocol he's been on, and possibly with fewer side effects. Always hungry for knowledge, he's just now at the stage of learning more about these most recent options.

If Duane wants to commit to his care, giving himself the same high quality of attention he gives to others, then he'll need to learn to prioritize himself, *without* the guilt. He'll need to know that he's worth paying attention to, worth his doctor's time and concern, and worth the very best in available treatment. He'll need to learn to look inward, and listen to what works best for his body. By educating himself, he'll become knowledgeable and better able to support and encourage his goals and choices. He may end up on the exact treatment plan he's currently using, but at least he will understand better what he's doing and why, and will be able to believe in it wholeheartedly. Or, he may adjust his medication with his physician's supervision, after developing a more thorough understanding of newer therapies and a more communicative relationship with him. Perhaps he'll begin to augment his health by alternative means, asking questions and finding holistic answers. Along the way, what Duane will be learning most of all is how to trust his own judgment.

That may just be the best thing yet for his overall well-being, both physically and mentally.

Given Duane's fondness for meditation and hypnotherapy, one of the tools he is using as part of his psychological care is a meditation to help him develop a trust in himself, and to find a calm, centered way of listening to his own needs. He often uses a meditation similar to the one that follows, and finds it beneficial for guiding him to that place of quiet and inner wisdom.

The Meditation

This meditation may be read slowly by a friend, or silently to oneself.

Take a nourishing, cleansing deep breath. And release. And another. Release. As you continue to breathe, think about how important to your overall well-being your breath is. It is your source of life, your energy, your strength. Breathe. And feel yourself become clearer, more centered, and relaxed.
   Pause.

Breathe into your center. Feel that place where you can be grounded and solid. Trust your breath to fill your center with life, with clarity and energy. Fill your center almost to overflowing with the clean, nourishing breath of life.

Pause.

Let your entire body benefit from your breath. Feel the air that enters your body as it flows to all parts of your head, your neck, your back, torso, arms, hands, legs, and feet. Breathe life into every part of your body.

Pause.

Now let your mind relax. Let your thoughts settle. Let your entire being become calmer, more at peace . . . at peace with yourself, the world, and everyone in it.

Pause.

Notice how your breath continues to flow without your conscious thought or effort. Notice how your heart still pumps, your lungs still work, every cell in your being functioning in harmony with every other cell. Without any extra effort by you, your body is performing exactly as it needs to.

You can trust your body to work beautifully in harmony and precision. It does all it can to keep you healthy and keep your systems working together as one. Even during illness, your body is checking and re-checking its efforts to keep you well.

Pause.

Your mind is part of your body, part of the whole. Let your mind be free of tension, free of unwanted stress. Body and mind, working together in harmony, keeping you safe, centered, and well.

Turn inward, now, and notice what your body-mind is telling you. Focus in on any and all messages your body-mind is offering. Listen. Quietly listen.

Pause.

What do you hear?

Let your awareness come to your needs, any of them . . . all of them. What are your needs? They are made clear to you, just by your listening.

Pause.

Breathe. Trust your inner voice. It is a vital part of who you are. Let yourself commit to listening, ever more carefully, every day. Trust your inner voice. Care for it. Nourish it with your breath. Trust . . . care . . . nourish.

Trust . . . care . . . nourish.

Breathe and know you are in good hands with yourself. Trust your breath. Care for yourself. Nourish yourself. You are well.

You are well.

You are well.

PART THREE

Growing on from Here

If you can dream it, you can do it.
—Walt Disney

Chapter 19

Self-Nurturance

*As long as we focus on the outside
there will always be an empty,
hungry, lost place inside
that needs to be filled.*

—Shakti Gawain

Students in medical school are taught a physiological fact that provides a wonderful metaphor for healthy self-care: The first task of the heart is to pump blood to itself.

In my presentations to care-providers, counselors, mental health volunteers, families, and others working in HIV, I discuss something called "healthy selfishness." Such a term usually raises a few eyebrows on those who hear it for the first time, so conditioned are we to think of anything associated with the word *selfish* as negative. Yet, healthy selfishness has become a concept that has grown tremendously in importance, not only for people caring for others, but as a widely accepted philosophy on healthy living in general.

Much like the heart, if we are to be of any use to others—be they people entrusted to us during their illness, or those who make up our everyday friendships—we must first make sure that we are in a condition that allows us to be available. Being available means being able to be present; to listen and really hear, and to be fully *there*, in the moment. So *there* that anyone in your company can feel your support as tangible as a favorite security blanket.

Being available means that your mind and body are quietly focused. Your mind is not off making up the week's shopping list and your body is not closed off, tightened—indicating that you'd rather be somewhere else. Your mind is wrapped around the relationship in the room and your body language is in agreement: *nothing is more important than being here with you in this moment.*

Too often when we think that we are listening—to a friend, for instance—we are really engaging only a very small part of ourselves in the conversation. We half-listen, perhaps we smile and nod a few times, and if asked later what it was that we were agreeing to, we'd be hard-pressed to say! We're not fully there. We engage part way, while the rest of us is engaged in what we therapists call "narcissistic withdrawal," the tendency—during times of stress or boredom—for the ego to check out, to leave and go off to do whatever it is that's on our minds. We may be thinking about going out for a cigarette, how nice it would be to take a walk in the park, or we're daydreaming about a date for later that evening. No matter what form the withdrawal takes, the result is the same: We're not *there.*

Sometimes our presence is needed for urgent matters, such as when a health-care provider is on duty. Sometimes a loved one simply needs a strong shoulder to cry on. Maybe a friend just wants to talk. But for whatever *external* reason our presence is requested, the *internal* reason is fairly constant: someone wants to feel cared about; that he or she matters; that he or she is not alone in the world, at least for a moment. A good listener's presence accomplishes all that and more.

Being present and available to another human being requires a wholeness, a feeling of being filled enough within, in order to be able to share, significantly and intimately, with another. If a friend were hungry, you'd probably share your food. If a co-worker's car broke down, you'd most likely offer a ride. If a relative were suddenly homeless, you'd perhaps open up your home. But being able to share your *self* with another person?

That requires something more of you: It requires being *whole* enough. It's less tangible than a meal, car, or house, and in that intangibility lies its mystery. Yet, we all know how good it feels when someone is really present for us, even if we can't quite put the feeling into words. To know that someone is *there* is a marvelous shot in the arm for one's self-esteem. The message is: I must be worth this person's time and attention!

Life can be chaotic. While we're driving, we're thinking of a million things that have to be done once we arrive at our destination. While we're on the phone, we're cooking. While we're in a business meeting, we're thinking about the weekend. Once the weekend comes, we have scores of chores to do in the yard, the house, the car, with the neighbors, with friends, with family . . . on and on. It seems almost impossible to get time for oneself, to devote energy to the nurturance and preservation of our own being.

Maybe we plan a vacation and once we're there, we busy ourselves with the same running, talking, thinking, and doing that we allow to occupy us at home. But now, we're doing these things with palm trees in the background, or Mickey Mouse ears on our heads. So nurturance still doesn't happen, it just costs us more!

Life can also be overwhelming. When we are not paying attention, we find that the list of day-to-day demands on our schedule, energy, and talents seems to grow of its own volition, totally outside of our conscious awareness: a partner's needs, a child's needs, a parent's needs, tasks to be finished, goals to accomplish, new projects to begin . . . health issues, work issues, money issues, family issues. When we do stop to take a breath, we wonder, *how did this happen to us?*

So, the question becomes: How can we each allow ourselves to be there, to be present, focused, and available in this moment, no matter how many others are vying for our attention, no matter how many directions we are pulled, no matter what we feel we simply must attend to?

This is where self-nurturance comes in.

Think about this: Many of us try very hard to please others.

What do we do to try and please ourselves? How do we take good care of ourselves? Do we think enough of ourselves, do we think we are important enough (read: is your self-esteem high enough) to handle *ourselves* with care, love, and attention? Healthy selfishness means that you know you matter; and it's not just lip service, it's put into practice, *by you*. It means that you give yourself enough life-affirming messages in what you do, how you think, how you prioritize your own well-being. What is enough? That is determined by listening to your needs!

Let's look at a couple of positive examples.

I had the privilege of knowing a dear friend who worked in HIV education. He was, therefore, devoted to teaching others how to take good care of themselves. Monday through Friday, he was teaching people how to stay healthy and alive, literally.

One thing my friend enjoyed was to have a big bouquet of fresh flowers in his apartment. Such an extravagance on a limited, nonprofit income! But he decided that having those fresh-cut flowers in his environment was worth cutting corners someplace else in his budget. So each Sunday, he'd walk to the corner florist, and purchase a big new batch of fragrant blooms. He loved to come home to their smell, their color, and their sheer beauty. It helped *him* to feel alive, vibrant and connected with nature, and so, those flowers provided him a big, empowering message, *I'm worth it!*, on a weekly basis. For him, that Sunday walk to the florist was like a comforting hug. For him, this was self-nurturance.

Recently I needed to have some oral surgery performed to have a difficult tooth extracted, which would require me to be put under, as they say. Never having had such an experience myself (but having heard some horror stories!), I was understandably apprehensive. Although I enjoyed my first meeting with the oral surgeon and considered him a well-trained professional, still, I hardly knew him. All I really knew was that he had an expensive high-rise office and lots of diplomas on the wall. Moderately reassuring at best. And here I was, about to be knocked out, rendered completely helpless at the hands of him and his staff, as they permanently removed a tiny part of my body!

Aside from asking all the medical questions I needed, I decided to prepare myself with as much care and attention as I could. For several days prior to the surgery I meditated, with the goal being reduced anxiety, so that not only would I come to look forward to the procedure, one that would make me a healthier person, but also so that my physical body would relax and cooperate during the operation, and afterward during recovery. I wanted my mind to help my body as much as it could, and, being no fan of pain, I wanted the recuperative process to go well, with minimal discomfort and maximum healing.

Also for several days prior, I took extra vitamins, including those with herbs that are known to be helpful to the immune system, and exercised a bit more than usual. In case I wasn't feeling up to strenuous activity in the days to come, I wanted my body to feel as though it was in good shape, not being neglected in the least. I didn't want my mind to promote guilt, just because I wasn't on the treadmill during recovery!!

I also stayed in good communication with the doctor's staff, following their preoperative guidelines and asking any questions that would come up for me. I had friends lined up should I need anything following the surgery, the cupboard was stocked with soup (and the freezer with ice cream!), and all the primary people in my life knew what was going on.

So, by the surgery date, I was in good mental and physical health, anxieties at bay, confidence heightened, ready for a new experience. Quite a change in attitude from my initial apprehension!

Sure enough, by the time I was done with the surgery and on my way back to the dental office for my postoperative checkups, I was experiencing rapid healing, minimal discomfort, and a profound sense that all my preparations, physical and mental, were well worth it.

This episode was not a dress rehearsal, it was a piece of my life. Though a relatively minor moment in the grand scheme of things, for me it was very real. I didn't want to have a haphazard, ill-prepared-for experience marked by neglect or carelessness. I wanted to have a full experience, conscious of all my feelings, and one that included plenty of care and attention to my needs. Healthy selfishness. What began in dreaded anticipation became an experience that included positive self-nurturance with the accompanying rewards of good health.

The point of these stories is that there is a time to take care of others, and a time to take care of oneself. These two directions of energy can coexist in a healthy, conscious, mindful manner, or they can be cause for a stressful, chaotic life. If you desire to live healthy and well in your world, how can you do so by neglecting the organic machine that is your own person? Yet that's precisely what we tend to do. We put ourselves and our needs last to everyone else's, rendering us much less able to function effectively.

First and foremost, all your systems—mental, physical, and emotional—must work together harmoniously, as a gestalt, in order to handle whatever ongoing, increasing or changing demands your life might include. Metaphorically speaking, it's like being attuned enough to unexpectedly switch lanes on the freeway in order to avoid an accident, or having to come to a sudden stop because a child has run out into the street. This requires your vigilant attention and the cooperation of all your senses. Without such attention, life can too easily catch you by surprise and feel overwhelming, frustrating, and lacking in any elements of growth or even fun. At the more disabling end of the spectrum, people experience ulcers, heart attacks, and strokes because they're not paying attention!

A former long-term client of mine was having some difficulty balancing the demands of her professional and personal lives. With a highly responsible position in a big-city law firm, a significant other, and two small sons to take care of, the demands on her time and talents were extraordinary. In addition, she did volunteer work that was very important to her spiritual well-being, but was lately feeling overwhelming and unrewarding. It felt as if there simply wasn't enough of her to go around. So although there wasn't any part of her life that she was willing to give up, she understood that she couldn't continue the juggling act the way it was without a tremendous increase in stress and its accompanying ramifications: a possible decline in health, moodiness, a short temper, anxiety, depression, and a general lack of enjoyment and excitement about her life.

She began to think about putting some of her caretaking skills and her resourcefulness toward the betterment of her *own* well-being. While she was responsible for the professional and/or personal well-being of many others, she knew that there must be a way to strike a balance between her obligations to other people and her (thus far neglected) obligation to herself. She began, for the first time in her life, to think about what she needed in order to take better care of herself and feel a healthier balance to her life. She understood, intellectually, that she would be less able to continue taking care of the people in her life that mattered the most to her—her partner and children—if she continued to neglect herself. Now she needed to find a way to actualize this self-care.

What she realized is that she was missing the companionship of her girlfriends, many of whom were long-term and dear friends from college. She had always found these friendships to be both nurturing and fun; they were very important to her mental health and the balance of her life.

She gradually reduced some of her responsibilities at work and also reached a compromise with her significant other regarding their child-care needs, so that she could spend some quality time with these friends. She built into her schedule a way to have a gals-only lunch with several of them each week, and also to attend a yoga class one night a week with a few others. In this way, she was getting out of the office more, attending to her physical and mental well-being through both yoga and highly enjoyable companionship, and prioritizing some regular, quality contact with her support system. It was a process that took several months to refine, but the payoff for her is tremendous: lowered stress, feeling less isolation at work and home, improved mental and physical energy, and a satisfying degree of stimulating conversation with like-minded adults. She creatively found ways to self-nurture, and thereby gave herself a message of positive self-worth: *My happiness and well-being are as important as that of those around me.*

Life does come with a pause button. We just have to remember to push it!

I am reminded of the words by Rabindranath Tagore: "The butterfly counts not months but moments and has time enough."

Learning to nurture oneself in everyday living is a way to honor one's true self. True self refers to who we are in our quiet moments. Simply put, it refers to our truth. When we peel off the layers that are sometimes necessary in order to survive in our day-to-day world, we are left with a true self. Not the work self that needs to be efficient and task-oriented; not the social self that requires charm and pleasant conversation, whether we feel like conversing or not; not the various other public selfs that have to make adjustments many times throughout the day, in order to do, to accomplish, to succeed, to manage, but the inner and personal true self of who we are at our very core, with all its wisdom, serenity, centeredness, and genuine feelings.

The true self is that part of us, that identity, which wears no armor. It stands alone, it sometimes thinks profoundly, and very often it feels deeply. It is what we were born with and what we die with, without all those costumes we wear in between. The true self is the self from which all the others grow. It is the home of our genuineness, and our very human-ness. The true self, like a beautiful and valuable flower, needs attention, care, and nurturance.

One of the best ways I've found to identify the true self, as well as to learn to self-nurture, is through meditation. Meditation allows one the quiet and introspection that lets a person connect with his or her inner being. Through meditation, we can reach that place of centeredness, that peace, where we find out who we really are. No tests, no deadlines, no façades. When we are alone with and in touch with the inner being, we can actualize our ability to reach toward those places hiding behind the other selfs. We can touch our genuineness, our honesty. We can be ourselves. We can simply *be*.

Just by going to that place, we nurture that place. It receives our attention. We are *there*. Nothing is more important. We wrap our minds around it. We engage our hearts. We become fully enraptured in the fine art of being. We come home to ourselves. We breathe. We live. We *are*.

The Meditation

This meditation may be read slowly by a friend, or silently to oneself.

Breathe, and enjoy the benefits of the breath. Breathe slowly, rapidly, deeply or shallowly . . . whatever you want. Breathe in order to feel good, alive. Breathe in order to be aware of the breath. Play with your breath. Breathe for the sheer fun of it.
Pause.
Now let your awareness come to the peaceful feeling of simply breathing. Doing absolutely nothing, worrying about nothing. Feeling free. Unencumbered. Just breathe and be.
Breathe and be.
Pause.
Imagine now that all your responsibilities have vanished. All your fears are gone. All your worries have evaporated. There is no one demanding anything of you. There is nothing you have to do. Treat yourself to this delicious freedom.
Pause.
Let yourself be. Simply be. Breathe into just being. Breathe.
Now allow your mind to focus on this thought: I am fully and wholly who I am. I am fully and wholly my truth. Repeat this to yourself several times. I am fully and wholly who I am. I am fully and wholly my truth.
I am fully and wholly who I am. I am fully and wholly my truth.
Long pause.
You are a unique creation.
You have the ability to know yourself as no one else can.
What is your truth?
Pause.

Make a commitment to yourself: Take the time for growth, for nurturance . . .

Breathe nurturing energy into every cell of your being.

Pause.

Commit to ever-increasing awareness about who you are . . .

Breathe acceptance into your process.

Pause.

Commit to nonjudgmental honesty . . .

Breathe and allow yourself unconditional love.

Pause.

There is no one like you. You are unique.

Breathe in love . . . wrap this love around your heart.

Let your relationship with yourself bloom.

Accept your uniqueness, unconditionally. Celebrate your uniqueness.

Celebrate being human.

Celebrate being exactly who you are!

Chapter 20

Self-Assessments

To thine own self be true.
—William Shakespeare

The following three self-assessment exercises are presented as an accompaniment to several of the topics covered in this book. They are created with the express purpose of helping you to achieve a better understanding of what your particular issues may be; to help you move from a general knowledge of an issue to a specific application in your life. These exercises are designed for increased insight in the areas of self-esteem, family dynamics, and relationships.

How you choose to utilize them is, of course, totally up to you. I've used these exercises in the self-esteem seminars I lead and have seen them make a profound impact on people's level of insight, helping them to get more in touch with their feelings and the issues of their past. I've seen these exercises provide a motivational jumping-off point for lively group discussions. Some people have told me that they do the exercises with a partner together at home.

The first one, the Self-Esteem Awareness Exercise, is designed to help move your thinking from "all-or-nothing" toward a more manageable and workable understanding of self-esteem. Then, it is intended to help you get more in touch with the specific parts of yourself, and how each part fares with regard to your own self-worth. It may be illuminating for you to see what you discover about yourself, especially the *feelings* you possess about who you are.

The second, Understanding Family Dynamics, is an exercise that's intended as a starting-off point toward greater awareness of the early formation of your feelings, especially your feelings of self-worth. Until we stop to look more closely at our individual histories, we may not appreciate the birth of certain emotional patterns. Families shape these patterns early in a person's development. Knowing oneself means knowing one's beginnings.

Last, the Relationship Exercise is a way to help you gain clarity with your relationship landscape—what you bring to a relationship, what you want in a relationship, and what the difficulties are for you when it comes to having the type of relationship you desire. On the surface, it may sound simplistic, but we humans have a tendency to forge ahead blindly, without *really* taking stock of our internal needs and desires. Healthy relationships require self-awareness and perspective.

If you're currently working on any of these topics in your own therapy, then you may find these exercises to be helpful additions to the issues and ideas that are being stirred up for you, the ones that are most alive for you now. If you are not in therapy, then these assessments can help open some doors of understanding for you, as you begin the process of greater self-awareness and valuable insight.

Self-Esteem Awareness Exercise

Self-esteem is not an either-or proposition. Rather than think in all-or-nothing terms—where we have *either* good self-esteem *or* low self-esteem—it is far more helpful to look at the different parts of our lives and the different identities that comprise who we are. In this way, we can begin to identify, specifically, where we need to work on our feelings of self-worth.

Use the following terms: **terrific / good / fair / low / very low**

A. How would you rate your self-esteem when you are:

At home: _____

At work: _____

In a relationship: _____

Single: _____

With friends: _____

With family members*: _____ _____

_____ _____ _____

B. How do you feel about yourself as a:

Son/daughter: _____

Sibling: _____

Lover: _____

Productive member
   of society: _____

Friend: _____

Other(s): _____ _____

Total # of: terrifics _____ *goods* _____ *fairs* _____
lows _____ *very lows* _____

*Your level of self-esteem may be different with different relatives, i.e., parents, grandparents, siblings. Feel free to differentiate. Use more space as needed.

What have you learned about yourself? Any surprises?

_____

_____

_____

In what area(s) do you feel it would be most helpful for you to begin working on your self-esteem? How might you accomplish this?

_____

_____

_____

Understanding Family Dynamics

We were born perfect little bundles of love. What the heck happened? Much of who we are, what we feel, and how we think is due to the type of upbringing we experienced. Childhood messages can continue to cause unhappiness, feelings of low self-worth, and other difficulties long into adulthood. Once we *identify* these messages, *examine* them, and begin to *work through* them, we can then learn to discard those which no longer serve us and replace them with healthier messages. Healthier internal messages lead to healthier life choices. This is a process referred to as "re-parenting." This exercise is one way to begin that process. Use it as a starting point toward greater self-understanding and growth.

As an adult, the feelings I am *least* comfortable with are:

_____

The feelings I am *most* comfortable with are:

_____

I deal with anger by:

_____

I deal with sadness or disappointment by:

_____

I express my joy by:

_____

I am most comfortable when:

_____

When I was a child, my family's way to deal with anger was:

_____

My family's way to deal with disappointment was:

_____

The way I was shown affection was:

_____

My *positive* feelings of self-worth came from:

_____

My feelings of *low* self-worth came from:

_____

My family *was/was not* homophobic, as displayed by:

_____

I wish that, as a child, I had been given:

_____

In raising a child of my own to have healthy self-esteem, I would make sure that:

_____

Relationship Exercise

Think about your past and current relationships and friendships, especially your romantic/sexual/intimate involvements. Perhaps there is something that feels familiar in all your relationships, and yet, is cause for unhappiness or pain. Perhaps you keep coming up against the same issues or obstacles over and over. Or perhaps you keep wishing for one thing, but getting another. Some patterns you may be aware of, and others may elude you. Some may be causing you unhappiness, anxiety, depression, feelings of low self-worth, etc.

Our relationship frustrations are often the result of blind spots, those areas of ourselves marked by unawareness and unanswered questions: "Why do I keep doing this?" "What makes me feel this way?" "Why do I keep having this same experience?" Use this exercise to help you understand yourself better . . . the kind of partner you are, the kind of partner you desire, and why.

A. What are the top five qualities you bring to a relationship?

1. _____
2. _____
3. _____
4. _____
5. _____

B. What are the top five qualities you want your partner to possess?

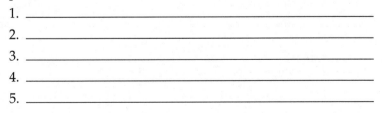

1. _____
2. _____
3. _____
4. _____
5. _____

C. What do you feel are your primary obstacles to meeting the kind of person you want to meet?

_____

_____

D. What areas do you have difficulty in when it comes to making love last?

_____

_____

E. What similarities do you notice among your most recent relationships?

_____

_____

F. What similarities do you notice among your (nonsexual) friendships?

_____

_____

G. What works well for you in relationships, and what would you like to change? First, regarding *yourself*:

In relationships, I do this well:

_____

_____

I would like to change this about myself as a partner:

_____

_____

Regarding the *other person:*
In relationships, I like it when he/she:

_____

_____

I would like for this to be different:

_____

_____

H. What have you learned about yourself and your relationship patterns?

_____

_____

_____

I. Is there any difference between what you *want* and what you are *ready for*?

Elaborate:

_____

_____

_____

J. What might you need (to do) in order to have healthier relationships in your life?

_____

_____

_____

K. How might you best begin to accomplish the changes you desire in your relationships?

_____

_____

_____

Chapter 21

Unity in the Community: Resources

There are 600 million gay people in the world, and add to that siblings, parents, and friends, and something's on the move.

—Walter Righter, retired Episcopal bishop

If you are seeking health care, for yourself or for someone you care about, an easily accessed listing of HIV services, general health services, and women's health services may be found in the front of your phone book. Also, a local hospital's HIV treatment unit, if it has one, would have brochures and phone numbers that may be helpful. Even if they do not have an HIV unit, any hospital would have a social worker on staff who would be able to direct you, as would a free clinic or women's health clinic in your area, or in the nearest major city.

Locating specifically gay- and lesbian-oriented resources, however, may require more effort and creativity, especially if you live in outlying communities. You could begin your search for gay and lesbian services, support groups, counseling, health care, social events, etc., through a national or local gay magazine or newspaper. Check with a large newspaper stand or major bookstore in a metropolitan area near you. If you know of a gay restaurant, bar, or club in your town or city, they often have free gay/lesbian publications available by the door. Gay businesses and groups advertise in these publications.

Most major cities have a gay and lesbian center of some sort, everything from the world's largest, in Los Angeles, to a small but events-packed storefront, like the one I found in London. Even smaller towns often have a phone number or two in the phone book for local gay groups. Your local university or community college may likely have a gay student union, and perhaps—depending on what part of the country you live in—your neighborhood library may carry issues of some gay publications. Of course, there are a great many gay, lesbian, bisexual, and transgender Web sites on the Internet.

The following is a listing of national, state and 800 numbers and Web site addresses of helpful organizations which you can use as a starting point. Usually an organization has at least some information about other groups, so when you reach a friendly voice, feel free to ask questions. Funding for nonprofit agencies is always tenuous at best, so it's unfortunate, but often the case, that 800 number helplines and various community/grass roots agencies run out of money. This list, therefore, cannot be guaranteed, although it is accurate and up to date at the time of publication.

America Responds to AIDS (ARTA)/National AIDS Hotline: 1-800-342-AIDS (2437); TTY: 1-800-243-7889

Bisexual Support Services: 1-800-585-9368

Childhelp U.S.A. (child abuse): 1-800-422-4453

Gay & Lesbian Alliance Against Defamation: 1-800-GAY-MEDIA; http://www.glaad.org

Gay & Lesbian National Hotline: 1-888-843-4564; http://www.glnh.org

Missing Children Help Center: 1-800-872-5437

The National AIDS Information Clearinghouse: 1-800-458-5231; TTY/TDD: 1-800-243-7012

PFLAG (Parents, Friends, & Family of Lesbians and Gays): http://www.pflag.org

Runaway Hotline: 1-800-231-6946

Transgender Forum: http://www.transgender.org

Universal Fellowship of Metropolitan Community Churches: http://www.ufmcc.com
World Congress of Gay and Lesbian Jewish Organizations: http://www.wcgljo.org/wcgljo
Youth Crisis Line: 1-800-843-5200

STATE-BY-STATE AIDS PROGRAMS/HEALTH CLINICS:

AIDS Task Force of Alabama: 205-781-6448
Alaskan AIDS Assistance Association: 907-263-2050
(Arizona) Tucson AIDS Project: 520-322-6226
Arkansas AIDS Foundation: 501-375-0352
(California) AIDS Project Los Angeles: 800-922-2437
   San Fransisco AIDS Foundation: 415-863-AIDS
   Shanti (L.A.): 213-962-8197
   Shanti Project (S.F.) 415-864-2273
Colorado AIDS Project: 303-837-0166
   Gay, Lesbian, Bisexual Community Center of CO: 303-831-6268
(Connecticut) AIDS Project (Hartford): 860-951-4833
   AIDS Project (New Haven): 203-624-0947
(Delaware) AIDS Delaware: 302-652-6776
(District of Columbia) Whitman-Walker Clinic: 202-322-5295
(Florida) Miami AIDS Project: 305-243-3838
(Georgia) AID-Atlanta: 404-876-9944
(Hawaii) Life Foundation: 808-521-2437
Idaho AIDS Foundation: 208-345-2277
(Illinois) AIDS Foundation Chicago: 312-922-2322
   Horizon Community Services: 773-871-5777
Indiana Community AIDS Action Network: 317-920-3190
Iowa Dept. of Public Health AIDS Prevention Program: 515-281-6801
(Kansas) Topeka AIDS Project: 913-232-3100
(Kentucky) AIDS Volunteer: 606-278-7494
(Louisiana) New Orleans AIDS Task Force: 504-945-4000

(Maine) The AIDS Project: 207-775-1267

(Maryland) Health Education Resource Organization: 410-685-1180

(Massachusetts) AIDS Action Committee: 617-437-6200

(Michigan) The AIDS Project: 313-876-0980

Minnesota AIDS Project: 612-341-2060

Mississippi HIV Education and Prevention Program: 601-960-7723

(Missouri) HIV/STD Information Hotline: 800-533-2437

(Montana) Yellowstone AIDS Project: 406-245-2029

Nebraska AIDS Project: 402-342-6367

(Nevada) AID for AIDS of Nevada: 702-382-2326

New Hampshire AIDS Foundation: 603-623-0710

(New Jersey) Essex County AIDS Project: 201-565-0300

New Mexico AIDS Services, Albuquerque: 505-266-0911
  Santa Fe: 505-820-2437

(North Carolina) The AIDS Service Agency: 919-834-2437
  Metrolina AIDS Project: 704-333-1435
  Onslow County AIDS Task Force: 910-346-0915
  Triad Health Project: 919-275-1654

North Dakota State Department of Health: 701-328-2378

(Ohio) AIDS Volunteers of Cincinnati: 513-421-2437
  Columbus AIDS Task Force: 614-488-2437
  AIDS Task Force of Greater Cleveland: 216-621-0766

(Oklahoma) HIV Resource Center: 918-749-4194
  Shanti/Tulsa: 918-749-7898

(Oregon) Cascade AIDS Project: 503-223-5907

(Pennsylvania) Action AIDS: 215-981-0088
  We the People Living with AIDS: 215-545-6868

(Puerto Rico) AIDS Central Office, P.R. Dept. of Health: 787-766-1616

(Rhode Island) Project AIDS: 401-831-5522

South Carolina AIDS Education Network: 803-736-1171

South Dakota Dept. of Health: 605-773-3364

Tennessee Dept. of Health AIDS Program: 615-741-7500
  AIDS Response: 423-450-2437

(Texas) AIDS Foundation of Houston: 713-623-6796

AIDS Services of Austin: 512-451-2273
Dallas AIDS Resource Center: 214-521-5124
Texas Dept. of Health AIDSLINE: 512-490-2500
Utah AIDS Foundation: 801-487-2323
Vermont Cares: 802-863-2437
(Virginia) Richmond AIDS Info Network: 804-358-2437
Virgin Islands-St. Thomas HIV Project: 809-774-3168
(Washington) Northwest AIDS Foundation: 206-329-6923
Shanti/Seattle: 206-322-0279
(West Virginia) Mountain State AIDS Network: 304-292-9000
Wisconsin AIDS Resource Center: 414-273-1991
Wyoming AIDS Project: 307-237-7833

Chapter 22

Conclusion: Whose Choice Is It, Anyway?

Life is a cabaret, old chum.
—Cabaret

While coming out is in many ways the beginning of something new—a new chapter of life, a new degree of honesty with oneself and others—it is also a lifelong process. And it occurs in ways we often don't even think about.

We deal with coming out every time we meet someone new, whether we choose to verbalize our sexual orientation out loud, or we simply consider in our minds whether this new person is to be let in on a most personal and intimate truth. Or perhaps we communicate our identity (and desire) through nonverbal body language—a wink, a smile or a knowing glance: gaydar.

And in reality, we come out in other ways, all the time, throughout all stages of life. As our changing identities emerge, we arrive at forks in the road where we are faced with opportunities to confront our new selves, how we wish to proceed and what to do about who we are becoming.

My friend Jim lived at home with his parents and siblings during high school, then moved away and waited tables to put himself through college. After college, he became a teacher. Soon he was involved in a long-term relationship. Then he began writing articles for educational magazines. He split with his partner. Now he's moved clear across the country, bought a home, and is seeing someone new. So, forgetting for the moment the nuances that accompany anyone's day-to-day living, and looking only at the broad brush strokes of his life, Jim has been a son, sibling, student, waiter, teacher, lover, writer, divorcé, traveler and homeowner.

With each of his life-stages he has, consciously or unconsciously, adopted an identity and a set of feelings around that identity. He's also viewed himself privately, and discussed himself publicly, in terms that identify and correspond to that particular moment of life. *What do I do? I'm a teacher.* Or, *Hello, I'm Jim and this is my lover, Frank.* Or, *I'm a new homeowner applying for a loan.* Or, *Hi, I'm single. Want to go for coffee?* He "comes out" every step along the way, with a new identity, facing new challenges and obstacles and surprises and wonders. And all during the process he feels combinations of excitement, dread, anxiety, depression, hopelessness, hopefulness, confusion, courage, joy, anticipation, serenity, happiness . . . he feels alive. He *feels.*

Each step of life requires courage, whether we are coming out to our parents, or coming into our own as professionals in our chosen fields. And with each moment, we have the choice to proceed consciously, or to sleepwalk through our own existence. We can use our own sound judgments, listening to our conscience and sage inner voice, or we can let others decide for us who we are to be, and how we should proceed.

By our choices, we define ourselves. And at each decision-making intersection, we show ourselves—and everyone around us—what we are made of.

How we *feel* about ourselves during the journey, our self-esteem, is always there, sitting right in the front row, watching the show. It becomes an ongoing, supremely important task of living, then, to pay attention to our self-esteem. To know when it's solid and strong, and to consider the necessary repairs when it's low and weak. To know oneself really implies knowing one's sense of self-worth. *How I feel about myself, as I walk through each and every day of my life, is perhaps the single most consistent, on-*

going mark of my being conscious, a task to which I choose to stay vigilant. It is me. And I am worth such attention.

Who have you been? Who are you now? And who are you willing to become? The answers not only carry with them the feelings you have about yourself, but are also *determined* by such feelings. If you feel yourself worthy, competent, able, lovable and genuine, no matter what negative messages have reached you regarding your self-worth, then you are free to be whomever you so choose. You are free, with literally an endless, new and rewarding road to travel. And the opportunities for further growth present themselves all along the way, in forms both joyous and painful. Serendipitous lessons are *always* there to be learned! You can choose to learn them. It is your life, after all.

Perhaps one of life's greatest lessons is that no one else gets to decide how you feel about yourself—with all your abilities, loves, desires and experiences—without your permission. If your family wants you to be straight, but you know you are gay, they choose your life for you only with your participation. Your parents have their own lives to lead, and all the feelings about themselves that go along with it. Do they get to lead *your* life, too, thereby dictating all of *your* accompanying feelings?

Your lover makes you feel inadequate with your participation. Your minister expresses homophobia to the congregation only with the attention of his audience. Some doctors refuse to treat AIDS patients, homophobes snicker behind your back, schools ban same-sex dances and the religious right blows hot air . . . only with permission. If there's no one there to listen, does the falling tree make any sound?

Where will your journey take you, what choices are you willing to make, how courageous do you wish to be, and can you see yourself as *worth* a life of bliss? Are you able to commit to your own process, vigilantly growing into the empowerment that you deserve? Because healthy self-esteem *is* a commitment.

This life is yours, the community is your tribe, and your limitations need only be set by you. Now it's up to you. Your growth and the actualization of your potential as a loving and genuine person is a lifelong investment, an investment that you alone have the power to make. Who will you be, to yourself . . . to other people . . . with your family . . . in society? Your own vision for yourself is the one that matters most.

May you become all you wish to be. The journey is just beginning.

Have you found your life distasteful?
My life did, and does, smack sweet.
Was your youth of pleasure wasteful?
Mine I save and hold complete.
Do your joys with age diminish?
When mine fail me, I'll complain.
Must in Death your daylight finish?
My sun sets to rise again.

—Robert Browning

About the Author

Dr. Richard L. Pimental-Habib is a counselor and psychotherapist, and holds a doctorate in clinical hypnotherapy with an emphasis in mind-body medicine. His masters level graduate training was in psychodynamic psychotherapy, developmental psychoanalytic psychology, and marriage, family, and child counseling. His undergraduate work was in fine arts, at the University of California.

Dr. Pimental-Habib is in private practice in Los Angeles, specializing in gay and lesbian issues, relationships, HIV/AIDS, families, loss and grief, addiction and recovery, wellness, and mind-body medicine. He volunteers as a consultant for several HIV-response agencies throughout the Los Angeles area; he leads seminars on gay and lesbian self-esteem, wellness through meditation, and bereavement; and he educates peer counselors to work in HIV mental health. As a bereavement counselor for the country's first AIDS hospice, he designed a one-year follow-up bereavement program that continues to serve as the model for such programs nationwide.

Dr. Pimental-Habib has written several professional papers on HIV-related grief and grief counseling, has been a regular columnist for a variety of gay and lesbian publications, and writes for national parenting magazines. *Empowering the Tribe* is his first book of nonfiction.

He lives in Los Angeles and New England with his two highly meditative cats. You can visit his Web site at *http://www.outwork. com/members/drrph*